Practical ethics

Practical ethics

PETER SINGER

CAMBRIDGE UNIVERSITY PRESS

CAMBRIDGE

LONDON   NEW YORK   NEW ROCHELLE
MELBOURNE   SYDNEY

Published by the Press Syndicate of the University of Cambridge
The Pitt Building, Trumpington Street, Cambridge CB2 1RP
32 East 57th Street, New York, NY 10022, USA
296 Beaconsfield Parade, Middle Park, Melbourne 3206, Australia

First published 1979

Set, printed and bound in Great Britain by
Fakenham Press Limited, Fakenham, Norfolk

Library of Congress Cataloguing in Publication Data

Singer, Peter.
Practical ethics.

Includes bibliographical references and index.
1. Ethics. 2. Social ethics. I. Title.
BJ1012.S49   170   79–52328

ISBN 0 521 22920 0 hard covers
ISBN 0 521 29720 6 paperback

CONTENTS

PREFACE

Practical ethics covers a wide area. We can find ethical ramifications in most of our choices, if we look hard enough. This book does not attempt to cover the whole area. The problems it deals with have been selected on two grounds: relevance, and the extent to which philosophical reasoning can contribute to discussion of them.

I regard an ethical issue as relevant if it is one that any thinking person must face. Some of the issues discussed in this book confront us daily: what are our personal responsibilities towards the poor? Are we justified in treating animals as nothing more than machines producing flesh for us to eat? And why should we bother about acting in accordance with moral principles anyway? Other problems, like abortion and euthanasia, fortunately are not everyday decisions for most of us; but they are issues which can arise at some time in our lives. They are also issues of current concern about which any active participant in our society's decision-making process needs to reflect.

The extent to which an issue can usefully be discussed philosophically depends on the kind of issue it is. Some issues are controversial largely because there are facts in dispute. For example, whether experiments in genetic engineering using recombinant DNA ought to go ahead seems to hang largely on whether they pose a serious risk to public health through the escape of new bacteria to which we have no resistance. Philosophers lack the expertise to tackle this question. In other cases, however, the facts are clear and accepted by both sides; it is conflicting ethical views that give rise to disagreement over what to do. Then the kind of reasoning and analysis that philosophers practise really can make a difference. The issues discussed in this book are ones in which ethical, rather than factual, disagreement plays a major role. The potential contribution of philosophers to discussions of these issues is therefore considerable.

In writing this book I have not hesitated to make use of my own previously published articles and books. Thus Chapter 3 is based on my book, *Animal Liberation* (New York Review/Random House, 1975) although it also takes account of objections made since the book appeared. Sections of Chapter 8 restate arguments from 'Famine, Affluence and Morality', *Philosophy and Public Affairs*, vol. 1 (1972) and from 'Reconsidering the Famine Relief Argument' in Peter Brown and Henry Shue (eds.) *Food Policy: The Responsibility of the United States in the Life and Death Choices* (New York, The Free Press, 1977). Portions of Chapter 9 draw on *Democracy and Disobedience* (Oxford, Clarendon Press, 1973).

H. J. McCloskey, Derek Parfit and Robert Young provided useful comments on a draft version of the book. Robert Young's ideas also entered into my thinking at an earlier stage, when we jointly taught a course on these topics at La Trobe University. The chapter on euthanasia, in particular, owes much to his ideas, though he may not agree with everything in it. Going back further still, my interest in ethics was stimulated by H. J. McCloskey, whom I was fortunate to have as a teacher during my undergraduate years; while the mark left by R. M. Hare, who taught me at Oxford, is apparent in the ethical foundations underlying the positions taken in this book. Jeremy Mynott, of Cambridge University Press, encouraged me to write the book and helped to shape and improve it as it went along. It remains only to thank Jean Archer for typing up the final version with her usual efficiency and good humour.

Oxford, February 1979   Peter Singer

Note to the reader

To give an uncluttered text, notes, references and suggested further reading are provided by chapter on pp. 221–33.

1

About ethics

This book is about practical ethics, that is about the application of ethics or morality – I shall use the words interchangeably – to practical issues like the treatment of racial minorities, equality for women, the use of animals for food and research, abortion, euthanasia and the obligation of the wealthy to help the poor. No doubt the reader will want to get on to these issues without delay; but there are some preliminaries which must be dealt with at the start. In order to have a useful discussion *within* ethics, it is necessary to say a little *about* ethics so that we have a clear understanding of what we are doing when we discuss ethical questions. This first chapter therefore sets the stage for the remainder of the book. In order to prevent it growing into an entire volume itself, it is brief and at times dogmatic. I cannot take the space properly to consider all the different conceptions of ethics that might be opposed to the one I shall defend; but this chapter will at least serve to reveal the assumptions on which the remainder of the book is based.

What ethics is not

Some people think that morality is now out of date. They regard morality as a system of nasty puritanical prohibitions, mainly designed to stop people having fun. Traditional moralists who claim to be the defenders of morality, when they are only defending one particular moral code, rather than morality as such, have been allowed to pre-empt the field to such an extent that when a newspaper headline reads BISHOP ATTACKS DECLINING MORAL STANDARDS we expect to read yet again about promiscuity, homosexuality, pornography and so on, and not about corporations bribing government officials, or the puny amounts we give as overseas aid to poorer nations.

So the first thing ethics is not, is a set of prohibitions particularly concerned with sex. Sex raises no special moral issues at all. Decisions about sex may involve considerations of honesty, concern for others, prudence and so on, but there is nothing special about sex in this respect, for the same could be said of decisions about driving a car. (In fact the moral issues raised by driving a car, both from an environmental and from a safety point of view, are much more serious than those raised by having sex.) Accordingly this book contains no discussion of sexual morality. There are more important ethical issues to be considered.

The second thing that ethics is not, is an ideal system which is all very noble in theory but no good in practice. The reverse of this is closer to the truth: an ethical judgment that is no good in practice must suffer from a theoretical defect as well, for the whole point of ethical judgments is to guide practice.

People sometimes believe that ethics is inapplicable to the real world because they believe that ethics is a system of short and simple rules like 'Do not lie', 'Do not steal', and 'Do not kill'. It is not surprising that those who hold this model of ethics should also believe that ethics is not suited to life's complexities. In unusual situations, simple rules conflict; and even when they do not, following a rule can lead to disaster. It may normally be wrong to lie, but if you were living in Nazi Germany and the Gestapo came to your door looking for Jews, it would surely be right to deny the existence of the Jewish family hiding in your attic.

Like the failure of a restrictive sexual morality, the failure of an ethic of simple rules must not be taken as a failure of ethics as a whole. It is only a failure of one view of ethics, and not even an irremediable failure of that view. Those who think that ethics is a system of rules – the deontologists – can rescue their position by finding more complicated and more specific rules which do not conflict with each other, or by ranking the rules in some hierarchical structure to resolve conflicts between them. Moreover there is a long-standing approach to ethics which is quite untouched by the complexities which make simple rules difficult to apply. This is the teleological or consequentialist view. Consequentialists start not with moral rules but with goals. They assess actions by the extent to which they further these goals. The best-known, though not the only, consequentialist theory is utilitarianism. The classical utilitarian regards an action as right if it produces as much or more of an increase in the happiness of all affected by it than any alternative action, and wrong if it does not.

The consequences of an action vary according to the circumstances in which it is performed. Hence a utilitarian can never properly be accused of a lack of realism, or of a rigid adherence to ideals in defiance of practical experience. The utilitarian will judge lying bad in some circumstances and good in others, depending on its consequences.

The third thing ethics is not, is something intelligible only in the context of religion. I shall treat ethics as entirely independent of religion.

Some theists say that ethics cannot do without religion because the very meaning of 'good' is nothing other than 'what God approves'. Plato refuted a similar claim more than two thousand years ago by arguing that if the gods approve of some actions it must be because those actions are good, in which case it cannot be the gods' approval that makes them good. The alternative view makes divine approval entirely arbitrary: if the gods had happened to approve of torture and disapprove of helping our neighbours, torture would have been good and helping our neighbours bad. Some modern theists have attempted to extricate themselves from this type of dilemma by maintaining that God is good and so could not possibly approve of torture; but these theists are caught in a trap of their own making, for what can they possibly mean by the assertion that God is good? That God is approved of by God?

Traditionally the more important link between religion and ethics was that religion was thought to provide a reason for doing what is right, the reason being that those who are virtuous will be rewarded by an eternity of bliss while the rest roast in hell. Not all religious thinkers have accepted this: Immanuel Kant, a most pious Christian, scorned anything that smacked of a self-interested motive for obeying the moral law. We must obey it, he said, for its own sake. Nor do we have to be Kantians to dispense with the motivation offered by traditional religion. There is a long line of thought which finds the source of ethics in the attitudes of benevolence and sympathy for others that most people have. This is, however, a complex topic and since it is the subject of the final chapter of this book I shall not pursue it here. It is enough to say that our everyday observation of our fellows clearly shows that ethical behaviour does not require belief in heaven and hell.

The fourth, and last claim about ethics that I shall deny in this opening chapter is that ethics is relative or subjective. At least, I shall deny these claims in some of the senses in which they are often made. This point requires a more extended discussion than the other three.

Let us take first the often-asserted idea that ethics is relative to the society one happens to live in. This is true in one sense and false in another. It is true that, as we have already seen in discussing consequentialism, actions that are right in one situation because of their good consequences may be wrong in another situation because of their bad consequences. Thus casual sexual intercourse may be wrong when it leads to the existence of children who cannot be adequately cared for, and not wrong when, because of the existence of effective contraception, it does not lead to reproduction at all. But this is only a superficial form of relativism. While it suggests that a specific principle like 'Casual sex is wrong' may be relative to time and place, it says nothing against such a principle being objectively valid in certain specified circumstances, or against the universal applicability of a more general principle like 'Do what increases happiness and reduces suffering.'

The more fundamental form of relativism became popular in the nineteenth century when data on the moral beliefs and practices of far-flung societies began pouring in. To the strict reign of Victorian prudery the knowledge that there were places where sexual relations between unmarried people were regarded as perfectly wholesome brought the seeds of a revolution in sexual attitudes. It is not surprising that to some the new knowledge suggested, not merely that the moral code of nineteenth-century Europe was not objectively valid, but that no moral judgment can do more than reflect the customs of the society in which it is made.

Marxists adapted this form of relativism to their own theories. The ruling ideas of each period, they said, are the ideas of its ruling class, and so the morality of a society is relative to its dominant economic class, and thus indirectly relative to its economic basis. So they triumphantly refuted the claims of feudal and bourgeois morality to objective, universal validity. But this raises a problem: if all morality is relative, what is so special about communism? Why side with the proletariat rather than the bourgeoisie?

Engels dealt with this problem in the only way possible, by abandoning relativism in favour of the more limited claim that the morality of a society divided into classes will always be relative to the ruling class, although the morality of a society without class antagonisms could be a 'really human' morality. This is no longer relativism at all, but Marxism still, in a confused sort of way, provides the impetus for a lot of woolly relativist ideas.

The problem that led Engels to abandon relativism defeats ordinary ethical relativism as well. Anyone who has thought about an ethical decision knows that being told what our society thinks we ought to do does not settle our decision. We have to reach our own decision. The beliefs and customs we were brought up with may exercise great influence on us, but once we start to reflect upon them we can decide whether to act in accordance with them, or go against them.

The opposite view – that ethics is always relative to a particular society – has most implausible consequences. If our society disapproves of slavery, while another society approves of it, we have no basis to choose between these conflicting views. Indeed, on a relativist analysis there is really no conflict – when I say slavery is wrong I am really only saying that my society disapproves of slavery, and when the slaveowners from the other society say that slavery is right, they are only saying that their society approves of it. Why argue? Obviously we could both be speaking the truth.

Worse still, the relativist cannot satisfactorily account for the nonconformist. If 'slavery is wrong' means 'my society disapproves of slavery' then someone who lives in a society which does not disapprove of slavery is, in claiming that slavery is wrong, making a simple factual error. An opinion poll could demonstrate the error of an ethical judgment. Would-be reformers are therefore in a parlous situation: when they set out to change the ethical views of their fellow-citizens they are *necessarily* mistaken; it is only when they succeed in winning most of the society over to their own views that those views become right.

These difficulties are enough to sink ethical relativism; ethical subjectivism at least avoids making nonsense of the valiant efforts of would-be moral reformers, for it makes ethical judgments depend on the approval or disapproval of the person making the judgment, rather than that person's society. There are other difficulties, though, that at least some forms of ethical subjectivism cannot overcome.

If those who say that ethics is subjective mean by this that when I say that cruelty to animals is wrong I am really only saying that I disapprove of cruelty to animals, they are faced with an aggravated form of one of the difficulties of relativism: the inability to account for ethical disagreement. What was true for the relativist of disagreement between people from different societies is for the subjectivist true of disagreement between any two people. I say cruelty to animals is wrong: someone else says it is not wrong. If this means that I disapprove of cruelty to animals and someone else does not, both statements may be true and so there is nothing to argue about.

Other theories often described as 'subjectivist' are not open to this objection. Suppose someone maintains that ethical judgments are neither true nor false because they do not describe anything – neither objective moral facts, nor one's own subjective states of mind. This theory might hold that, as C. L. Stevenson suggested, ethical judgments express attitudes, rather than decribe them, and we disagree about ethics because we try, by expressing our own attitude, to bring our listeners to a similar attitude. Or it might be, as R. M. Hare has urged, that ethical judgments are prescriptions and therefore more closely related to commands than to statements of fact. On this view we disagree because we care about what people do. Those features of ethical argument that imply the existence of objective moral standards can be explained away by maintaining that this is some kind of error – perhaps the legacy of the belief that ethics is a God-given system of law, or perhaps just another example of our tendency to objectify our personal wants and preferences. J. L. Mackie has defended this view.

Provided they are carefully distinguished from the crude form of subjectivism which sees ethical judgments as descriptions of the speaker's attitudes, these are plausible accounts of ethics. In their denial of a realm of ethical facts which is part of the real world, existing quite independently of us, they are no doubt correct; but does it follow from this that ethical judgments are immune from criticism, that there is no role for reason or argument in ethics and that, from the standpoint of reason, any ethical judgment is as good as any other? I do not think it does, and none of the three philosophers referred to in the previous paragraph denies reason and argument a role in ethics, though they disagree as to the significance of this role.

This issue of the role that reason can play in ethics is the crucial point raised by the claim that ethics is subjective. The non-existence of a mysterious realm of objective ethical facts need not concern us, as long as it does not imply the non-existence of ethical reasoning. It may even help, since if we could arrive at ethical judgments only by intuiting these strange ethical facts, ethical argument would be more difficult still. So what has to be shown to put practical ethics on a sound basis is that ethical reasoning is possible. Here the temptation is to say simply that the proof of the pudding lies in the eating, and the proof that reasoning is possible in ethics is to be found in the remaining chapters of this book, in which we do reason about ethics; but this is not entirely satisfactory. From a theoretical point of view it is unsatisfactory because we might find ourselves reasoning about ethics without really understanding how this can happen; and from a practical point of view it is unsatisfactory because our reasoning is more likely to go astray if we lack a grasp of its foundations. I shall therefore attempt to say something about how we can reason in ethics.

What ethics is: one view

What follows is a sketch of a view of ethics which allows reason an important role in ethical decisions. It is not the only possible view of ethics, but it is a plausible view. Once again, however, I shall have to pass over qualifications and objections worth a chapter to themselves. To those who think these undiscussed objections defeat the position I am advancing I can only say, again, that this whole chapter may be treated as no more than a statement of the assumptions on which this book is based. In that way it will at least assist in giving a clear view of what I take ethics to be.

What is it to make a moral judgment, or to argue about an ethical issue, or to live according to ethical standards? How do moral judgments differ from other practical judgments? Why do we regard a woman's decision to have an abortion as raising an ethical issue, but not her decision to change her job? What is the difference between a person who lives by ethical standards and one who doesn't?

All these questions are related, so we only need to consider one of them; but to do this we need to say something about the nature of ethics. Suppose that we have studied the lives of a number of different people, and we know a lot about what they do, what they believe, and so on. Can we then decide which of them are living by ethical standards and which are not?

We might think that the way to proceed here is to find out who believes it wrong to lie, cheat, steal and so on, and does not do any of these things, and who has no such beliefs, and shows no such restraint in their actions. Then those in the first group would be living according to ethical standards and those in the second group would not be. But this procedure mistakenly assimilates two distinctions: the first is the distinction between living according to (what we judge to be) the right ethical standards and living according to (what we judge to be) mistaken ethical standards; the second is the distinction between living according to some ethical standards, and living according to no ethical standards at all. Those who lie and cheat, but do not believe what they are doing to be wrong, may be living according to ethical standards. They may believe, for any of a number of possible reasons, that it is right to lie, cheat, steal and so on. They are not living according to conventional ethical standards, but they may be living according to some other ethical standards.

This first attempt to distinguish the ethical from the non-ethical was mistaken, but we can learn from our mistakes. We found that we must concede that those who hold unconventional ethical beliefs are still living according to ethical standards, *if they believe, for any reason, that it is right to do as they are doing*. The italicized condition gives us a clue to the answer we are seeking. The notion of living according to ethical standards is tied up with the notion of defending the way one is living, of giving a reason for it, of justifying it. Thus people may do all kinds of things we regard as wrong, yet still be living according to ethical standards, if they are prepared to defend and justify what they do. We may find the justification inadequate, and may hold that the actions are wrong, but the attempt at justification, whether successful or not, is sufficient to bring the person's conduct within the domain of the ethical as opposed to the non-ethical. When, on the other hand, people cannot put forward any justification for what they do, we may reject their claim to be living according to ethical standards, even if what they do is in accordance with conventional moral principles.

We can go further. If we are to accept that a person is living according to ethical standards, the justification must be of a certain kind. For instance, a justification in terms of self-interest alone will not do. When Macbeth, contemplating the murder of Duncan, admits that only 'vaulting ambition' drives him to do it, he is admitting that the act cannot be justified ethically. 'So that I can be king in his place' is not a weak attempt at an ethical justification for assassination; it is not the sort of reason that counts as an ethical justification at all. Self-interested acts must be shown to be compatible with more broadly based ethical principles if they are to be ethically defensible, for the notion of ethics carries with it the idea of something bigger than the individual. If I am to defend my conduct on ethical grounds, I cannot point only to the benefits it brings me. I must address myself to a larger audience.

From ancient times, philosophers and moralists have expressed the idea that ethical conduct is acceptable from a point of view that is somehow *universal*. The 'Golden Rule' attributed to Moses tells us to go beyond our own personal interests and 'do unto others as we would have them do unto us'. The same idea of putting oneself in the position of another is involved in the Christian commandment that we love our neighbour as ourself. The Stoics held that ethics derives from a universal natural law. Kant developed this idea into his famous formula: 'Act only on that maxim through which you can at the same time will that it should become a universal law.' Kant's theory has itself been modified and developed by R. M. Hare, who sees 'universalizability' as a logical feature of moral judgments. The eighteenth-century British philosophers Hutcheson, Hume and Adam Smith appealed to an imaginary 'impartial spectator' as the test of a moral judgment, and this theory has its modern version in the Ideal Observer Theory. Utilitarians, from Jeremy Bentham to J. J. C. Smart, take it as axiomatic that in deciding moral issues 'each counts for one and none for more than one'; while John Rawls, a leading contemporary critic of utilitarianism, incorporates essentially the same axiom into his own theory by deriving basic ethical principles from an imaginary choice in which those choosing do not know whether they will be the ones who gain or lose by the principles they select. Even Continental philosophers like the existentialist Jean-Paul Sartre and the Marxist Jürgen Habermas, who differ in many ways from their English-speaking colleagues – and from each other – agree that ethics is in some sense universal.

One could argue endlessly about the merits of each of these characterizations of the ethical; but what they have in common is more important than their differences. They agree that the justification of an ethical principle cannot be in terms of any partial or sectional group. Ethics takes a universal point of view. This does not mean that a particular ethical judgment must be universally applicable. Circumstances alter causes, as we have seen. What it does mean is that in making ethical judgments we go beyond our own likes and dislikes. From an ethical point of view the fact that it is I who benefit from, say, a more equal distribution of income and you, say, who lose by it, is irrelevant. Ethics requires us to go beyond 'I' and 'you' to the universal law, the universalizable judgment, the standpoint of the impartial spectator or ideal observer, or whatever we choose to call it.

Can we use this universal aspect of ethics to derive an ethical theory which will give us guidance about right and wrong? Philosophers from the Stoics to Hare and Rawls have attempted this. No attempt has met with general acceptance. The problem is that if we describe the universal aspect of ethics in bare, formal terms, a wide range of ethical theories, including quite irreconcilable ones, are compatible with this notion of universality; if, on the other hand, we build up our description of the universal aspect of ethics so that it leads us ineluctably to one particular ethical theory, we shall be accused of smuggling our own ethical beliefs into our definition of the ethical – and this definition was supposed to be broad enough, and neutral enough, to encompass all serious candidates for the status of 'ethical theory'. Since so many others have failed to overcome this obstacle to deducing an ethical theory from the universal aspect of ethics, it would be foolhardy to attempt to do so in a brief introduction to a work with a quite different aim. Nevertheless I shall propose something only a little less ambitious. The universal aspect of ethics, I suggest, does provide a persuasive, although not conclusive, reason for taking a broadly utilitarian position.

My reason for suggesting this is as follows. In accepting that ethical judgments must be made from a universal point of view, I am accepting that my own interests cannot, simply because they are *my* interests, count more than the interests of anyone else. Thus my very natural concern that my own interests be looked after must, when I think ethically, be extended to the interests of others. Now, imagine that I am trying to decide between two possible courses of action – any example would do. Imagine, too, that I am deciding in a complete ethical vacuum, that I know nothing of any ethical considerations – I am, we might say, in a pre-ethical stage of thinking. How would I make up my mind? One thing that would be still relevant would be how the possible courses of action will affect my interests. Indeed, if we define 'interests' broadly enough, so that we count anything people desire as in their interests (unless it is incompatible with another desire or desires) then it would seem that at this pre-ethical stage, *only* one's own interests can be relevant to the decision.

Suppose I then begin to think ethically, to the extent of recognizing that my own interests cannot count for more, simply because they are my own, than the interests of others. In place of my own interests, I now have to take account of the interests of all those affected by my decision. This requires me to weigh up all these interests and adopt the course of action most likely to maximize the interests of those affected. Thus I must choose the course of action which has the best consequences, on balance, for all affected. This is a form of utilitarianism. It differs from classical utilitarianism in that 'best consequences' is understood as meaning what, on balance, furthers the interests

of those affected, rather than merely what increases plea
and reduces pain. (It has, however, been suggested that classical utilitarians like Bentham and John Stuart Mill used
'pleasure' and 'pain' in a broad sense which allowed them to
include achieving what one desired as a 'pleasure' and the
reverse as a 'pain'. If this interpretation is correct, the difference
between classical utilitarianism and utilitarianism based on
interests disappears.)

What does this show? It does not show that utilitarianism can
be deduced from the universal aspect of ethics. There are other
ethical ideals – like individual rights, the sanctity of life, justice,
purity and so on – which are universal in the required sense, and
are, at least in some versions, incompatible with utilitarianism.
It does show that we very swiftly arrive at an *initially* utilitarian
position once we apply the universal aspect of ethics to simple,
pre-ethical decision making. This, I believe, places the onus of
proof on those who seek to go beyond utilitarianism. The
utilitarian position is a minimal one, a first base which we reach
by universalizing self-interested decision making. We cannot, if
we are to think ethically, refuse to take this step. If we are to be
persuaded that we should go beyond utilitarianism and accept
non-utilitarian moral rules or ideals, we need to be provided
with good reasons for taking this further step. Until such
reasons are produced, we have some grounds for remaining
utilitarians.

This tentative argument for utilitarianism corresponds to the
way in which I shall discuss practical issues in this book. I am
inclined to hold a utilitarian position, and to some extent the
book may be taken as an attempt to indicate how a consistent
utilitarianism would deal with a number of controversial problems. But I shall not take utilitarianism as the only ethical
position worth considering. I shall try to show the bearing of
other views, of theories of rights, of justice, of the sanctity of life,
and so on, on the problems discussed. In this way readers will be
able to come to their own conclusions about the relative merits
of utilitarian and non-utilitarian approaches, and about the
whole issue of the role of reason and argument in ethics.

2

Equality and its implications

The basis of equality

The present century has seen dramatic changes in moral attitudes. Most of these are still controversial. Abortion, universally prohibited twenty years ago, is now legal in many countries, but even where it is legal it is still opposed by substantial and respected sections of the population. The same is true of changes in attitudes to extra-marital sex, homosexuality, pornography, euthanasia, and suicide. Great as the changes have been, no new consensus has been reached. The issues remain controversial and it is possible to defend either side without jeopardizing one's intellectual or social standing.

Equality seems to be different. The change in attitudes to inequality – especially racial inequality – has been no less sudden and dramatic than the change in attitudes to sex, but it has been more complete. Racist assumptions shared by most Europeans at the turn of the century are now totally unacceptable, at least in public life. A poet could not now write of 'lesser breeds without the law', and retain – indeed enhance – his reputation, as Rudyard Kipling did in 1897. This does not mean that there are no longer any racists, but only that they must disguise their racism if their views and policies are to have any chance of general acceptance. The principle that all humans are equal is now part of the prevailing political and ethical orthodoxy. But what, exactly, does it mean and why do we accept it?

Once we go beyond the agreement that blatant forms of racial discrimination are wrong, once we question the basis of the principle that all humans are equal and seek to apply this principle to particular cases, the consensus starts to weaken. One sign of this is the furore over the claims made by Arthur Jensen, Professor of Educational Psychology at the University of California, Berkeley and H. J. Eysenck, Professor of Psychology at the University of London, about genetically based variations in intelligence between different races. Many of the most forceful opponents of Jensen and Eysenck assume that these claims, if sound, would justify racial discrimination. Are they right? Similar questions can be asked about research into differences between males and females.

Another issue requiring us to think about the principle of equality is 'reverse discrimination'. Some philosophers and lawyers have argued that the principle of equality requires that when allocating jobs or university places we should ensure places are given to members of oppressed minorities. Others have contended that the same principle of equality rules out any discrimination on racial grounds, whether for or against the worst-off members of society.

We can only answer these questions if we are clear about what it is we intend to say, and can justifiably say, when we assert that all humans are equal. Hence the need for an inquiry into the ethical foundations of the principle of equality.

When we say that all humans are equal, irrespective of race or sex, what exactly are we claiming? Racists, sexists and other opponents of equality have often pointed out that, by whatever test we choose, it simply is not true that all humans are equal. Some are tall, some are short; some are good at mathematics, others are poor at it; some can run 100 metres in ten seconds, some take fifteen or twenty; some would never intentionally hurt another being, others would kill a stranger for $100 if they could get away with it; some have emotional lives which touch the heights of ecstasy and the depths of despair, while others live on a more even plane, relatively untouched by what goes on around them ... and so we could go on. The plain fact is that humans differ, and the differences apply to so many characteristics that the search for a factual basis on which to erect the principle of equality seems hopeless.

John Rawls has suggested, in his influential book *A Theory of Justice*, that equality can be founded on the natural characteristics of human beings, provided we select what he calls a 'range property'. Suppose we draw a circle on a piece of paper. Then all points within the circle – this is the 'range' – have the property of being within the circle, and they have this property equally. Some points may be closer to the centre and others nearer the edge, but all are, equally, points inside the circle. Similarly, Rawls suggests, the property of 'moral personality' is a property which virtually all humans possess, and all humans who possess this property possess it equally. By 'moral personality' Rawls does not mean 'morally good personality'; he is using 'moral' in contrast to 'amoral'. A moral person, Rawls says, must have a sense of justice. More broadly, one might say that to be a moral person is to be the kind of person to whom one can make moral appeals, with some prospect that the appeal will be heeded.

Rawls maintains that moral personality is the basis of human equality, a view which derives from his 'contract' approach to justice. The contract tradition sees ethics as a kind of mutually beneficial agreement – roughly, 'Don't hit me and I won't hit you.' Hence only those capable of appreciating that they are not being hit, and of restraining their own hitting accordingly, are within the sphere of ethics.

There are problems with using moral personality as the basis of equality. One objection is that moral personality is, unlike being inside a circle, a matter of degree. Some people are highly sensitive to issues of justice and ethics generally; others, for a variety of reasons, have only a very limited awareness of such principles. The suggestion that being a moral person is the minimum necessary for coming within the scope of the principle of equality still leaves it open just where this minimal line is to be drawn. Nor is it intuitively obvious why, if moral personality is so important, we should not have grades of moral status, with rights and duties corresponding to the degree of refinement of one's sense of justice.

Still more serious is the objection that it is not true that all humans are moral persons, even in the most minimal sense. Infants and small children, along with some mentally defective humans, lack the required sense of justice. Shall we then say that all humans are equal, except for very young or mentally defective ones? This is certainly not what we ordinarily understand by the principle of equality. If this revised principle implies that we may disregard the interests of very young or mentally defective humans in ways that would be wrong if they were older or more intelligent, we would need far stronger arguments to induce us to accept it. (Rawls deals with infants and children by including *potential* moral persons along with actual ones within the scope of the principle of equality. But this is an *ad hoc* device, confessedly designed to square his theory with our ordinary moral intuitions, rather than something for which independent arguments can be produced. Moreover although Rawls admits that those with irreparable mental defects 'may present a difficulty' he offers no suggestions towards the solution of this difficulty.)

So the possession of 'moral personality' does not provide a satisfactory basis for the principle that all humans are equal. I doubt that any natural characteristic, whether a 'range property' or not, can fulfil this function, for I doubt that there is any morally significant property which all humans possess equally.

There is another possible line of defence for the belief that there is a factual basis for a principle of equality which prohibits racism and sexism. We can admit that humans differ as individuals, and yet insist that there are no morally significant differences between the races and sexes. Knowing that someone is black or white, female or male, does not enable us to draw conclusions about her or his intelligence, sense of justice, depth of feelings, or anything else that would entitle us to treat her or him as less than equal. The racist claim that whites are superior to blacks in these capacities is in this sense false. The differences between individuals do not adhere to racial lines, and some blacks are superior to some whites in all these respects. The same is true of the parallel sexist stereotype which sees women as more emotional, less rational, less aggressive and less enterprising than men. Obviously this is not true of women as a whole. Some women are less emotional, more rational, more aggressive and more enterprising than some men.

The fact that humans differ as individuals, not as races or sexes, is important and we shall return to it when we come to discuss the implications of the claims made by Jensen, Eysenck and others; yet it provides neither a satisfactory principle of equality, nor an adequate defence against a more sophisticated opponent of equality than the blatant racist or sexist. Suppose that someone proposes that people should be given intelligence tests and then classified into higher or lower status categories on the basis of the results. Perhaps those who scored above 125 would be a slave-owning class; those scoring between 100 and 125 would be free citizens but lack the right to own slaves; while those scoring below 100 would be made the slaves of those who had scored above 125. A hierarchical society of this sort seems as abhorrent as one based on race or sex; but if we base our support for equality on the factual claim that differences between individuals cut across racial and sexual boundaries, we have no grounds for opposing this kind of inegalitarianism. For this hierarchical society would be based on real differences between people.

We can reject this 'hierarchy of intelligence' and similar fantastic schemes only if we are clear that the claim to equality does not rest on intelligence, moral personality, rationality or similar matters of fact. There is no logically compelling reason for assuming that a difference in ability between two people justifies any difference in the amount of consideration we give to their interests. Equality is a basic ethical principle, not an assertion of fact. We can see this if we return to our earlier discussion of the universal aspect of ethical judgments.

We saw in the previous chapter that when I make an ethical

judgment I must go beyond a personal or sectional point of view and take into account the interests of all those affected. This means that we weigh up interests, considered simply as interests and not as my interests, or the interests of Australians, or of whites. This provides us with a basic principle of equality: the principle of equal consideration of interests.

The essence of the principle of equal consideration of interests is that we give equal weight in our moral deliberations to the like interests of all those affected by our actions. This means that if only X and Y would be affected by a possible act, and if X stands to lose more than Y stands to gain, it is better not to do the act. We cannot, if we accept the principle of equal consideration of interests, say that doing the act is better, despite the facts described, because we are more concerned about Y than we are about X. What the principle really amounts to is: an interest is an interest, whoever's interest it may be.

We can make this more concrete by considering a particular interest, say the interest we have in the relief of pain. Then the principle says that the ultimate moral reason for relieving pain is simply the undesirability of pain as such, and not the undesirability of X's pain, which might be different from the undesirability of Y's pain. Of course, X's pain might be more undesirable than Y's pain because it is more painful, and then the principle of equal consideration would give greater weight to the relief of X's pain. Again, even where the pains are equal, other factors might be relevant, especially if others are affected. If there has been an earthquake we might give priority to the relief of a doctor's pain so she can treat other victims. But the doctor's pain itself counts only once, and with no added weighting. The principle of equal consideration of interests acts like a pair of scales, weighing interests impartially. True scales favour the side where the interest is stronger or where several interests combine to outweigh a smaller number of similar interests; but they take no account of whose interests they are weighing.

From this point of view race is irrelevant to the consideration of interests; for all that counts are the interests themselves. To give less consideration to a specified amount of pain because that pain was experienced by a black would be to make an arbitrary distinction. Why pick on race? Why not on whether a person was born in a leap year? Or whether there is more than one vowel in her surname? All these characteristics are equally irrelevant to the undesirability of pain from the universal point of view. Hence the principle of equal consideration of interests shows straightforwardly why the most blatant forms of racism, like that of the Nazis, are wrong. For the Nazis were concerned only for the welfare of members of the 'Aryan' race, and the sufferings of Jews, Gypsies and Slavs were of no concern to them.

The principle of equal consideration of interests is sometimes thought to be a purely formal principle, lacking in substance and too weak to exclude any inegalitarian practice. We have already seen, however, that it does exclude racism and sexism, at least in their most blatant forms. If we look at the impact of the principle on the imaginary hierarchical society based on intelligence tests we can see that it is strong enough to provide a basis for rejecting this more sophisticated form of inegalitarianism too.

The principle of equal consideration of interests prohibits making our readiness to consider the interests of others depend on their abilities or other characteristics, apart from the characteristic of having interests. It is true that we cannot know where equal consideration of interests will lead us until we know what interests people have, and this may vary according to their abilities or other characteristics. Consideration of the interests of mathematically gifted children may lead us to teach them advanced mathematics at an early age, which for different children might be entirely pointless or positively harmful. But the basic element, the taking into account of the person's interests, whatever they may be, must apply to everyone, irrespective of race, sex or scores on an intelligence test. Enslaving those who score below a certain line on an intelligence test would not – barring extraordinary and implausible beliefs about human nature – be compatible with equal consideration.

Intelligence has nothing to do with many important interests that humans have, like the interest in avoiding pain, in developing one's abilities, in satisfying basic needs for food and shelter, in enjoying friendly and loving relations with others, and in being free to pursue one's projects without unnecessary interference from others. Slavery prevents the slaves from satisfying these interests as they would want to; and the benefits it confers on the slaveowners are hardly comparable in importance to the harm it does to the slaves.

So the principle of equal consideration of interests is strong enough to rule out an intelligence-based slave society as well as cruder forms of racism and sexism. It looks as if it may be a defensible form of the principle that all humans are equal, a form which we can use in discussing more controversial issues about equality. Before we go on to these topics, however, it will be useful to say a little more about the nature of the principle.

Equal consideration of interests is a minimal principle of equality in the sense that it does not dictate equal treatment. Take a relatively straightforward example of an interest, the interest in having physical pain relieved. Imagine that after an earthquake I come across two victims, one with a crushed leg, in agony, and one with a gashed thigh, in slight pain. I have only two shots of morphine left. Equal treatment would suggest that I give one to each injured person, but one shot would not do much to relieve the pain of the person with the crushed leg. She would still be in much more pain than the other victim, and even after I have given her one shot, giving her the second shot would bring greater relief than giving a shot to the person in slight pain. Hence equal consideration of interests in this situation leads to what some may consider an inegalitarian result: two shots of morphine for one person, and none for the other.

There is a still more controversial inegalitarian implication of the principle of equal consideration of interests. In the case above, although equal consideration of interests leads to unequal treatment, this unequal treatment is an attempt to produce a more egalitarian result. By giving the double dose to the more seriously injured person, we bring about a situation in which there is less difference in the degree of suffering felt by the two victims than there would be if we gave one dose to each. Instead of ending up with one person in considerable pain and one in no pain, we end up with two people in slight pain. This is in line with the principle of declining marginal utility, a principle well-known to economists, which states that for a given individual, a set amount of something is more useful when the individual has little of it than when he has a lot. If I am struggling to survive on 200 grammes of rice a day, and you provide me with an extra fifty grammes per day, you have improved my position significantly; but if I already have a kilo of rice per day, I probably couldn't care less about the extra fifty grammes. When marginal utility is taken into account the principle of equal consideration of interests inclines us towards an equal distribution of income, and to that extent the egalitarian will endorse its conclusions. What is likely to trouble the egalitarian about the principle of equal consideration of interests is that there are circumstances in which the principle of declining marginal utility does not hold or is overridden by countervailing factors.

We can vary the example of the earthquake victims to illustrate this. Let us say, again, that there are two victims, one more severely injured than the other, but this time we shall say that the more severely injured victim, A, has lost a leg and is in danger of losing a toe from her remaining leg; while the less severely injured victim, B, has an injury to her leg, but the limb can be saved. We have medical supplies for only one person. If we use them on the more severely injured victim the most we can do is save her toe, whereas if we use them on the less severely injured victim we can save her leg. In other words, we assume that the situation is: without medical treatment, A loses a leg and a toe, while B loses only a leg; if we give the treatment to A, A loses a leg and B loses a leg; if we give the treatment to B, A loses a leg and a toe, while B loses nothing.

Assuming that it is worse to lose a leg than it is to lose a toe (even when that toe is on one's sole remaining foot) the principle of declining marginal utility does not hold in this situation. We will do more to further the interests, impartially considered, of those affected by our actions if we use our limited resources on the less seriously injured victim than on the more seriously injured one. Therefore this is what the principle of equal consideration of interests leads us to do. Thus equal consideration of interests can, in special cases, widen rather than narrow the gap between two people at different levels of welfare. It is for this reason that the principle is a minimal principle of equality, rather than a thorough-going egalitarian principle. A more thorough-going form of egalitarianism would, however, be difficult to justify, both in general terms and in its application to special cases of the kind just described.

Minimal as it is, the principle of equal consideration of interests can seem too demanding in some cases. Can any of us really give equal consideration to the welfare of our family and the welfare of strangers? This question will be dealt with in Chapter 8, when we consider our obligations to assist those in need in poorer parts of the world. I shall try to show then that it does not force us to abandon the principle, although the principle may force us to abandon some other views we hold. Meanwhile we shall see how the principle assists us in discussing some of the controversial issues raised by demands for equality.

Equality and genetic diversity

In 1969 Arthur Jensen published a long article in the *Harvard Educational Review* entitled 'How Much Can We Boost IQ and Scholastic Achievement?' One short section of the article discussed the probable causes of the undisputed fact that – on average – American blacks do not score as well as American whites in standard IQ tests. Jensen summarized the upshot of this section as follows:

all we are left with are various lines of evidence, no one of which is definitive alone, but which, viewed altogether, make it a not unreasonable hypothesis that genetic factors are strongly implicated in the average negro–white intelligence difference. The preponderance of evidence is, in my opinion, less consistent with a strictly environmental hypothesis than with a genetic hypothesis, which, of course, does not exclude the influence of environment or its interaction with genetic factors.

This heavily qualified statement comes in the midst of a detailed review of a complex scientific subject, published in a scholarly journal. It would hardly have been surprising if it passed unnoticed by anyone but scientists working in the area of psychology or genetics. Instead it was widely reported in the popular press as an attempt to defend racism on scientific grounds. Jensen was accused of spreading racist propaganda, and likened to Hitler. His lectures were shouted down. Students demanded that he be dismissed from his university post, which was a relatively mild fate compared to other suggestions that appeared on the walls of university buildings. H. J. Eysenck and others who support Jensen's theories have received similar treatment, in Britain and Australia as well as in the USA.

The opposition to genetic explanations of alleged racial differences in intelligence is only one manifestation of a more general opposition to genetic explanations in other socially sensitive areas. It closely parallels, for instance, feminist hostility to the idea that there are biological factors behind male dominance; and it has obvious links with the intensity of feeling aroused by the new approach to the study of behaviour known as 'sociobiology'.

It would be inappropriate for me to attempt to assess the scientific merits of biological explanations of human behaviour in general, or of racial or sexual differences in particular. My concern is rather with the implications of these theories for the ideal of equality. For this purpose it is not necessary for us to establish whether the theories are right. All we have to ask is: suppose that Jensen is right. Does this mean that racism is defensible, and we have to reject the principle of equality? A similar question can be asked about the impact of theories of biological differences between the sexes. In neither case does the question assume that the theories are sound. It would be most unfortunate if our scepticism about such things led us to neglect these questions and then unexpected evidence turned up confirming the theories, with the result that a confused and unprepared public took them to have implications for the ideal of equality which they do not have.

I shall begin by considering the implications of the view that there is a difference in the average IQ of blacks and whites, and that genetic factors are responsible for at least a part of this difference. I shall then consider the impact of alleged differences in temperament and ability between the sexes.

Racial differences and racial equality

To date, almost all the discussion of alleged genetic differences in ability between the races has focused on differences in intelligence, particularly between American whites and American blacks. I shall follow this emphasis. But first a word of caution. When someone like Jensen talks of 'the average negro–white intelligence difference' what he really means is the average negro–white difference in scores on standard IQ tests. Now 'IQ' stands for 'Intelligence Quotient' but this does not mean that an IQ test really measures what we mean by 'intelligence' in ordinary contexts. Obviously there is some correlation between the two: if schoolchildren regarded by their teachers as highly intelligent did not generally score better on IQ tests than schoolchildren regarded as below normal intelligence, the tests would have to be changed – as indeed they were changed in the past. But this does not show how close the correlation is, and since our ordinary concept of intelligence is vague, there is no way of telling. Some psychologists have attempted to overcome this difficulty by simply defining 'intelligence' as 'what intelligence tests measure' but this merely introduces a new concept of 'intelligence', which is easier to measure than our ordinary notion, but may be quite different in meaning. Since 'intelligence' is a word in everyday use, to use the same word in a different sense is a sure path to confusion. What we should talk about, then, is 'the average negro–white IQ difference' since this is all that the available evidence can possibly support.

The distinction between intelligence and scores on IQ tests has led some to conclude that IQ is of no importance; this is the opposite, but equally erroneous, extreme to the view that IQ is identical with intelligence. IQ is important in our society. One's IQ is a factor in one's prospects of improving one's occupational status, income or social class. If there are genetic factors in racial differences in IQ, there will be genetic factors in racial differences in occupational status, income and social class. So if we are interested in equality we cannot ignore IQ.

When whites and blacks are given IQ tests, whites tend to get higher scores than blacks. The average white score is 100, the average black score around 85. These findings, although limited to comparisons of American blacks and whites, are not seriously disputed. What is hotly disputed is whether the difference is primarily to be explained by heredity or by environment – in other words, whether it reflects an innate difference between whites and blacks, or whether it is due to the deprived social and educational situation in which many blacks find themselves. (We should note that Jensen and others arguing for the genetic hypothesis accept that environmental factors do influence the difference in scores, although they believe this influence to be a minor one, not accounting for more than a third of the 15 point gap.)

Let us suppose that the genetic hypothesis turns out to be correct (making this supposition, as I have said, not because we believe it is correct but in order to explore its implications); what would be the implications of a genetically based difference of 10–15 points in the average IQs of whites and blacks? I believe that the implications of this supposition are less drastic than they are often supposed to be, and give no comfort to genuine racists. I have three reasons for this view.

First, the genetic hypothesis does not imply that we should reduce our efforts to overcome the environmental disadvantage which black children have in their homes and their schools. Admittedly, if the genetic hypothesis is correct, these efforts will not bring about a situation in which whites and blacks have equal IQs. Even if it were possible to eliminate all environmental disadvantages, the average white IQ would be about 10 points higher than the average black IQ. But this is no reason for accepting a gap of 15 points, or a situation in which blacks are hindered by their environment from doing as well as they can. Indeed, one could well argue for the opposite conclusion: that if IQ is important, blacks should have a superior environment in order to compensate for the position of disadvantage from which they start.

Second, the fact that the average IQ of whites is 15 points higher than that of blacks does not allow anyone to say that all whites have higher IQs than blacks – this is clearly false – or that any particular individual white has a higher IQ than a particular individual black – this will often be false. The point is that these figures are averages and say nothing about individuals. Many blacks score higher than the average white and many whites score below the average black. So whatever the cause of the difference in average IQs, it provides no justification for racial segregation in education or any other field. It remains true that individual blacks and whites must be treated as individuals, irrespective of their race.

The third reason why the genetic hypothesis gives no support for racism is the most fundamental of the three. It is simply that, as we saw earlier, the principle of equality is not based on any actual equality which all people share. I have argued that the only defensible basis for the principle of equality is equal consideration of interests, and I have also suggested that the most important human interests – like the interest in avoiding pain, in developing one's abilities, in satisfying basic needs for food and shelter, in enjoying warm personal relationships, in being free to pursue one's projects without interference, and many others – are not affected by differences in intelligence. We can be even more confident that they are not affected by differences in IQ. Thomas Jefferson, who drafted the ringing assertion of equality with which the American Declaration of Independence begins, knew this. In reply to an author who had endeavoured to refute the then common view that negroes lack intelligence, he wrote:

Be assured that no person living wishes more sincerely than I do, to see a complete refutation of the doubts I have myself entertained and expressed on the grade of understanding allotted to them by nature, and to find that they are on a par with ourselves ... but whatever be their degree of talent, it is no measure of their rights. Because Sir Isaac Newton was superior to others in understanding, he was not therefore lord of the property or person of others.

Jefferson was right. Equal status does not depend on intelligence. Racists who maintain the contrary are in peril of being forced to kneel before the next genius they encounter.

These three reasons suffice to show that claims that for genetic reasons blacks are not as good as whites at IQ tests do not provide grounds for denying the moral principle that all humans are equal. The third reason, however, has further ramifications which we shall follow up after discussing differences between the sexes.

Sexual differences and sexual equality
Recent discussions of alleged psychological differences between blacks and whites have focused on IQ. IQ has not been an issue in debates over psychological differences between females and males. On general IQ tests there are no consistent differences in the average scores of females and males. But IQ tests measure a range of different abilities, and when we break the results down according to the type of ability measured, we do find significant differences between the sexes. There is solid evidence to show that females have greater verbal ability than males. This involves not merely living up to the popular female stereotype of being more talkative, but also being better able to understand complex pieces of writing and being more creative with words. Males, on the other hand, appear to have greater mathematical ability, and also do better on tests involving what is known as 'visual–spatial' ability. An example of a task requiring visual–spatial ability is one in which the subject is asked to find a shape, say a square, which is embedded or hidden in a more complex design.

We shall discuss the significance of these relatively minor differences in intellectual abilities shortly. There is also one major non-intellectual characteristic in respect of which there is a marked difference between the sexes: aggression. Studies conducted on children in several different cultures have borne out what parents have long suspected: boys are more likely to play roughly, attack each other and fight back when attacked, than girls. Males are readier to hurt others than females; a tendency reflected in the fact that almost all violent criminals are male. It has been suggested that aggression is associated with competitiveness, and the drive to dominate others and get to the top of whatever pyramid one is a part of.

These are the major psychological differences which have been observed between females and males. What is the origin of these differences? Once again the rival explanations are environmental versus biological, nurture versus nature. Although this question of origin is important in some special contexts I shall suggest that it is often given *too* much importance by feminists who assume that the case for women's liberation rests on acceptance of the environmental side of the controversy. What is true of racial discrimination holds here too: discrimination can be shown to be wrong whatever the origin of the known psychological differences. But first let us look briefly at the rival explanations.

Anyone who has had anything to do with children will know that in all sorts of ways children learn that the sexes have different roles. Boys get trucks or guns for their birthday presents: girls get dolls or brush and comb sets. Girls are put into frilly pink dresses and told how nice they look: boys are dressed in jeans and praised for their physical strength. Children's books portray fathers going out to work while mothers clean the house and cook the dinner. It is surprising how little influence the feminist movement of the last ten years has had on all this.

Social conditioning exists, certainly, but does it explain the existence of differences between the sexes? It is, at best, an incomplete explanation. We still need to know *why* our society – and not just ours, but practically every human society – should shape children in this way. The usual feminist answer is that in earlier, simpler societies, the sexes had different roles because

women had to breast-feed their children during the long period
before weaning. This meant that the women stayed put while
the men went out to get food. As a result females evolved a more
social and emotional character, while males became tougher
and more aggressive. Because physical strength and aggression
were the ultimate forms of power in these simple societies, males
became dominant. The sex roles that exist today are, feminists
contend, an inheritance from these simpler circumstances,
an inheritance which became obsolete once technology made
it possible for the weakest person to operate a crane which
lifts fifty tons, or fire a missile which kills millions. Nor do
women have to be tied to home and children in the way they
used to be, since, except for a short period around the birth of
her children, a woman can combine motherhood and a
career.

The alternative view is that while social conditioning plays
some role in determining psychological differences between the
sexes, biological factors are also at work. The evidence for this
view is particularly strong in respect of aggression. Eleanor
Emmons Maccoby and Carol Nagy Jacklin, whose book *The
Psychology of Sex Differences* is the most thorough review of the
field yet published, give four grounds for their belief that the
greater aggression of males has a biological component: (1)
Males are more aggressive than females in all human societies in
which the difference has been studied. (2) Similar differences
are found in humans and in apes and other closely related
animals. (3) The differences are found in very young children, at
an age when there is no evidence of any social conditioning in
this direction (indeed Maccoby and Jacklin found some evidence that boys are *more* severely punished for showing aggression than girls). (4) Aggression has been shown to vary according to the level of sex hormones and females become more
aggressive if they receive male hormones.

The evidence for a biological basis of the differences in visual–spatial ability is a little more complicated, but it consists
largely of genetic studies which suggest that this ability is influenced by a recessive sex-linked gene. As a result, it is estimated,

approximately 50% of males have a genetic advantage in situations demanding visual–spatial ability, but only 25% of females have this advantage.

Evidence for and against a biological factor in the superior verbal ability of females and the superior mathematical ability of males is, at present, too weak to suggest a conclusion one way or the other.

Adopting the strategy we used before in discussing race and IQ, I shall not go further into the evidence for and against these biological explanations of differences between males and females. Instead I shall ask what the implications of the biological hypotheses would be.

The differences in the intellectual strengths and weaknesses of the sexes cannot explain more than a minute proportion of the difference in positions that males and females hold in our society. It might explain why, for example, there should be *more* males than females in professions like architecture and engineering, professions which, perhaps, require visual–spatial ability; but even in these professions, the magnitude of the differences in numbers cannot be explained by the genetic theory of visual–spatial ability. This theory suggests that half as many females are as genetically advantaged in this area as males, which would account for the lower average scores of females in tests of visual–spatial ability, but cannot account for the fact that there are not merely twice as many males as females in architecture and engineering, but at least ten times as many, and in most countries, even more. Moreover, if superior visual–spatial ability explains the male dominance of architecture and engineering, why isn't there a corresponding female dominance of professions requiring high verbal ability? It is true that there are more women journalists than engineers, and probably more women have achieved lasting fame as novelists than in any other area of life; yet female journalists and television commentators are heavily outnumbered by males, outside specifically 'women's subjects' like cookery and child care. So even if one accepts biological explanations for the patterning of these abilities, one can still argue that women do not have the same opportunities as men to make the most of the abilities they have.

What of differences in aggression? One's first reaction might be that feminists should be delighted with the evidence on this point – what better way could there be of showing the superiority of females than their greater reluctance to hurt others? But the fact that most violent criminals are male may be only one side of greater male aggression. The other side could be greater male competitiveness, ambition, and drive to achieve power. This would have different, and for feminists less welcome, implications. An American sociologist, Steven Goldberg, has built a provocatively entitled book, *The Inevitability of Patriarchy*, around the thesis that the biological basis of greater male aggression will always make it impossible to bring about a society in which women have as much political power as men. From this claim it is easy to move to the view that women should accept their inferior position in society and not strive to compete with males, or to bring up their daughters to compete with males in these respects; instead women should return to their traditional sphere of looking after the home and children. It is these conclusions which have aroused the hostility of some feminists to biological explanations of male dominance.

As in the case of race and IQ, the moral conclusions alleged to follow from the biological theories do not really follow from them at all. Similar arguments apply.

First, whatever the origin of psychological differences between the sexes, social conditioning can emphasize or soften these differences. As Maccoby and Jacklin stress, the biological bias towards, say, male visual–spatial superiority is really a greater natural readiness to learn these skills. Where women are brought up to be independent their visual–spatial ability is much higher than when they are kept at home and dependent on males. This is no doubt true of other differences as well. Hence feminists may well be right to attack the way in which we encourage girls and boys to develop in distinct directions, even if this encouragement is not itself responsible for creating psychological differences between the sexes, but only reinforces innate predispositions.

Second, whatever the origin of psychological differences between the sexes, they exist only when averages are taken, and some females are more aggressive and have better visual–spatial ability than some males. We have seen that the genetic hypothesis offered in explanation of male visual–spatial superiority itself suggests that a quarter of all females will have greater natural visual–spatial ability than half of all males. Our own observations should convince us that there are females who are also more aggressive than some males. So, biological explanations or not, we are never in a position to say: 'You're a woman, so you can't become an engineer', or 'Because you are female, you will not have the drive and ambition needed to succeed in politics.' Nor should we assume that no male can possibly have sufficient gentleness and warmth to stay at home with the children while their mother goes out to work. We must assess people as individuals, not merely lump them into 'female' and 'male' if we are to find out what they are really like; and we must keep the roles occupied by females and males flexible if people are to be able to do what they are best suited for.

The third reason is, like the previous two, parallel to the reasons I have given for believing that a biological explanation of racial differences in IQ would not justify racism. The most important human interests are no more affected by differences in aggression than they are by differences in intelligence. Less aggressive people have the same interest in avoiding pain, developing their abilities, having adequate food and shelter, enjoying good personal relationships, and so on, as more aggressive people. There is no reason why more aggressive people ought to be rewarded for their aggression with higher salaries and the ability to provide better for these interests.

Since aggression, unlike intelligence, is not generally regarded as a desirable trait, the male chauvinist is hardly likely to deny that greater aggression in itself provides no ethical justification of male supremacy. He may, however, offer it as an explanation, rather than a justification, of the fact that males hold most of the leading positions in politics, business, the universities and other areas in which people of both sexes compete for power and status. He may then go on to suggest that this shows that the status quo is merely the result of competition between males and females under conditions of equal opportunity. Hence, it is not, he may say, unfair. This suggestion raises the further ramifications of biological differences between people which, as I said at the close of our discussion of the race and IQ issue, need to be followed up in more depth.

From equality of opportunity to equality of consideration

In our society large differences in income and social status are commonly thought to be all right, so long as they were brought into being under conditions of equal opportunity. The idea is that there is no injustice in Jill earning $100,000 and Jack earning $10,000, as long as Jack had his chance to be where Jill is today. Suppose that the difference in income is due to the fact that Jill is a doctor whereas Jack is a farm worker. This would be acceptable if Jack had the same opportunity as Jill to be a doctor, and this is taken to mean that Jack was not kept out of medical school because of his race, or religion or something similar – in effect, if Jack's school results had been as good as Jill's, he would have been able to study medicine, become a doctor and earn $100,000 a year. Life, on this view, is a kind of race in which it is fitting that the winners should get the prizes, so long as all get an equal start. The equal start represents equality of opportunity and this, some say, is as far as equality should go.

To say that Jack and Jill had equal opportunities to become a doctor, because Jack would have got into medical school if his results had been as good as Jill's, is to take a superficial view of equal opportunity which will not stand up to further probing. We need to ask *why* Jack's results were not as good as Jill's. Perhaps his education up to that point had been inferior – bigger classes, less qualified teachers, inadequate resources and so on. If so he was not competing on equal terms with Jill after all.

Genuine equality of opportunity requires us to ensure that schools give the same advantages to everyone.

Making schools equal would be difficult enough, but it is the easiest of the tasks that await a thorough-going proponent of equal opportunity. Even if schools are the same, some children will be favoured by the kind of home they come from. A quiet room to study, plenty of books, and parents who encourage their child to do well at school could explain why Jill succeeds where Jack, forced to share a room with two younger brothers and put up with his father's complaints that he is wasting his time with books instead of getting out and earning his keep, does not. But how does one equalize a home? Or parents? Unless we are prepared to abandon the traditional family setting and bring up our children in communal nurseries, we can't.

This might be enough to show the inadequacy of equal opportunity as an ideal of equality, but the ultimate objection – the one which connects with our previous discussion of equality – is still to come. Even if we did rear our children communally, as on a *kibbutz* in Israel, they would inherit different abilities and character traits, including different levels of aggression and different IQs. Eliminating differences in the child's environment would not affect differences in genetic endowment. True, it might reduce the disparity between, say, IQ scores, since it is likely that, at present, social differences accentuate genetic differences; but the genetic differences would remain and on most estimates they are a major component of the existing differences in IQ. (Remember that we are now talking of *individuals*. We do not know if race affects IQ, but there is little doubt that differences in IQ between individuals of the same race are, in part, genetically determined.)

So equality of opportunity is not an attractive ideal. It rewards the lucky, who inherit those abilities that allow them to pursue interesting and lucrative careers. It penalizes the unlucky, whose genes make it very hard for them to achieve similar success.

We can now fit our earlier discussion of race and sex differences into a broader picture. Whatever the facts about the social or genetic basis of racial differences in IQ, removing social disadvantages will not suffice to bring about an equal or a just distribution of income – not an equal distribution, because those who inherit the abilities associated with high IQ will continue to earn more than those who do not; and not a just distribution because distribution according to the abilities one inherits is based on an arbitrary form of selection which has nothing to do with what people deserve or need. The same is true of visual–spatial ability and aggression, if these do lead to higher incomes or status. If, as I have argued, the basis of equality is equal consideration of interests, and the most important human interests have little or nothing to do with these factors, there is something questionable about a society in which income and social status correlate to a significant degree with them.

When we pay people high salaries for programming computers and low salaries for cleaning offices we are, in effect, paying people for having a high IQ, and this means that we are paying people for something largely determined before they are born and almost wholly determined before they reach an age at which they are responsible for their actions. From the point of view of justice and utility there is something wrong here. Both would be better served by a society which adopted the famous Marxist slogan: 'From each according to his ability, to each according to his needs.' If this could be achieved the differences between the races and sexes would lose their social significance. Only then would we have a society truly based on the principle of equal consideration of interests.

Is it realistic to aim at a society which rewards people according to their needs rather than their IQ, aggression or other inherited abilities? Don't we have to pay people more to be doctors or lawyers or university professors, to do the intellectually demanding work which is essential for our well-being?

There are difficulties in paying people according to their needs rather than their inherited abilities. If one country attempts to introduce such a scheme while others do not, the result is likely to be some kind of 'brain drain'. We can already see this, on a small scale, in the number of scientists and doctors emigrating from Britain to the United States, Canada and Australia – which is not because Britain does pay people according to need rather than inherited abilities, but because these sections of the community, though relatively well-paid by British standards, would be much better paid in some other countries. If Britain were to make a serious attempt to equalize the salaries of doctors and manual workers, there can be no doubt that the number of doctors emigrating would greatly increase. This is part of the problem of 'socialism in one country'. Marx expected the socialist revolution to be a world-wide one. When the Russian Marxists found that their revolution had not sparked off the anticipated world revolution, they had to adapt Marxist ideas to this new situation. They did so by harshly restricting freedom, including the freedom to emigrate. These restrictions still exist, in the Soviet Union and other communist states. Without them, and despite the considerable pay differentials which still exist in these nations,* there would very likely be an enormous outflow of skilled people to the capitalist nations, which reward skill more highly. But if 'socialism in one country' requires making the country an armed camp, with border guards keeping watch on the citizens within as well as the enemy without, socialism may not be worth the price.

To allow these difficulties to lead us to the conclusion that we can do nothing to improve the distribution of income that now exists in capitalist countries would, however, be too pessimistic. For one thing, the Western world now has, to a large extent, a common culture. If a trend towards a more equal distribution of income exists in some Western nations, it is very likely to spread to others, thus reducing the incentive for migration. For another, there is, in the more affluent Western nations, a good deal of scope for reducing pay differentials before the point is

* According to one observer, salary differentials in China are quite steep, in some areas steeper than in Western nations. For instance, a full professor gets almost seven times as much as a junior lecturer, whereas in Britain, Australia or the US the ratio is more like three to one. See Simon Leys, *Chinese Shadows* (New York, 1977).

reached at which people begin to think of emigrating. This is, of course, especially true of those countries, like the United States, where pay differentials are presently very great. It is here that pressure for a more equitable distribution can best be applied.

What of the problems of redistribution within a single nation? There is a popular belief that if we did not pay people a lot of money to be doctors or university professors, they would not undertake the studies required to achieve these positions. I do not know what evidence there is in support of this assumption, but it seems to me highly dubious. My own salary is considerably higher than the salaries of the people employed by the university to mow the lawns and keep the grounds clean, but if our salaries were identical I would still not want to swap positions with them – although their jobs are a lot more pleasant than some lowly-paid work. Nor do I believe that my doctor would jump at a chance to change places with his receptionist if their salaries did not differ. It is true that my doctor and I have had to study for several years to get where we are, but I at least look back on my student years as one of the most enjoyable periods of my life.

Although I do not think it is because of the money that people choose to become doctors rather than receptionists, there is one qualification to be made to the suggestion that payment should be based on need rather than ability. It must be admitted that the prospect of earning more money sometimes leads people to make greater efforts to use the abilities they have, and these greater efforts can benefit patients, customers, students, or the public as a whole. It might therefore be worth trying to reward *effort*, which would mean paying people more if they worked near the upper limits of their abilities, whatever those abilities might be. This, however, is quite different from paying people for the level of ability they happen to have, which is something they cannot themselves control. As Jeffrey Gray, a psychologist at Oxford University, has written, the evidence for genetic control of IQ suggests that to pay people differently for 'upper class' and 'lower class' jobs is 'a wasteful use of resources in the guise of "incentives" which either tempt people to do what is beyond their powers or reward them more for what they would do anyway'.

We have, up to now, been thinking of people like university professors, who are paid by the government, and doctors, whose incomes are determined either by government bodies, where there is some kind of national health service, or by the government protection given to professional associations like a medical association, which enables the profession to exclude anyone who might seek to advertise his services at a lower cost. These incomes are therefore already subject to government control, and could be altered without drastically changing the powers of government. The private business sector of the economy is a different matter. Business people who are quick to seize an opportunity will, under any private enterprise system, make more money than their rivals or, if they are employed by a large corporation, may be promoted faster. Taxation can help to redistribute some of this income, but there are limits to how effective a steeply progressive tax system can be – there almost seems to be a law to the effect that the higher the rate of tax, the greater the amount of tax avoidance.

So do we have to abolish private enterprise if we are to eliminate undeserved wealth? That suggestion raises issues too large to be discussed here; but it can be said that private enterprise has a habit of reasserting itself under the most inhospitable conditions. Communist societies still have their black markets, and if you want your plumbing fixed swiftly it can be advisable to pay a bit extra on the side. Only a radical change in human nature – a decline in acquisitive and self-centred desires – could overcome the tendency for people to find a way around any system which suppresses private enterprise. Since no such change in human nature is in sight we shall probably continue to pay most to those with inherited abilities, rather than those who have the greatest needs. To hope for something entirely different is unrealistic. On the other hand to work for wider recognition of the principle of payment according to needs and effort rather than inherited ability is both realistic and, I believe, right.

Reverse discrimination

The preceding section suggested that moving to a more egalitarian society in which differences of income are reduced is ethically desirable but likely to prove difficult. Short of bringing about general equality, we might at least attempt to ensure that where there are important differences in income, status and power, women and racial minorities should not be on the worse end in numbers disproportionate to their numbers in the community as a whole. Inequalities between whites may be no more justifiable than those between blacks and whites, or males and females, but when these inequalities coincide with an obvious difference between people like the differences between blacks and whites or males and females, they do more to produce a divided society with a sense of superiority on the one side and a sense of inferiority on the other. Racial and sexual inequality may therefore have a more divisive effect than other forms of inequality. It may also do more to create a feeling of hopelessness among the inferior group, since their sex or their race is not the product of their own actions and there is nothing they can do to change it.

How are racial and sexual equality to be achieved within an inegalitarian society? We have seen that equality of opportunity is practically unrealizable, and if it could be realized might allow innate differences in aggression or IQ unfairly to determine membership of the upper strata. One way of overcoming these obstacles is to go beyond equality of opportunity and give preferential treatment to members of disadvantaged groups. This is reverse discrimination. It may be the best hope of reducing long-standing inequalities; yet it appears to offend against the principle of equality itself. Hence it is controversial.

Reverse discrimination is most often used in education and employment. Education is a particularly important area, since it has an important influence on one's prospects of earning a high income, holding a satisfying job, and achieving power and status in the community. Moreover in the United States education has been at the centre of the dispute over reverse discrimination because of Supreme Court cases over university admission procedures involving reverse discrimination. These cases have arisen because white males were denied admission to courses although their academic records and admission test scores were better than those of some black students admitted. The universities did not deny this; they sought to justify it by explaining that they operated admission schemes intended to help disadvantaged students.

The leading case, so far as United States law is concerned, is *Regents of the University of California vs. Bakke*. Alan Bakke applied for admission to the medical school of the University of California at Davis. In an attempt to increase the number of members of minority groups who attended medical school, the university reserved 16 out of every 100 places for students belonging to a disadvantaged minority. Since these students would not have won so many places in open competition, fewer white students were admitted than there would have been without this reservation. Some white students denied places would certainly have been offered them if, scoring as they did on the admission tests, they had been black. Bakke was among these white students and on being rejected he sued the university. Let us take this case as a standard case of reverse discrimination. Is it defensible?

I shall start by putting aside one argument sometimes used to justify reverse discrimination. It is sometimes said that if, say, 16% of the population is black, and yet only 2% of doctors are black, this is sufficient evidence that, somewhere along the line, our community discriminates against blacks. (Similar arguments have been mounted in support of claims of sexual discrimination.) Our discussion of the genetics versus environment debate indicates why this argument is inconclusive. It *may* be the case that blacks are, *on average*, less gifted for the kind of study one must do to become a doctor. I am not saying that this is true, or even probable, but it cannot be ruled out at this stage. So a disproportionately small number of black doctors is not in itself proof of discrimination against blacks. (Just as the disproportionately large number of black athletes in the US Olympic

team is not in itself proof of discrimination against whites.)
There might, of course, be other evidence suggesting that the
small number of black doctors really is the result of discrimination; but this would need to be shown. In the absence of positive
evidence of discrimination against blacks, it is not possible to
justify reverse discrimination on the grounds that it merely
redresses the balance of discrimination existing in the community.

Another way of defending a decision to accept a black student
in preference to a white student who scored higher in admission
tests would be to argue that standard tests do not give an
accurate indication of ability when one student has been
severely disadvantaged. This is in line with the point made in
the last section about the impossibility of achieving equal
opportunity. Education and home background presumably
influence test scores. A student with a background of deprivation who scores 55% in an admission test may have better
prospects of graduating in minimum time than another student
who scores 70%. Adjusting test scores on this basis would not
mean admitting black students in preference to better-qualified
white students. It would reflect a decision that the disadvantaged students really were better qualified than the whites. This
is not racial discrimination.

The University of California could not attempt this defence,
for its medical school at Davis had simply reserved 16% of
places for minority students. The quota did not vary according
to the ability displayed by minority applicants. This may be in
the interests of ultimate equality, but it is undeniably racial
discrimination.

In this chapter we have seen that the only possible basis for
the claim that all humans are equal is the principle of equal
consideration of interests. That principle outlaws forms of racial
and sexual discrimination which give less weight to the interests
of those discriminated against. Could Bakke claim that in rejecting his application the medical school gave less weight to his
interests that to those of black students?

We have only to ask this question to appreciate that university admission is not normally a result of consideration of the interests of each applicant. It depends rather on matching the applicants against standards which the university draws up with certain policies in mind. Take the most straightforward case: admission rigidly governed by scores on an intelligence test. Suppose those rejected by this procedure complained that their interests had been given less consideration than the interests of applicants of higher intelligence. The university would reply that its procedure did not take the applicants' interests into account at all, and so could hardly give less consideration to the interests of one applicant than it gave to others. We could then ask the university why it used intelligence as the criterion of admission. It might say, first, that to pass the examinations required for graduation takes a high level of intelligence. There is no point in admitting students unable to pass, for they will not be able to graduate. They will waste their own time and the university's resources. Secondly, the university may say, the higher the intelligence of our graduates, the more useful they are likely to be to the community. The more intelligent our doctors, the better they will be at preventing and curing disease. Hence the more intelligent the students a medical school selects, the better value the community gets for its outlay on medical education.

This particular admission procedure is of course one-sided; a good doctor must have other qualities in addition to a degree of intelligence. It is only an example, however, and that objection is not relevant to the point I am using the example to make. This point is that no one objects to intelligence as a criterion for selection in the way that they object to race as a criterion; yet those of higher intelligence admitted under an intelligence-based scheme have no more of an intrinsic right to admission than those admitted by reverse discrimination. Higher intelligence, I have argued before, carries with it no right or justifiable claim to more of the good things our society offers. If a university admits students of higher intelligence it does so not in consideration of their greater interest in being admitted, nor in recognition of their right to be admitted, but because it favours goals which it believes will be advanced by this admission procedure. So if this same university should adopt new goals and use reverse discrimination to promote them, applicants who would have been admitted under the old procedure cannot claim that the new procedure violates their right to be admitted, or treats them with less respect than others. They had no special claim to be admitted in the first place; they were the fortunate beneficiaries of the old university policy. Now that this policy has changed others benefit, not they. If this seems unfair, it is only because we had become accustomed to the old policy.

So reverse discrimination cannot be justifiably condemned on the grounds that it violates the rights of university applicants, or treats them with less than equal consideration. There is no inherent right to admission, and equal consideration of the interests of applicants is not involved in normal admission tests. If reverse discrimination is open to objection it must be because the goals it seeks to advance are bad, or because it will not really promote these goals.

The principle of equality might be a ground for condemning the goals of a racially discriminatory admissions procedure. When universities discriminate against already disadvantaged minorities we suspect that the discrimination really does result from less concern for the interests of the minority. Almost certainly this was why universities in the American South excluded blacks until segregation was held to be unconstitutional. Here, in contrast to the reverse discrimination situation, those rejected could justifiably claim that their interests were not being weighed equally with the interests of whites who were admitted. Other explanations may have been offered, but they were surely specious.

Opponents of reverse discrimination have not objected to the goals of social equality and greater minority representation in the professions. They would be hard put to do so. Equal consideration of interests supports moves towards equality because of the principle of diminishing marginal utility, because it relieves the feeling of hopeless inferiority that can exist when members of one race or sex are always worse off than members of another race or the other sex, and because severe inequality between races means a divided community with consequent racial tension.

Within the overall goal of social equality, greater minority representation in professions like law and medicine is desirable for several reasons. Members of minority groups are more likely to work among their own people than whites, and this may help to overcome the scarcity of doctors and lawyers in poor neighbourhoods where most members of disadvantaged minorities live. They may also have a better understanding of the problems disadvantaged people face than any outsider would have. Black and female doctors and lawyers can serve as role models to other blacks and females, breaking down the unconscious mental barriers against aspiring to such positions. Finally, white male students may themselves learn more about the attitudes of blacks and women, and thus become better doctors and lawyers, if their fellow students include members of these groups.

Opponents of reverse discrimination are on stronger ground when they claim that reverse discrimination will not promote equality. As Justice Powell said, in the *Bakke* case, 'Preferential programs may only reinforce common stereotypes holding that certain groups are unable to achieve success without special protection.' To achieve real equality, it might be said, blacks and women must win their places on their merits. As long as blacks get into law school more easily than whites, black law graduates will be regarded as inferior – including those who would have got in under open competition.

There is also a long-term objection to reverse discrimination as a means to equality. In the present social climate we may be confident that race will be taken into account only to benefit disadvantaged minorities; but will this climate last? Should old-fashioned racism return, won't our approval of racial quotas now make it easier to turn them against minority groups? Can we really expect the introduction of racial distinctions to advance the goal of the elimination of racial distinctions?

These practical objections raise difficult factual issues.

Though they were referred to in the *Bakke* case, they have not been central in the American legal battles over reverse discrimination. Judges are properly reluctant to decide cases on factual grounds on which they have no special expertise. Alan Bakke won his case chiefly on the grounds that the US Civil Rights Act of 1964 provides that no person shall, on the grounds of colour, race or national origin, be excluded from any activity receiving Federal financial assistance. A bare majority of the judges held that this excluded all discrimination, benign or not. They added, however, that there would be no objection to a university including race as one among a number of factors, like athletic or artistic ability, work experience, demonstrated compassion, a history of overcoming disadvantage, or leadership potential. The court thus effectively allowed universities to choose their student body in accord with their own goals, so long as they did not use quotas.

That is now the law in the United States. From an ethical, rather than a legal, point of view the distinction between quotas and other ways of giving preference to disadvantaged groups may be less significant. The important point is that reverse discrimination, whether by quotas or some other method, is not contrary to any sound principle of equality and does not violate any rights of those excluded by it. Properly applied, it is in keeping with equal consideration of interests, in its aspirations at least. The only real doubt is whether it will work. We cannot yet tell. In the absence of more promising alternatives it seems worth a try.

Before concluding this chapter I should mention a minor instance of reverse discrimination to be found in this book. Feminists often object to the use of the pronoun 'he' to include both males and females in sentences like: 'If someone were to deny this, he would have to argue ...' Grammarians have replied that the use of the masculine in this instance is a matter of gender, rather than sex – a subtle distinction more easily observed in French or German where tables and chairs can be masculine or feminine, than in English where all males are masculine, females feminine and the rest, barring ships perhaps, neuter. Whatever its origin, however, the use of 'he' does bring to mind males rather than females, so serving to perpetuate the unconscious idea that most writing is about males. And it is surely not just a coincidence that in a male-dominated society we use the male term to include the female, rather than the other way around. I propose a simple remedy. Let us for a time use 'she' to include both females and males. It may jar at first, but we will soon get used to it – and it is much more elegant than the cumbersome 'she or he' or 'she/he' some people have adopted in a valiant effort to avoid sexism. Once 'she' is as naturally read to include the male as 'he' is now read to include the female, we can start using whichever pronoun we please. That is a piece of reverse discrimination that violates no rights, ethical or legal.

Equality for animals?

Racism and speciesism

In the previous chapter I gave reasons for believing that the fundamental principle of equality, on which the equality of all human beings rests, is the principle of equal consideration of interests. Only a basic moral principle of this kind can allow us to defend a form of equality which embraces all human beings, with all the differences that exist between them. I shall now contend that while this principle does provide an adequate basis for human equality, it provides a basis which cannot be limited to humans. In other words I shall suggest that, having accepted the principle of equality as a sound moral basis for relations with others of our own species, we are also committed to accepting it as a sound moral basis for relations with those outside our own species – the nonhuman animals.

This suggestion may at first seem bizarre. We are used to regarding the oppression of blacks and women as among the most important moral and political issues facing the world today. These are serious matters, worthy of the time and energy of any concerned person. But animals? Surely the welfare of animals is in a different category altogether, a matter for old ladies in tennis shoes to worry about. How can anyone waste their time on equality for animals when so many humans are denied real equality?

This attitude reflects a popular prejudice against taking the interests of animals seriously – a prejudice no better founded than the prejudice of white slaveowners against taking the interests of blacks seriously. It is easy for us to criticize the prejudices of our grandfathers, from which our fathers freed themselves. It is more difficult to distance ourselves from our own beliefs, so that we can dispassionately search for prejudices among them. What is needed now is a willingness to follow the arguments where they lead, without a prior assumption that the issue is not worth attending to.

The argument for extending the principle of equality beyond our own species is simple, so simple that it amounts to no more than a clear understanding of the nature of the principle of equal consideration of interests. We have seen that this principle implies that our concern for others ought not to depend on what they are like, or what abilities they possess (although precisely what this concern requires us to do may vary according to the characteristics of those affected by what we do). It is on this basis that we are able to say that the fact that some people are not members of our race does not entitle us to exploit them, and similarly the fact that some people are less intelligent than others does not mean that their interests may be disregarded. But the principle also implies that the fact that beings are not members of our species does not entitle us to exploit them, and similarly the fact that other animals are less intelligent than we are does not mean that their interests may be disregarded.

We saw in the previous chapter that many philosophers have advocated equal consideration of interests, in some form or other, as a basic moral principle. Few recognized that the principle has applications beyond our own species. One of the few who did was Jeremy Bentham, the founding father of modern utilitarianism. In a forward-looking passage, written at a time when black slaves in the British dominions were still being treated much as we now treat nonhuman animals, Bentham wrote:

The day *may* come when the rest of the animal creation may acquire those rights which never could have been withholden from them but by the hand of tyranny. The French have already discovered that the blackness of the skin is no reason why a human being should be abandoned without redress to the caprice of a tormentor. It may one day come to be recognised that the number of the legs, the villosity of the skin, or the termination of the *os sacrum*, are reasons equally insufficient for abandoning a sensitive being to the same fate. What else is it that should trace the insuperable line? Is it the faculty of reason, or perhaps the faculty of discourse? But a full-grown horse or dog is beyond comparison a more rational, as well as a more conversable animal, than an infant of a day, or a week, or even a month, old. But suppose they were otherwise, what would it avail? The question is not, Can they reason? nor Can they *talk*? but, *Can they suffer?*

In this passage Bentham points to the capacity for suffering as the vital characteristic that entitles a being to equal consideration. The capacity for suffering – or more strictly, for suffering and/or enjoyment or happiness – is not just another characteristic like the capacity for language, or for higher mathematics. Bentham is not saying that those who try to mark 'the insuperable line' that determines whether the interests of a being should be considered happen to have selected the wrong characteristic. The capacity for suffering and enjoying things is a prerequisite for having interests at all, a condition that must be satisfied before we can speak of interests in any meaningful way. It would be nonsense to say that it was not in the interests of a stone to be kicked along the road by a schoolboy. A stone does not have interests because it cannot suffer. Nothing that we can do to it could possibly make any difference to its welfare. A mouse, on the other hand, does have an interest in not being tormented, because it will suffer if it is.

If a being suffers, there can be no moral justification for refusing to take that suffering into consideration. No matter what the nature of the being, the principle of equality requires that its suffering be counted equally with the like suffering – in so far as rough comparisons can be made – of any other being. If a being is not capable of suffering, or of experiencing enjoyment or happiness, there is nothing to be taken into account. This is why the limit of sentience (using the term as a convenient, if not strictly accurate, shorthand for the capacity to suffer or experience enjoyment or happiness) is the only defensible boundary of concern for the interests of others. To mark this boundary by some characteristic like intelligence or rationality would be to mark it in an arbitrary way. Why not choose some other characteristic, like skin colour?

Racists violate the principle of equality by giving greater weight to the interests of members of their own race when there is a clash between their interests and the interests of those of another race. White racists do not accept that pain is as bad when it is felt by blacks as when it is felt by whites. Similarly those I would call 'speciesists' give greater weight to the interests of members of their own species when there is a clash between their interests and the interests of those of other species. Human speciesists do not accept that pain is as bad when it is felt by pigs or mice as when it is felt by humans.

That, then, is really the whole of the argument for extending the principle of equality to nonhuman animals; but there may be some doubts about what this equality amounts to in practice. In particular, the last sentence of the previous paragraph may prompt some people to reply: 'Surely pain felt by a mouse just is not as bad as pain felt by a human. Humans have much greater awareness of what is happening to them, and this makes their suffering worse. You can't equate the suffering of, say, a person dying slowly from cancer, and a laboratory mouse undergoing the same fate.'

I fully accept that in the case described the human cancer victim normally suffers more than the nonhuman cancer victim. This in no way undermines the extension of equal consideration of interests to nonhumans. It means, rather, that we must take care when we compare the interests of different species. In some situations a member of one species will suffer more than a member of another species. In this case we should still apply the principle of equal consideration of interests but the result of so doing is, of course, to give priority to relieving the greater suffering. A simpler case may help to make this clear.

If I give a horse a hard slap across its rump with my open hand, the horse may start, but it presumably feels little pain. Its skin is thick enough to protect it against a mere slap. If I slap a baby in the same way, however, the baby will cry and presumably does feel pain, for its skin is more sensitive. So it is worse to slap a baby than a horse, if both slaps are administered with equal force. But there must be some kind of blow – I don't know exactly what it would be, but perhaps a blow with a heavy stick – that would cause the horse as much pain as we cause a baby by slapping it with our hand. That is what I mean by 'the same amount of pain' and if we consider it wrong to inflict that much pain on a baby for no good reason then we must, unless we are speciesists, consider it equally wrong to inflict the same amount of pain on a horse for no good reason.

There are other differences between humans and animals that cause other complications. Normal adult human beings have mental capacities which will, in certain circumstances, lead them to suffer more than animals would in the same circumstances. If, for instance, we decided to perform extremely painful or lethal scientific experiments on normal adult humans, kidnapped at random from public parks for this purpose, adults who entered parks would become fearful that they would be kidnapped. The resultant terror would be a form of suffering additional to the pain of the experiment. The same experiments performed on nonhuman animals would cause less suffering since the animals would not have the anticipatory dread of being kidnapped and experimented upon. This does not mean, of course, that it would be *right* to perform the experiment on animals, but only that there is a reason, which is not speciesist, for preferring to use animals rather than normal adult humans, if the experiment is to be done at all. It should be noted, however, that this same argument gives us a reason for preferring to use human infants – orphans perhaps – or retarded humans for experiments, rather than adults, since infants and retarded humans would also have no idea of what was going to happen to them. So far as this argument is concerned nonhuman animals and infants and retarded humans are in the same category; and if we use this argument to justify experiments on nonhuman animals we have to ask ourselves whether we are also prepared to allow experiments on human infants and retarded adults. If we make a distinction between animals and these humans, how can we do it, other than on the basis of a morally indefensible preference for members of our own species?

There are many areas in which the superior mental powers of normal adult humans make a difference: anticipation, more detailed memory, greater knowledge of what is happening, and so on. These differences explain why a human dying from cancer is likely to suffer more than a mouse. It is the mental anguish which makes the human's position so much harder to bear. Yet these differences do not all point to greater suffering on the part of the normal human being. Sometimes animals may suffer *more* because of their more limited understanding. If, for instance, we are taking prisoners in wartime we can explain to them that while they must submit to capture, search, and confinement they will not otherwise be harmed and will be set free at the conclusion of hostilities. If we capture a wild animal, however, we cannot explain that we are not threatening its life. A wild animal cannot distinguish an attempt to overpower and confine from an attempt to kill; the one causes as much terror as the other.

It may be objected that comparisons of the sufferings of different species are impossible to make, and that for this reason when the interests of animals and humans clash the principle of equality gives no guidance. It is probably true that comparisons of suffering between members of different species cannot be made precisely. Nor, for that matter, can comparisons of suffering between different human beings be made precisely. Precision is not essential. As we shall see shortly, even if we were to prevent the infliction of suffering on animals only when the interests of humans will not be affected to anything like the extent that animals are affected, we would be forced to make radical changes in our treatment of animals that would involve our diet, the farming methods we use, experimental procedures in many fields of science, our approach to wildlife and to hunting, trapping and the wearing of furs, and areas of entertainment like circuses, rodeos, and zoos. As a result, a vast amount of suffering would be avoided.

So far I have said a lot about the infliction of suffering on animals, but nothing about killing them. This omission has been deliberate. The application of the principle of equality to the infliction of suffering is, in theory at least, fairly straight-forward. Pain and suffering are bad and should be prevented or minimized, irrespective of the race, sex, or species of the being that suffers. How bad a pain is depends on how intense it is and how long it lasts, but pains of the same intensity and duration are equally bad, whether felt by humans or animals. When we come to consider the value of life, we cannot say quite so confidently that a life is a life, and equally valuable, whether it is a human life or an animal life. It would not be speciesist to hold that the life of a self-aware being, capable of abstract thought, of planning for the future, of complex acts of communication, and so on, is more valuable than the life of a being without these capacities. (I am not saying whether this view is justifiable or not; only that it cannot simply be rejected as speciesist, because it is not on the basis of species itself that one life is held to be more valuable than another.) The value of life is a notoriously difficult ethical question, and we can only arrive at a reasoned conclusion about the comparative value of human and animal life after we have discussed the value of life in general. This is a topic for a separate chapter. Meanwhile there are important conclusions to be derived from the extension beyond our own species of the principle of equal consideration of interests, irres-pective of our conclusions about the value of life.

Speciesism in practice

Animals as food
For most people in modern, urbanized societies, the principal form of contact with nonhuman animals is at meal times. The use of animals for food is probably the oldest and the most widespread form of animal use. There is also a sense in which it is the most basic form of animal use, the foundation stone on which rests the belief that animals exist for our pleasure and convenience.

If animals count in their own right, our use of animals for food becomes questionable – especially when animal flesh is a luxury rather than a necessity. Eskimos living in an environment where they must kill animals for food or starve, might be justified in claiming that their interest in surviving overrides that of the animals they kill. Most of us cannot defend our diet in this way. Citizens of industrialized societies can easily obtain an adequate diet without the use of animal flesh. The overwhelming weight of medical evidence indicates that animal flesh is not necessary for good health or longevity. Nor is it an efficient way of producing food, since most of the animals consumed in industrialized societies have been fattened on grains and other foods which we could have eaten directly. When we feed these grains to animals, only about 10% of the nutritional value remains as meat for human consumption. So, with the exception of animals raised entirely on grazing land unsuitable for crops, animals are eaten neither for health, nor to increase our food supply. Their flesh is a luxury, consumed because people like its taste.

In considering the ethics of the use of animal flesh for human food in industrialized societies, we are considering a situation in which a relatively minor human interest must be balanced against the lives and welfare of the animals involved. The principle of equal consideration of interests does not allow major interests to be sacrificed for minor interests.

The case against using animals for food is at its strongest when animals are made to lead miserable lives so that their flesh can be made available to humans at the lowest possible cost. Modern forms of intensive farming apply science and technology to the attitude that animals are objects for us to use. In order to have meat on the table at a price that people can afford, our society tolerates methods of meat production that confine sentient animals in cramped, unsuitable conditions for the entire duration of their lives. Animals are treated like machines that convert fodder into flesh, and any innovation that results in a higher 'conversion ratio' is liable to be adopted. As one authority on the subject has said, 'cruelty is acknowledged only when profitability ceases'. To avoid speciesism we must stop these practices. Our custom is all the support that factory farmers need. The decision to cease giving them that support may be difficult, but it is less difficult than it would have been for a white Southerner to go against the traditions of his society and free his slaves; if we do not change our dietary habits, how can we censure those slaveholders who would not change their own way of living?

These arguments apply to animals who have been reared in factory farms – which means that we should not eat chicken, pork or veal, unless we know that the meat we are eating was not produced by factory farm methods. The same is true of eggs, unless they are specifically sold as 'free range'.

These arguments do not take us all the way to a vegetarian diet, since some animals, for instance sheep and beef cattle, still graze freely outdoors. This could change. In America cattle are often fattened in crowded feedlots, and other countries are following suit. Meanwhile, back at the research station, scientists are trying out methods of raising lambs indoors, in wire cages. As long as sheep and cattle graze outdoors, however, arguments directed against factory farming do not imply that we should cease eating meat altogether.

The lives of free-ranging animals are undoubtedly better than those of animals reared in factory farms. It is still doubtful if using them for food is compatible with equal consideration of interests. One problem is, of course, that using them as food involves killing them – but this is an issue to which, as I have said, we shall return when we have discussed the value of life in the next chapter. Apart from taking their lives there are also many other things done to animals in order to bring them cheaply to our dinner table. Castration, the separation of mother and young, the breaking up of herds, branding, transporting, and finally the moments of slaughter – all of these are likely to involve suffering and do not take the animals' interests into account. Perhaps animals could be reared on a small scale without suffering in these ways, but it does not seem economical or practical to do so on the scale required for feeding our large urban populations. In any case, the important question is not whether animal flesh *could* be produced without suffering, but whether the flesh we are considering buying *was* produced without suffering. Unless we can be confident that it was, the principle of equal consideration of interests implies that it was wrong to sacrifice important interests of the animal in order to satisfy less important interests of our own; consequently we should boycott the end result of this process.

For those of us living in cities where it is difficult to know how the animals we might eat have lived and died, this conclusion brings us very close to a vegetarian way of life. I shall consider some objections to it in the final section of this chapter.

Experimenting on animals
Perhaps the area in which speciesism can most clearly be observed is the use of animals in experiments. Here the issue stands out starkly, because experimenters often seek to justify experimenting on animals by claiming that the experiments lead us to discoveries about humans; if this is so, the experimenter must agree that human and nonhuman animals are similar in crucial respects. For instance, if forcing a rat to choose between starving to death and crossing an electrified grid to obtain food tells us anything about the reactions of humans to stress, we must assume that the rat feels stress in this kind of situation.

People sometimes think that all animal experiments serve vital medical purposes, and can be justified on the grounds that they relieve more suffering than they cause. This comfortable belief is mistaken. Drug companies test new shampoos and cosmetics they are intending to market by dripping concentrated solutions of them into the eyes of rabbits. Food additives, including artificial colourings and preservatives, are tested by what is known as the LD_{50} – a test designed to find the 'Lethal Dose', or level of consumption which will make 50% of a sample of animals die. In the process nearly all of the animals are made very sick before some finally die and others pull through. These tests are not necessary to prevent human suffering: we already have enough shampoos and food colourings. There is no need to develop new ones which might be dangerous.

Nor can all university experiments be defended on the grounds that they relieve more suffering than they inflict. Three experimenters at Princeton University kept 256 young rats without food or water until they died. They concluded that young rats under conditions of fatal thirst and starvation are much more active than normal adult rats given food and water. In a well-known series of experiments that has been going on for more than 15 years, H. F. Harlow of the Primate Research Center, Madison, Wisconsin, has been rearing monkeys under conditions of maternal deprivation and total isolation. He found that in this way he could reduce the monkeys to a state in which, when placed among normal monkeys, they sat huddled in a corner in a state of persistent depression and fear. Harlow has also produced monkey mothers so neurotic that they smash their infant's face into the floor and rub it back and forth.

In these cases, and many others like them, the benefits to humans are either non-existent or very uncertain; while the losses to members of other species are certain and real. Hence the experiments indicate a failure to give equal consideration to the interests of all beings, irrespective of species.

In the past, argument about animal experimentation has often missed this point because it has been put in absolutist terms: would the opponent of experimentation be prepared to let thousands die from a terrible disease which could be cured by experimenting on one animal? This is a purely hypothetical question, since experiments do not have such dramatic results, but so long as its hypothetical nature is clear, I think the question should be answered affirmatively – in other words, if one, or even a dozen animals had to suffer experiments in order to save thousands, I would think it right and in accordance with equal consideration of interests that they should do so. This, at any rate, is the answer a utilitarian must give. Those who believe in absolute rights might hold that it is always wrong to sacrifice one being, whether human or animal, for the benefit of another. In that case the experiment should not be carried out, whatever the consequences.

To the hypothetical question about saving thousands of people through a single experiment on an animal, opponents of speciesism can reply with a hypothetical question of their own: would experimenters be prepared to perform their experiments on orphaned humans with severe and irreversible brain damage if that were the only way to save thousands? (I say 'orphaned' in order to avoid the complication of the feelings of the human parents.) If experimenters are not prepared to use orphaned humans with severe and irreversible brain damage, their readiness to use nonhuman animals seems to discriminate on the basis of species alone, since apes, monkeys, dogs, cats and even mice and rats are more intelligent, more aware of what is happening to them, more sensitive to pain, and so on, than many brain-damaged humans barely surviving in hospital wards and other institutions. There seems to be no morally relevant characteristic that such humans have which nonhuman animals lack. Experimenters, then, show bias in favour of their own species whenever they carry out experiments on nonhuman animals for purposes that they would not think justified them in using human beings at an equal or lower level of sentience, awareness, sensitivity, and so on. If this bias were eliminated the number of experiments performed on animals would be greatly reduced.

Other forms of speciesism

I have concentrated on the use of animals as food and in research, since these are examples of large-scale, systematic speciesism. They are not, of course, the only areas in which the principle of equal consideration of interests, extended beyond the human species, has practical implications. There are many other areas which raise similar issues, including the fur trade, hunting in all its different forms, circuses, rodeos, zoos and the pet business. Since the philosophical questions raised by these issues are not very different from those raised by the use of animals as food and in research, I shall leave it to the reader to apply the appropriate ethical principles to them.

Some objections

This book is not the first occasion on which I have put forward the position for which I have argued in this chapter. On previous occasions I have encountered a variety of questions and objections, some straightforward and predictable, some more subtle and unexpected. In this final section of the chapter I shall attempt to answer the most important of these objections. I shall begin with the more straightforward ones.

How do we know that animals can feel pain?

We can never directly experience the pain of another being, whether that being is human or not. When I see my daughter fall and scrape her knee, I know that she feels pain because of the way she behaves – she cries, she tells me her knee hurts, she rubs the sore spot, and so on. I know that I myself behave in a somewhat similar – if more inhibited – way when I feel pain, and so I accept that my daughter feels something like what I feel when I scrape my knee.

The basis of my belief that animals can feel pain is similar to the basis of my belief that my daughter can feel pain. Animals in pain behave in much the same way as humans do, and their behaviour is sufficient justification for the belief that they feel pain. It is true that, with the exception of those apes who have been taught to communicate by sign language, they cannot actually say that they are feeling pain – but then when my daughter was a little younger she could not talk either. She found other ways to make her inner states apparent, however, so demonstrating that we can be sure that a being is feeling pain even if the being cannot use language.

To back up our inference from animal behaviour, we can point to the fact that the nervous systems of all vertebrates, and especially of birds and mammals, are fundamentally similar. Those parts of the human nervous system that are concerned with feeling pain are relatively old, in evolutionary terms. Unlike the cerebral cortex, which developed only after our ancestors diverged from other mammals, the basic nervous system evolved in more distant ancestors common to ourselves and the other 'higher' animals. This anatomical parallel makes it likely that the capacity of animals to feel is similar to our own.

It is significant that none of the grounds we have for believing that animals feel pain hold for plants. We cannot observe behaviour suggesting pain – sensational claims to the contrary have not been substantiated – and plants do not have a centrally organized nervous system like ours.

Animals eat each other, so why shouldn't we eat them?
This might be called the Benjamin Franklin Objection. Franklin recounts in his *Autobiography* that he was for a time a vegetarian but his abstinence from animal flesh came to an end when he was watching some friends prepare to fry a fish they had just caught. When the fish was cut open, it was found to have a smaller fish in its stomach. 'Well', Franklin said to himself, 'if you eat one another, I don't see why we may not eat you' and he proceeded to do so.

Franklin was at least honest. In telling this story, he confesses that he convinced himself of the validity of the objection only after the fish was already in the frying pan and smelling 'admirably well'; and he remarks that one of the advantages of being a 'reasonable creature' is that one can find a reason for whatever one wants to do. The replies that can be made to this objection are so obvious that Franklin's acceptance of it does testify more to his love of fried fish than his powers of reason. For a start, most animals that kill for food would not be able to survive if they did not, whereas we have no need to eat animal flesh. Next, it is odd that humans, who normally think of the behaviour of animals as 'beastly' should, when it suits them, use an argument that implies we ought to look to animals for moral guidance. The decisive point, however, is that nonhuman animals are not capable of considering the alternatives open to them or of reflecting on the ethics of their diet. Hence it is impossible to hold the animals responsible for what they do, or to judge that because of their killing they 'deserve' to be treated in a similar way. Those who read these lines, on the other hand, must consider the justifiability of their dietary habits. You cannot evade responsibility by imitating beings who are incapable of making this choice.

Sometimes people point to the fact that animals eat each other in order to make a slightly different point. This fact suggests, they think, not that animals deserve to be eaten, but rather that there is a natural law according to which the stronger prey upon the weaker, a kind of Darwinian 'survival of the fittest' in which by eating animals we are merely playing our part.

This interpretation of the objection makes two basic mistakes, one a mistake of fact and the other an error of reasoning. The factual mistake lies in the assumption that our own consumption of animals is part of the natural evolutionary process. This might be true of a few primitive cultures which still hunt for food, but it has nothing to do with the mass production of domestic animals in factory farms.

Suppose that we did hunt for our food, though, and this was part of some natural evolutionary process. There would still be an error of reasoning in the assumption that because this process is natural it is right. It is, no doubt, 'natural' for women to produce an infant every year or two from puberty to menopause, but this does not mean that it is wrong to interfere with this process. We need to know the natural laws which affect us in order to estimate the consequences of what we do; but we do not have to assume that the natural way of doing something is incapable of improvement.

Differences between humans and animals

That there is a huge gulf between humans and animals was unquestioned for most of the course of Western civilization. The basis of this assumption has been undermined by Darwin's discovery of our animal origins and the associated decline in the credibility of the story of our Divine Creation, made in the image of God with an immortal soul. Some have found it difficult to accept that the differences between us and the other animals are differences of degree rather than kind. They have searched for ways of drawing a line between humans and animals. To date these boundaries have been shortlived. For instance it used to be said that only humans used tools. Then it was observed that the Galapagos woodpecker used a cactus thorn to dig insects out of crevices in trees. Next it was suggested that even if other animals *used* tools, humans are the only *tool-making* animals. But Jane Goodall found that chimpanzees in the jungles of Tanzania chewed up leaves to make a sponge for sopping up water, and trimmed the leaves off branches to make tools for catching insects. The use of language was another boundary line – but now chimpanzees and gorillas have learnt the sign language of the deaf and dumb, and there is evidence that whales and dolphins have a complex language of their own.

If these attempts to draw the line between humans and animals had fitted the facts of the situation, they would still not carry any moral weight. That a being does not use language or make tools is hardly a reason for ignoring its suffering. Some philosophers have claimed that there is a more profound difference. They have claimed that animals cannot think or reason, and that accordingly they have no conception of themselves, no self-consciousness. They live from instant to instant, and do not see themselves as distinct entities with a past and a future. Nor do they have autonomy, the ability to choose how to live one's life. It has been suggested that autonomous, self-conscious beings are in some way much more valuable, more morally significant, than beings who live from moment to moment, without the capacity to see themselves as distinct beings with a past and a future. Accordingly the interests of autonomous, self-conscious beings ought normally to take priority over the interests of other beings.

I shall not now consider whether some nonhuman animals are self-conscious and autonomous. The reason for this omission is that I do not believe that, in the present context, much depends on this question. We are now considering only the application of the principle of equal consideration of interests. In the next chapter, when we discuss questions about the value of life, we shall see that there are reasons for holding that self-consciousness is crucial; and we shall then investigate the evidence for self-consciousness in nonhuman animals. Meanwhile the more important issue is: does the fact that a being is self-conscious entitle it to some kind of priority of consideration?

The claim that self-conscious beings are entitled to prior consideration is compatible with the principle of equal consideration of interests if it amounts to no more than the claim that something which happens to a self-conscious being can cause it to suffer more (or be happier, as the case may be) than if the being were not self-conscious. This might be because the self-conscious creature has greater awareness of what is happening, can fit the event into the overall framework of a longer time period, and so on. But this is a point I granted at the start of this chapter (pp. 52–3, above) and provided it is not carried to ludicrous extremes – like insisting that if I am self-conscious and a veal calf is not, depriving me of veal causes more suffering than depriving the calf of its freedom to walk, stretch and eat grass – it is not denied by the criticisms I made of animal experimentation and factory farming.

It would be a different matter if it were claimed that, even when a self-conscious being did not suffer *more* than a being that was merely sentient, its suffering was more *important* because it was a more valuable type of being. This introduces non-utilitarian claims of value – claims which do not derive simply from taking a universal standpoint in the manner described in the final section of Chapter 1. Since the argument for utilitarianism developed in that section was admittedly tentative, I cannot use that argument to rule out all non-utilitarian values. Nevertheless we are entitled to ask *why* self-conscious beings should be considered more valuable and in particular why the alleged greater value of a self-conscious being should result in preferring the lesser interests of a self-conscious being to the greater interests of a merely sentient being, even where the self-consciousness of the former being is not itself at stake. This last point is an important one, for we are not now considering cases in which the lives of self-conscious beings are at risk but cases in which self-conscious beings will go on living, their

faculties intact, whatever we decide. In these cases if the existence of self-consciousness does not affect the nature of the
interests under comparison, it is not clear why we should drag
self-consciousness into the discussion at all, any more than we
should drag species, race or sex into similar discussions.
Interests are interests, and ought to be given equal consideration whether they are the interests of human or nonhuman
animals, self-conscious or non-self-conscious animals.

There is another possible reply to the claim that self-
consciousness, or autonomy, or some similar characteristic, can
serve to distinguish human from nonhuman animals: recall that
there are mentally defective humans who have less claim to be
self-conscious or autonomous than many nonhuman animals. If
we use these characteristics to place a gulf between humans and
other animals, we place these unfortunate humans on the other
side of the gulf; and if the gulf is taken to mark a difference in
moral status, then these humans would have the moral status of
animals rather than humans.

This reply, which has been dubbed 'the argument from
marginal cases' (because grossly defective humans are thought
of as being at the margins of humanity) is very forceful, because
most of us find horrifying the idea of using mentally defective
humans in painful experiments, or fattening them for gourmet
dinners. But some philosophers have argued that these consequences would not really follow from the use of a characteristic
like self-consciousness or autonomy to distinguish humans from
other animals. I shall consider three of these attempts.

The first suggestion is that mental defectives who do not
possess the capacities which mark the normal human off from
other animals should nevertheless be treated as if they did
possess these capacities, since they belong to a species, members
of which normally do possess them. The suggestion is, in other
words, that we treat individuals not in accordance with their
actual qualities, but in accordance with the qualities normal for
their species.

It is interesting that this suggestion should be made in
defence of treating members of our species better than members

of another species, when it would be firmly rejected if it were used to justify treating members of our race or sex better than members of another race or sex. In the previous chapter, when discussing the impact of possible differences in IQ between blacks and whites, I made the obvious point that whatever the difference between the *average* scores for blacks and whites, some blacks score better than some whites, and so we ought to treat blacks and whites as individuals and not according to the average score for their race, whatever the explanation of that average might be. If we accept this we must reject the suggestion that when dealing with mentally defective humans we grant them the status or rights normal for their species. For what is the significance of the fact that this time the line is to be drawn around the species rather than around the race or sex? We cannot insist that beings be treated as individuals in the one case, and as members of a group in the other. Membership of a species is no more relevant in these circumstances than membership of a race or sex.

A second suggestion is that although mental defectives may not possess higher capacities than other animals, they are nonetheless human beings, and as such we have special relations with them that we do not have with other animals. As one reviewer of my book on this subject put it: 'Partiality for our own species, and within it for much smaller groupings is, like the universe, something we had better accept ... The danger in [an] attempt to eliminate partial affections is that it may remove the source of all affections.'

This argument ties morality too closely to our affections. Of course some people may have a closer relationship with the most gravely retarded human than they do with any nonhuman animal, and it would be absurd to tell them that they should not feel this way. They simply do, and as such there is nothing good or bad about it. The question is whether our moral obligations to a being should be made to depend on our feelings in this manner. Notoriously, some human beings have a closer relationship with their cat than with their neighbours. Would those who tie morality to affections accept that these people are justified in saving their cats from a fire before they save their neighbours? And even those who are prepared to answer this question affirmatively would, I trust, not want to go along with racists who could argue that because white people have more natural relationships with and greater affection towards other whites, it is all right for whites to give preference to the interests of other whites over the interests of blacks. Ethics does not demand that we eliminate personal relationships and partial affections, but it does demand that when we act we assess the moral claims of those affected by our actions independently of our feelings for them.

The third suggestion invokes the widely-used 'slippery slope' argument. The idea of this argument is that once we take one step in a certain direction we shall find ourselves on a slippery slope and shall slither further than we wished to go. In the present context the argument is used to suggest that we need a clear line to divide those beings we can experiment upon, or fatten for dinner, from those we cannot. Species membership makes a nice sharp dividing line, whereas levels of self-consciousness, autonomy or sentience do not. Once we allow that a grossly retarded human being has no higher moral status than an animal we have begun our descent down a slope, the next level of which is denying rights to social misfits, and the bottom of which is a totalitarian government disposing of anyone it does not like by classifying them as mentally defective.

The slippery slope argument is important in some contexts, but it cannot bear too much weight. If we believe that, as I have argued in this chapter, the special status we now give to humans allows us to ignore the interests of billions of sentient creatures, we should not be deterred from trying to rectify this situation by the mere possibility that the principles on which we base this attempt will be misused by evil rulers for their own ends. And it is no more than a possibility. The change I have suggested might make no difference to our treatment of humans, or it might even improve it.

In the end, no ethical line that is arbitrarily drawn can be secure. It is better to find a line that can be defended openly and honestly. When discussing euthanasia in Chapter 7 we shall see that a line drawn in the wrong place can have unfortunate results even for those placed on the higher, or human side of the line.

It is also important to remember that the aim of my argument is to elevate the status of animals rather than to lower the status of any humans. I do not wish to suggest that mentally defective humans should be force-fed with food colourings until half of them die – although this would certainly give us a more accurate indication of whether the substance was safe for humans than testing it on rabbits or dogs does. I would like our conviction that it would be wrong to treat mentally defective humans in this way to be transferred to nonhuman animals at similar levels of self-consciousness and with similar capacities for suffering. It is excessively pessimistic to refrain from trying to alter our attitudes on the grounds that we might start treating mental defectives with the same lack of concern we now have for animals, rather than give animals the greater concern that we now have for mental defectives.

Ethics and reciprocity

In the earliest surviving major work of moral philosophy in the Western tradition, Plato's *Republic*, there is to be found the following view of ethics:

> They say that to do injustice is, by nature, good; to suffer injustice, evil; but that there is more evil in the latter than good in the former. And so when men have both done and suffered injustice and have had experience of both, any who are not able to avoid the one and obtain the other, think that they had better agree among themselves to have neither; hence they begin to establish laws and mutual covenants; and that which is ordained by law is termed by them lawful and just. This, it is claimed, is the origin and nature of justice – it is a mean or compromise, between the best of all, which is to do injustice and not be punished, and the worst of all, which is to suffer injustice without the power of retaliation.

This was not Plato's own view; he put it into the mouth of Glaucon in order to allow Socrates, the hero of his dialogue, to refute it. It is a view which has never gained general acceptance, but has not died away either. Echoes of it can be found in the ethical theories of contemporary philosophers like John Rawls, Gilbert Harman and John Mackie; and it has been used, by these philosophers and others, to justify the exclusion of animals from the sphere of ethics, or at least from its core. For if the basis of ethics is that I refrain from doing nasty things to others as long as they don't do nasty things to me, I have no reason against doing nasty things to those who are incapable of appreciating my restraint and controlling their conduct towards me accordingly. Animals, by and large, are in this category. When I am surfing far out from shore and a shark attacks, my concern for animals will not help; I am as likely to be eaten as the next surfer, though he may spend every Sunday afternoon taking potshots at sharks from a boat. Since animals cannot reciprocate, they are, on this view, outside the limits of the ethical contract.

In assessing this conception of ethics we should distinguish between *explanations* of the origin of ethical judgments, and *justifications* of these judgments. The explanation of the origin of ethics in terms of a tacit contract between people for their mutual benefit is quite plausible (though not more plausible than a number of alternative accounts). But we could accept this account, as a historical explanation, without thereby committing ourselves to any views about the rightness or wrongness of the ethical system that has resulted. No matter how self-interested the origins of ethics may be, it is possible that once we have started thinking ethically we are led beyond these mundane premises. For we are capable of reasoning, and reason is not subordinate to self-interest. When we are reasoning about ethics we are using concepts that, as we saw in the first chapter of this book, take us beyond our own personal interest, or even the interest of some sectional group. According to the contract view of ethics, this universalizing process should stop at the boundaries of our community; but once the process has begun we may come to see that it would not be consistent with our other convictions to halt at that point. Just as the first mathematicians, who may have started counting in order to keep track of the number of people in their tribe, had no idea that they were taking the first steps along a path that would lead to the infinitesimal calculus, so the origin of ethics tells us nothing about where it will end.

When we turn to the question of justification we can see that contractual accounts of ethics have many problems. Clearly, such accounts exclude from the ethical sphere a lot more than nonhuman animals. Since permanent mental defectives are equally incapable of reciprocating, they must also be excluded. The same goes for infants and very young children; but the problems of the contractual view are not limited to these 'marginal cases'. The ultimate reason for entering into the ethical contract is, on this view, self-interest. Unless some additional universal element is brought in, one group of people has no reason to deal ethically with another if it is not in their interest to do so. If we take this seriously we shall have to revise our ethical judgments very drastically. For instance, the white slave traders who landed on a lonely part of the African coast and captured blacks to sell in America had no self-interested reason for treating blacks any better than they did. The blacks had no way of retaliating. If they had only been contractualists, the slave traders could have rebutted the abolitionists by explaining to them that ethics stops at the boundaries of the community, and since blacks are not part of their community they have no duties to them.

Nor is it only past practices that would be affected by taking the contractual model seriously. Though people often speak of the world today as a single community, there is no doubt that the power of people in, say, Chad, to reciprocate either good or evil that is done to them by, say, citizens of the United States is very limited. Hence it does not seem that the contract view provides for any obligations on the part of wealthy nations to poorer nations.

Most striking of all is the impact of the contract model on our attitude to future generations. 'Why should I do anything for posterity? What has posterity ever done for me?' would be the view we ought to take if only those who can reciprocate are within the bounds of ethics. There is no way in which those who will be alive in the year 2100 can do anything to make our lives better or worse. Hence if obligations only exist where there can be reciprocity, we need have no worries about problems like the disposal of nuclear waste. True, some nuclear wastes will still be deadly for a quarter of a million years; but as long as we put it in containers that will keep it away from us for 100 years, we have done all that ethics demands of us.

These examples should suffice to show that, whatever its origin, the ethics we have now does go beyond a tacit under-standing between beings capable of reciprocity, and the prospect of returning to such a basis is not appealing. Since no account of the origin of morality compels us to base our morality on reciprocity, and since no other arguments in favour of this conclusion have been offered, we should reject this view of ethics.

4

What's wrong with killing?

An oversimplified summary of the first three chapters of this book might read like this: the first chapter sets up a conception of ethics from which, in the second chapter, the principle of equal consideration of interests is derived; this principle is then used to illuminate problems about the equality of humans and, in the third chapter, applied to nonhuman animals.

Thus the principle of equal consideration of interests has been behind much of our discussion so far; but as I suggested in the previous chapter, the application of this principle when lives are at stake is less clear than when we are concerned with interests like avoiding pain and experiencing pleasure. In this chapter we shall look at some views about the value of life, and the wrongness of taking life, in order to prepare the ground for the following chapters in which we shall turn to the practical issues of killing animals, abortion and euthanasia.

Human life

People often say that life is sacred. They almost never mean what they say. They do not mean, as their words seem to imply, that life itself is sacred. If they did, killing a pig or pulling up a cabbage would be as abhorrent to them as the murder of a human being. When people say that life is sacred, it is human life they have in mind. But why should human life have special value?

In discussing the doctrine of the sanctity of human life I shall not take the term 'sanctity' in a specifically religious sense. The doctrine may well have a religious origin, as I shall suggest later in this chapter, but it is now part of a broadly secular ethic, and it is as part of this secular ethic that it is most influential today. Nor shall I take the doctrine as maintaining that it is *always* wrong to take human life, for this would imply absolute pacifism, and there are many supporters of the sanctity of human life who concede that we may kill in self-defence. We may take the doctrine of the sanctity of human life to be no more than a way of saying that human life has some very special value, a value quite distinct from the value of the lives of other living things.

The view that human life has unique value is deeply rooted in our society and is enshrined in our law. To see how far it can be taken, consider the following description of an actual case reported recently in an American medical journal:

A baby was born with Down's syndrome [also known as mongolism, a form of mental retardation], an obstruction in the intestine, and a congenital heart condition. The mother thought that the retarded infant would be impossible for her to care for and would have a destructive effect on her already shaky marriage. She therefore refused to give permission for surgery to remove the obstruction in the intestine. [Without surgery, the baby would soon die.] Thereupon a local child-welfare agency, invoking a child-abuse statute, obtained a court order directing that surgery be performed. After a complicated course of surgery and thousands of dollars worth of medical care, the infant was returned to the mother. In addition to her mental retardation, the baby's physical growth and development remained poor because of the heart condition. An enquiry eighteen months after the baby's birth revealed that the mother felt more than ever that she had been done a severe injustice.

In this case a human being was kept alive, against the wishes of her mother, and at a cost of thousands of dollars, despite the fact that she would never be able to live an independent life, or to think and talk as normal humans do. Contrast this with the casual way in which we take the lives of stray dogs, experimental monkeys and beef cattle. What justifies the difference?

In every society known to us there has been some prohibition on the taking of life. Presumably no society can survive if it allows its members to kill one another without restriction. Just who is protected, however, is a matter on which societies have differed. In many tribal societies the only serious offence is to kill an innocent member of the tribe itself – members of other tribes may be killed with impunity. In more sophisticated nation-states protection generally extends to all within the nation's territorial boundaries, although there have been cases – like slave-owning states – in which a minority was excluded. Nowadays most agree, in theory if not in practice, that, apart from special cases like self-defence, war, possibly capital punishment, and one or two other doubtful areas, it is wrong to kill human beings irrespective of their race, religion, class or nationality. The moral inadequacy of narrower principles, limiting the respect for life to a tribe, race or nation, is taken for granted; but the argument of the preceding chapter must raise doubts about whether the boundary of our species marks a more defensible limit to the protected circle.

At this point we should pause to ask what we mean by terms like 'human life' or 'human being'. These terms figure prominently in debates about, for example abortion. 'Is the fetus a human being?' is often taken as the crucial question in the abortion debate; but unless we think carefully about these terms such questions cannot be answered.

It is possible to give 'human being' a precise meaning. We can use it as equivalent to 'member of the species *homo sapiens*'. Whether a being is a member of a given species is something that can be determined scientifically, by an examination of the nature of the chromosomes in the cells of living organisms. In this sense there is no doubt that from the first moments of its existence a fetus conceived by human parents is a human being; and the same is true of the most grossly and irreparably retarded 'human vegetable'.

There is another use of the term 'human', one proposed by Joseph Fletcher, a Protestant theologian and a prolific writer on ethical issues. Fletcher has compiled a list of what he calls

'Indicators of Humanhood' which includes the following: self-awareness, self-control, a sense of the future, a sense of the past, the capacity to relate to others, concern for others, communication, and curiosity. This is the sense of the term which we have in mind when we praise someone by saying that she is 'a real human being' or shows 'truly human qualities'. In saying this we are not, of course, referring to the person's membership in the species *homo sapiens* which as a matter of biological fact is rarely in doubt; we are implying that human beings characteristically possess certain qualities, and this person possesses them to a high degree.

These two senses of 'human being' overlap but do not coincide. The fetus, the grossly retarded 'human vegetable', even the newborn infant – all are indisputably members of the species *homo sapiens*, but none are self-aware, have a sense of the future, or the capacity to relate to others. Hence the choice between the two senses can make an important difference to how we answer questions like 'Is the fetus a human being?'.

When choosing which words to use in a situation like this we should choose terms which will enable us to express our meaning clearly, and which do not prejudge the answer to substantive questions. To stipulate that we shall use 'human' in, say, the first of the two senses just described, and that therefore the fetus is a human being and abortion is immoral would not do. Nor would it be any better to choose the second sense and argue on this basis that abortion is acceptable. The morality of abortion is a substantive issue, the answer to which cannot depend on a stipulation about how we shall use words. In order to avoid begging any questions, and to make my meaning clear, I shall for the moment put aside the tricky term 'human' and substitute two different terms, corresponding to the two different senses of 'human'. For the first sense, the biological sense, I shall simply use the cumbersome but precise expression 'member of the species *homo sapiens*' while for the second sense I shall use the term 'person'.

This use of 'person' is itself, unfortunately, liable to mislead, since 'person' is often used as if it meant the same as 'human being'. Yet the terms are not equivalent; there could be a person who is not a member of our species. There could also be members of our species who are not persons. The word 'person' has its origin in the Latin term for a mask worn by an actor in classical drama. By putting on a mask the actor signified that he was acting a role. Subsequently 'person' came to mean one who plays a role in life, one who is an agent. According to the Oxford Dictionary one of the current meanings of the term is 'a self-conscious or rational being'. This sense has impeccable philosophical precedents. John Locke defines a person as 'A thinking intelligent being that has reason and reflection and can consider itself as itself, the same thinking thing, in different times and places.'

This definition makes 'person' close to what Fletcher meant by 'human', except that it selects two crucial characteristics – rationality and self-consciousness – as the core of the concept. Quite possibly Fletcher would agree that these two are central, and the others more or less follow from them. In any case, I propose to use 'person', in the sense of a rational and self-conscious being, to capture those elements of the popular sense of 'human being' which are not covered by 'member of the species *homo sapiens*'.

The value of the life of members of the species homo sapiens

With the clarification gained by our terminological interlude, and the argument of the preceding chapter to draw upon, this section can be very brief. The wrongness of inflicting pain on a being cannot depend on its species: nor can the wrongness of killing it. The biological facts upon which the boundary of our species is drawn do not have moral significance. To give preference to the life of a being simply because it is a member of our species would put us in the same position as racists who give preference to those who are members of their race.

This conclusion may seem obvious, for we have worked towards it gradually; but it differs strikingly from the prevailing attitude in our society, which as we have seen treats as sacred the lives of all members of our species. How is it that our society should have come to accept a view which bears up so poorly under critical scrutiny? A short historical digression may help to explain.

If we go back to the origins of Western civilization, to Greek or Roman times, we find that membership of *homo sapiens* was not sufficient to guarantee that one's life would be protected. There was no respect for the lives of slaves or other 'barbarians'; and even among the Greeks and Romans themselves, infants had no automatic right to life. Greeks and Romans killed deformed or weak infants by exposing them to the elements on a hilltop. Plato and Aristotle thought that the state should enforce the killing of deformed infants. The celebrated legislative codes said to have been drawn up by Lycurgus and Solon contained similar provisions. In this period an early death was clearly preferred to the prospect of a miserable existence.

Our present attitudes date from the coming of Christianity. There was a specific theological motivation for the Christian insistence on the importance of species membership: the belief that all born of human parents are immortal and destined for an eternity of bliss or for everlasting torment. With this belief, the killing of *homo sapiens* took on a fearful significance, since it consigned a being to his or her eternal fate. A second Christian doctrine which led to the same conclusion was the belief that since we are created by God we are his property, and to kill a human being is to usurp God's right to decide when we shall live and when we shall die. As Thomas Aquinas put it, taking a human life is a sin against God in the same way that killing a slave would be a sin against the master to whom the slave belonged. Nonhuman animals, on the other hand, were believed to have been placed by God under man's dominion, as recorded in the bible (*Genesis* I, 29 and IX, 1–3). Hence humans could kill nonhuman animals as they pleased, so long as they were not the property of another.

During the centuries of Christian domination of European thought the ethical attitudes based on these doctrines became part of the unquestioned moral orthodoxy of European civilization. Today the doctrines are no longer generally accepted, but the ethical attitudes to which they gave rise fit in with the deep-seated Western belief in the uniqueness and special privileges of our species, and have survived. Now that we are reassessing our specialist view of nature, however, it is also time to reassess our belief in the sanctity of the lives of members of our species.

The value of a person's life

We have broken down the doctrine of the sanctity of human life into two separate claims, one that there is special value in the life of a member of our species, and the other that there is special value in the life of a person. We have seen that the former claim cannot be defended. What of the latter? Is there special value in the life of a rational and self-conscious being, as distinct from a being that is merely sentient?

One line of argument for answering this question affirmatively runs as follows. A self-conscious being is aware of itself as a distinct entity, with a past and a future. (This, remember, was Locke's criterion for being a person.) A being aware of itself in this way will be capable of having desires about its own future. For example, a professor of philosophy may hope to write a book demonstrating the objective nature of ethics; a student may look forward to graduating; a child may want to go for a ride in an aeroplane. To take the lives of any of these people, without their consent, is to thwart their desires for the future. Killing a snail or a day-old infant does not thwart any desires of this kind, because snails and newborn infants are incapable of having such desires.

It may be said that when a person is killed we are not left with a thwarted desire in the same sense in which I have a thwarted desire when I am hiking through dry country and, pausing to ease my thirst, discover a hole in my waterbottle. In this case I have a desire which I cannot fulfil, and I feel frustration and discomfort because of the continuing and unsatisfied desire for water. When I am killed the desires I have for the future do not continue after my death, and I do not suffer from their non-fulfilment. But does this mean that preventing the fulfilment of these desires does not matter?

Classical utilitarianism, as expounded by the founding father of utilitarianism, Jeremy Bentham, and refined by later philosophers like John Stuart Mill and Henry Sidgwick, judges actions by their tendency to maximize pleasure or happiness and minimize pain or unhappiness. Terms like 'pleasure' and 'happiness' lack precision but it is clear that they refer to something that is experienced, or felt – in other words, to states of consciousness. According to classical utilitarianism, therefore, there is no direct significance in the fact that desires for the future go unfulfilled when people die. If you die instantaneously, whether you have any desires for the future makes no difference to the amount of pleasure or pain you experience. Thus for the classical utilitarian the status of 'person' is not *directly* relevant to the wrongness of killing.

Indirectly, being a person may be important for the classical utilitarian. Its importance arises in the following manner. If I am a person I have a conception of myself having a future. If I am also mortal, I will probably know that my future existence could be cut short. If I think that this is likely to happen at any moment, my present existence will be less enjoyable than if I do not think it is likely to happen for some time. If I learn that people like myself are very rarely killed, I will worry less. Hence the classical utilitarian can defend a prohibition on killing persons on the indirect ground that it will increase the happiness of people who would otherwise worry that they might be killed. I call this an *indirect* ground because it does not refer to any direct wrong done to the person killed, but rather to a consequence of it for other people. There is, of course, something odd about objecting to murder, not because of the wrong done to the victim, but because of the effect on others. One has to be a tough-minded classical utilitarian to be untroubled by this oddness. (Remember, though, that we are now only considering what is *especially* wrong about killing a *person*. The classical utilitarian can still regard killing as a wrong done to the victim, because it deprives the victim of her future happiness. This objection to murder will apply to any being likely to have a happy future, irrespective of whether the being is a person.) For

present purposes, however, the main point is that this indirect
ground does provide a reason for taking the killing of a person,
under certain conditions, more seriously than the killing of a
nonpersonal being. If a being is incapable of conceiving of itself
as existing over time, we need not take into account the possibility of it worrying about the prospect of its future existence
being cut short. It can't worry about this, for it has no conception of its own future.

I said that the indirect classical utilitarian reason for taking
the killing of a person more seriously than the killing of a
nonperson holds 'under certain conditions'. These conditions
are that the killing of the person may become known to other
persons, who derive from this knowledge a more gloomy estimate of their own chances of living to a ripe old age. It is of
course possible that a person could be killed in complete sec-
recy, so that no one else knew a murder had been committed.
Then this classical utilitarian reason against killing would not
apply.

That is, I think, the gist of what the classical utilitarian would
say about the distinction between killing a person and killing
some other type of being. There is, however, another version of
utilitarianism which gives more weight to the distinction. This
other version of utilitarianism judges actions, not by their tendency to maximize pleasure or minimize pain, but by the extent
to which they accord with the preferences of any beings affected
by the action or its consequences. This version of utilitarianism
is sometimes known as 'economic utilitarianism' because it is
the form of utilitarianism used by economists working in the
area known as 'welfare economics'; but a more accurate name
would be 'preference utilitarianism'. It is preference utilitarianism, rather than classical utilitarianism, that we reach by
universalizing our own interests in the manner described
in the opening chapter of this book – if, that is, we make the
plausible move of taking a person's interests to be what, on
balance and after reflection on all the relevant facts, a person
prefers.

According to preference utilitarianism, an action contrary to the preference of any being is, unless this preference is outweighed by contrary preferences, wrong. Killing a person who prefers to continue living is therefore wrong, other things being equal. That the victims are not around after the act to lament the fact that their preferences have been disregarded is irrelevant.

For preference utilitarians, taking the life of a person will normally be worse than taking the life of some other being, since a being which cannot see itself as an entity with a future cannot have a preference about its own future existence. This is not to deny that such a being might struggle against a situation in which its life is in danger, as a fish struggles to get free of the barbed hook in its mouth; but this indicates no more than a preference for the cessation of a state of affairs that is perceived as painful or threatening. Struggle against danger and pain does not suggest that the fish is capable of preferring its own future existence to non-existence. The behaviour of a fish on a hook suggests a reason for not killing fish by that method, but does not suggest a preference utilitarian reason against killing fish by a humane method.

Does a person have a right to life?

Although preference utilitarianism does provide a direct reason for not killing people, some may find the reason – even when coupled with the important indirect reasons which any form of utilitarianism will take into account – not sufficiently stringent. Even for preference utilitarianism, the wrong done to the person killed is merely one factor to be taken into account, and the preference of the victim could sometimes be outweighed by the preferences of others. Some say that the prohibition on killing people is more absolute than this kind of utilitarian calculation implies. Our lives, we feel, are things to which we have a *right*, and rights are not to be traded off against the preferences or pleasures of others.

I am not convinced that the notion of a moral right is a helpful or meaningful one, except when it is used as a shorthand way of referring to more fundamental moral considerations.

Nevertheless, since the idea that we have a 'right to life' is a popular one, it is worth asking whether there are grounds for attributing rights to life to persons, as distinct from other living beings.

Michael Tooley, a contemporary American philosopher, has argued that the only beings who have a right to life are those who can conceive of themselves as distinct entities existing over time – in other words, persons, as we have used the term. His argument is based on the claim that there is a conceptual connection between the desires a being is capable of having, and the rights which the being can be said to have. As Tooley puts it:

> The basic intuition is that a right is something that can be violated and that, in general, to violate an individual's right to something is to frustrate the corresponding desire. Suppose, for example, that you own a car. Then I am under a prima facie obligation not to take it from you. However, the obligation is not unconditional: it depends in part upon the existence of a corresponding desire in you. If you do not care whether I take your car, then I generally do not violate your right by doing so.

Tooley admits that it is difficult to formulate the connections between rights and desires precisely, because there are problem cases like people who are asleep or temporarily unconscious. He does not want to say that such people have no rights because they have, at that moment, no desires. Nevertheless, Tooley holds, the possession of a right must in some way be linked with the capacity to have the relevant desires, if not the actual desires themselves.

The next step is to apply this view about rights to the case of the right to life. To put the matter as simply as possible – more simply than Tooley himself does and no doubt *too* simply – if the right to life is the right to continue existing as a distinct entity, then the desire relevant to possessing a right to life is the desire to continue existing as a distinct entity. But only a being which is capable of conceiving itself as a distinct entity existing over time – that is, only a person – could have this desire. Therefore only a person could have a right to life.

This argument is incomplete. The connection between

having a right and having a capacity to desire whatever is the subject of the right should be clarified and defended. Nevertheless it seems plausible that the capacity to envisage one's own future should be a necessary condition of possessing a serious right to life. In any case I know of no better argument in defence of this alleged right than Tooley's.

People and respect for autonomy

To this point our discussion of the wrongness of killing people has focused on their capacity to envisage their future and have desires related to it. Another implication of being a person may also be relevant to the wrongness of killing. There is a strand of ethical thought, associated with Kant but including many modern writers who are not Kantians, according to which respect for autonomy is a basic moral principle. By 'autonomy' is meant the capacity to choose, to make and act on one's own decisions. Rational and self-conscious beings presumably have this ability, whereas beings who cannot consider the alternatives open to them are not capable of choosing in the required sense and hence cannot be autonomous. In particular, only a being who can grasp the difference between dying and continuing to live can autonomously choose to live. Hence killing a person who does not choose to die fails to respect that person's autonomy; and as the choice of living or dying is about the most fundamental choice anyone can make, the choice on which all other choices depend, killing a person who does not choose to die is the gravest possible violation of that person's autonomy.

Not everyone agrees that respect for autonomy is a basic moral principle, or a valid moral principle at all. Utilitarians do not respect autonomy for its own sake, although they might give great weight to a person's desire to go on living, either in a preference utilitarian way, or as evidence that the person's life was on the whole a happy one. But if we are preference utilitarians we must allow that a desire to go on living can be outweighed by other desires, and if we are classical utilitarians we must recognize that people may be utterly mistaken in their expectations of happiness. So a utilitarian, in objecting to the killing of a person, cannot place the same stress on autonomy as one who takes respect for autonomy as an independent moral principle. The classical utilitarian might have to accept that in some cases it would be right to kill a person who does not choose to die on the grounds that the person will otherwise lead a miserable life. We shall discuss actual cases which raise this issue shortly, in the chapter on euthanasia.

It may be helpful here to summarize our conclusions about the value of a person's life. We have seen that there are four possible reasons for holding that a person's life has some distinctive value over and above the life of a merely sentient being: the classical utilitarian concern with the effects of the killing on others; the preference utilitarian concern with the frustration of the victim's desires and plans for the future; the argument that the capacity to have desires about one's future is a necessary condition of a right to life; and respect for autonomy. Although a classical utilitarian would accept only the first, indirect, reason, and no utilitarian would accept more than the first two reasons, none of the four can be rejected out of hand. We shall therefore bear all four in mind when we turn to practical issues involving killing.

Before we do turn to practical questions about killing, however, we have still to consider claims about the value of life which are based neither on membership of our species, nor on being a person.

Conscious life

There are many beings who are conscious and capable of experiencing pleasure and pain, but are not rational and self-conscious and so not persons. Many nonhuman animals almost certainly fall into this category; so must newborn infants and some mental defectives. Exactly which of these lack self-consciousness is something we shall consider in the next chapters. If Tooley is right, those beings that do lack self-consciousness cannot be said to have a right to life, in the full sense of 'right'. Still, for other reasons, it might be wrong to kill them. In the present section we shall ask if the life of a being that is conscious but not self-conscious has value, and if so, how its value compares with the value of a person's life.

Should we value conscious life?

The most obvious reason for valuing the life of a being capable of experiencing pleasure or pain is the pleasure it can experience. If we value our own pleasures – like the pleasures of eating, of sex, of running at full speed and of swimming on a hot day – then the universal aspect of ethical judgments requires us to extend our positive evaluation of our own experience of these pleasures to the similar experiences of all who can experience them. But a being cannot experience pleasure if it is dead. Thus the fact that a being will experience pleasure in the future is a reason for saying that it would be wrong to kill it. Of course, a similar argument about pain points in the opposite direction, and it is only when we believe that the pleasure a being is likely to experience outweighs the pain it is likely to suffer, that this argument counts against killing. So what this amounts to is that we should not cut short a pleasant life.

This seems simple enough: We value pleasure, killing those who lead pleasant lives eliminates the pleasure they would otherwise experience, therefore such killing is wrong. But stating the argument in this way conceals something which, once noticed, makes the issue anything but simple. There are two ways of reducing the amount of pleasure in the world: one is to eliminate pleasures from the lives of those leading pleasant lives; the other is to eliminate those leading pleasant lives. The former leaves behind beings who experience less pleasure than they otherwise would have. The latter does not. This means that we cannot move automatically from a preference for a pleasant life rather than an unpleasant one, to a preference for a pleasant life rather than no life at all. For, it might be objected, being killed does not make us worse off; it makes us cease to exist. Once we have ceased to exist, we shall not miss the pleasure we would have experienced.

Perhaps this seems sophistical – an instance of the ability of academic philosophers to find distinctions without significance.

Well, then, consider the opposite case: a case not of reducing pleasure, but of increasing it. There are two ways of increasing the amount of pleasure in the world: one is to increase the pleasure of those who now exist; the other is to increase the number of those who will lead pleasant lives. If killing those leading pleasant lives is bad because of the loss of pleasure, then it would seem to be good to increase the number of those leading pleasant lives. We could do this by having more children, provided we could reasonably expect their lives to be pleasant, or by rearing large numbers of animals under conditions which would ensure that their lives would be pleasant. But would it really be good to create more pleasure by creating more pleased beings?

There seem to be two possible approaches to these perplexing issues. The first approach is simply to accept that it is good to increase the amount of pleasure in the world by increasing the number of pleasant lives, and bad to reduce the amount of pleasure in the world by reducing the number of pleasant lives. This approach has the advantage of being straightforward and clearly consistent, but it requires us to hold that if we could increase the number of beings leading pleasant lives without making others worse off, it would be good to do so. To see whether you are troubled by this conclusion, it may be helpful to consider a specific case. Imagine that a couple are trying to decide whether to have children. Suppose that so far as their own happiness is concerned, the advantages and disadvantages balance out. Children will interfere with their careers at a crucial stage of their professional lives, and they will have to give up their favourite recreation, cross-country skiing, for a few years at least. On the other hand they know that, like most parents, they will get joy and fulfilment from having children and watching them develop. Suppose that if others will be affected, the good and bad effects will cancel each other out. Finally, suppose that since the couple could provide their children with a good start in life, it is probable that their children will lead pleasant lives. Should the couple count the likely future pleasure of their children as a significant reason for having children? I doubt that many couples would, but if we accept this first approach, they should.

I shall call this approach the 'total' view since on this view we are concerned to increase the total amount of pleasure (and reduce the total amount of pain) and are indifferent whether this is done by increasing the pleasure of existing beings, or increasing the number of beings who exist.

The second approach is to count only beings who already exist, prior to the decision we are taking, or at least will exist independently of that decision. We can call this the 'prior existence' view. It denies that there is value in increasing pleasure by creating additional beings. The prior existence view is more in harmony with the intuitive judgment most people have (I think) that couples are under no moral obligation to have children whenever the children are likely to lead pleasant lives and no one else is adversely affected. But how do we square it with our intuitions about the reverse case, when a couple are considering having a child who, perhaps because it will inherit a genetic defect, would lead a thoroughly miserable life and die before its second birthday? We would think it wrong for a couple knowingly to conceive such a child; but if the pleasure a possible child will experience is not a reason *for* bringing it into the world, why is the pain a possible child will experience a reason *against* bringing it into the world? The prior existence view must either hold that there is nothing wrong with bringing a miserable being into the world, or explain the asymmetry between cases of possible children who are likely to have pleasant lives, and possible children who are likely to have miserable lives. Denying that it is bad knowingly to bring a miserable child into the world is hardly likely to appeal to those who adopted the prior existence view in the first place because it seemed more in harmony with our intuitive judgments than the total view; but a convincing explanation of the asymmetry is not easy to find. Perhaps the best one can say – and it is not very good – is that there is nothing *directly* wrong in conceiving a child who will be miserable, but once such a child exists, since its life can contain nothing but misery, we would reduce the amount of pain in the world by an act of euthanasia. But euthanasia is a more harrowing process for the parents and others involved than non-conception. Hence we have an indirect reason for not con-ceiving a child bound to have a miserable existence.

So is it wrong to cut short a pleasant life? We can hold that it is, on either the total view or the prior existence view, but our answers commit us to different things in each case. We can only take the prior existence approach if we accept that it is not wrong to bring a miserable being into existence – or else offer an explanation for why this should be wrong, and yet it not be wrong to fail to bring into existence a being whose life will be pleasant. Alternatively we can take the total approach, but then we must accept that it is also good to create more beings whose lives will be pleasant – and this has some odd practical implica-tions. Some of these implications we have already seen. Others will become evident in the next chapter.

Comparing the value of different lives

If we can give an affirmative – albeit somewhat shaky – answer to the question whether the life of a being that is conscious but not self-conscious has some value, can we also compare the value of different lives, at different levels of consciousness or self-consciousness? We are not, of course, going to attempt to assign numerical values to the lives of different beings, or even to produce an ordered list. The best that we could hope for is some idea of the principles which, when supplemented with the appropriate detailed information about the lives of different beings, might serve as the basis for such a list. But the most fundamental issue is whether we can accept the idea of ordering the value of different lives at all.

Some say that it is anthropocentric, even speciesist, to order the value of different lives in a hierarchical manner. If we do so we shall, inevitably, be placing ourselves at the top and other beings closer to us in proportion to the resemblance between them and ourselves. Instead we should recognize that from the points of view of the different beings themselves, each life is of equal value. It may be true that a person's life may include the study of philosophy while a mouse's life cannot; but the pleasures of a mouse's life are all that the mouse has, and can be presumed to mean as much to the mouse as the pleasures of a person's life mean to the person. We cannot say that the one is more or less valuable than the other.

Is it speciesist to judge that the life of a normal adult member of our species is more valuable than the life of a normal adult mouse? It would be possible to defend such a judgment only if we can find some neutral ground, some impartial standpoint from which we can make the comparison.

The difficulty of finding neutral ground is a very real practical difficulty, but I am not convinced that it presents an insoluble theoretical problem. I would frame the question we need to ask in the following manner. Imagine that I have the peculiar property of being able to turn myself into an animal, so that like Puck in *A Midsummer-Night's Dream* 'Sometimes a horse I'll be, sometimes a hound'. And suppose that when I am a horse, I really am a horse, with all and only the mental experiences of a horse, and when I am a human being I have all and only the mental experiences of a human being. Now let us make the additional supposition that I can enter a third state in which I remember exactly what it was like to be a horse and exactly what it was like to be a human being. What would this third state be like? In some respects – the degree of self-awareness and rationality involved, for instance – it might be more like a human existence than an equine one, but it would not be a human existence in every respect. In this third state, then, I could compare horse-existence with human-existence. Suppose that I were offered the opportunity of another life, and given the choice of life as a horse or as a human being, the lives in question being in each case about as good as horse or human lives can reasonably be expected to be on this planet. I would then be deciding, in effect, between the value of the life of a horse (to the horse) and the value of the life of a human (to the human).

Undoubtedly this scenario requires us to suppose a lot of things that could never happen, and some things that strain our imagination. The coherence of an existence in which one is neither a horse nor a human, but remembers what it was like to be both, might be questioned. Nevertheless I think I can make some sense of the idea of choosing from this position; and I am fairly confident that from this position, some forms of life would be seen as preferable to others.

If it is true that we can make sense of the choice between existence as a mouse and existence as a human, then – whichever way the choice would go – we can make sense of the idea that the life of one kind of animal possesses greater value than the life of another; and if this is so, then the claim that the life of every being has equal value is on very weak ground. We cannot defend this claim by saying that every being's life is all-important *for it*, since we have now accepted a comparison which takes a more objective – or at least intersubjective – stance and thus goes beyond the value of the life of a being considered solely from the point of view of that being.

So it would not necessarily be speciesist to rank the value of different lives in some hierarchical ordering. *How* we should go about doing this is another question, and I have nothing better to offer than the imaginative reconstruction of what it would be like to be a different kind of being. Some comparisons may be too difficult. We may have to say that we have not the slightest idea whether it would be better to be a fish or a snake; but then, we do not very often find ourselves forced to choose between killing a fish or a snake. Other comparisons might not be so difficult. In general it does seem that the more highly developed the conscious life of the being, the greater the degree of self-awareness and rationality, the more one would prefer that kind of life, if one were choosing between it and a being at a lower level of awareness. Perhaps that is the best that we can hope to say about this issue.

Non-conscious life

Up to now we have been considering the wrongness of taking life that is self-conscious, or at least conscious. For the sake of completeness we should also look briefly at the claim that it is always wrong to take life, other things being equal, because life itself has value, whether conscious or not.

The name most often associated with the view that all life has value is Albert Schweitzer. His ethic of 'reverence for life' is often praised, but less frequently explained or defended. The need for some explanation and defence may be indicated by the following quotation from Schweitzer's *Civilization and Ethics*. It is one of the few passages in which he attempts to argue in support of the ethical position with which his name is so often associated:

True philosophy must commence with the most immediate and comprehensive facts of consciousness. And this may be formulated as follows: 'I am life which wills to live, and I exist in the midst of life which wills to live' . . . Just as in my own will-to-live there is a yearning for more life, and for that mysterious exaltation of the will which is called pleasure, and terror in face of annihilation and that injury to the will-to-live which is called pain; so the same obtains in all the will-to-live around me, equally whether it can express itself to my comprehension or whether it remains unvoiced.

Ethics thus consists in this, that I experience the necessity of practising the same reverence for life toward all will-to-live, as toward my own. Therein I have already the needed fundamental principle of morality. It is *good* to maintain and cherish life; it is *evil* to destroy and to check life . . . A man is really ethical only when he obeys the constraint laid on him to help all life which he is able to succour, and when he goes out of his way to avoid injuring anything living. He does not ask how far this or that life deserves sympathy as valuable in itself, nor how far it is capable of feeling. To him life as such is sacred. He shatters no ice crystal that sparkles in the sun, tears no leaf from its tree, breaks off no flower, and is careful not to crush any insect as he walks. If he works by lamplight on a summer evening he prefers to keep the window shut and to breathe stifling air, rather than to see insect after insect fall on his table with singed and sinking wings.

It is not clear how we should interpret Schweitzer's position. The reference to the ice crystal is especially puzzling, for an ice crystal is not alive at all. Putting this aside, however, we must still ask whether by a 'will-to-live' Schweitzer means a conscious desire that exists, though it 'remains unvoiced' or something that is not merely unvoiced, but also unconscious and unfelt.

Can we understand the phrase 'will-to-live' in a sense which does not imply a conscious desire to live? We often talk about plants 'seeking' water or light 'so that' they can survive, but is this anything more than a metaphor? And once we admit that the 'will-to-live' of a plant is not a conscious will, is it still obvious that we ought to respect this 'will'? If a weed growing in my garden has no experiences at all, do I do anything wrong when I pull it out?

Not surprisingly, given the breadth of its coverage, the ethic of reverence for life cannot be absolute in its prohibitions. Schweitzer himself accepts the taking of one form of life to preserve another. His life as a doctor in Africa makes no sense except on the assumption that the lives of the human beings he was saving are more valuable than the lives of the germs and parasites he was destroying in their bodies, not to mention the plants and probably animals that those humans would kill and eat after Schweitzer had cured them. So, in practice, Schweitzer accepted a hierarchy of value with some forms of life taking precedence over others.

The idea of a hierarchy of value leaves open the possibility that when I weed my vegetable garden, the life of each weed I destroy has some value, though a value overridden by my own needs; but is there really any intrinsic value at all in the life of a weed? Suppose that we apply the test of imagining living the life of the weed I am about to pull out of my garden. I then have to imagine living a life with no conscious experiences at all. Such a life is a complete blank; I would not in the least regret the shortening of this subjectively barren form of existence. This test suggests, therefore, that the life of a being that has no conscious experiences is of no intrinsic value.

5

Taking life: animals

In the preceding chapter we examined some general principles about the value of life. In this and the following two chapters we shall draw from that discussion some conclusions about three cases of killing which have been the subject of heated debate: abortion, euthanasia and killing animals. Of these three the question of killing animals has probably aroused the least controversy; nevertheless, for reasons which will become clear later, it is impossible to defend a position on abortion and euthanasia without taking some view about the killing of nonhuman animals. So we shall look at that question first.

Can a nonhuman animal be a person?

We have seen that there are reasons for holding that the killing of a person is more seriously wrong than the killing of a being which is not a person. This is true whether we accept preference utilitarianism, Tooley's argument about the right to life, or the principle of respect for autonomy. Even a classical utilitarian would say that there may be indirect reasons why it is worse to kill a person. So in discussing the wrongness of killing nonhuman animals it is important to ask if any of them are persons.

It sounds odd to call an animal a person. This oddness may be no more than a symptom of our habit of keeping our own species sharply separated from others. In any case, we can avoid the linguistic oddness by rephrasing the question in accordance with our definition of 'person'. What we are really asking is whether any nonhuman animals are rational and self-conscious beings, aware of themselves as distinct entities with a past and a future.

Are animals self-conscious? Evidence that some animals, at least, are self-conscious has been provided by recent efforts to teach American Sign Language to apes. The ancient dream of teaching our language to another species was realized when two American scientists, Allen and Beatrice Gardner, guessed that the failure of previous attempts to teach chimpanzees to talk was due to the chimpanzees' lacking, not the intelligence required for using language, but the vocal equipment needed to reproduce the sounds of human language. The Gardners therefore decided to treat a young chimpanzee as if she were a human baby without vocal chords. They communicated with her, and with each other when in her presence, by using American Sign Language, a language widely used by deaf and dumb people.

The technique was a striking success. The chimpanzee, whom they called 'Washoe', now understands about 350 different signs, and is able to use correctly about 150 of them. She puts signs together to form simple sentences. As for self-consciousness, Washoe does not hesitate, when shown her own image in a mirror and asked 'Who is that?' to reply: 'Me, Washoe.' She also uses signs expressing future intentions.

Suppose that on the basis of such evidence we accept that Washoe and other chimpanzees (and more recently, gorillas) who have now been taught to use sign language are self-conscious. Are they exceptional among all the nonhuman animals in this respect, precisely because they can use language? Or is it merely that language enables these animals to demonstrate to us a characteristic which they, and other animals, possessed all along?

Some philosophers have argued that for a being to think it must be able to formulate its thoughts in words. Stuart Hampshire, for example, has written:

The difference here between a human being and an animal lies in the possibility of the human being expressing his intention and putting into words his intention to do so-and-so, for his own benefit or for the benefit of others. The difference is not merely that an animal in fact has no means of communicating, or of recording for itself, its intention, with the effect that no one can ever know what the intention was. It is a stronger difference, which is more correctly expressed as the senselessness of attributing intentions to an animal which has not the means to reflect upon, and to announce to itself or to others, its own future behaviour ... It would be senseless to attribute to an animal a memory that distinguished the order of events in the past, and it would be senseless to attribute to it an expectation of an order of events in the future. It does not have the concepts of order, or any concepts at all.

If Hampshire is right, no being without language can be a person. This applies, presumably, to young humans as well as to animals. Only those animals who can use a language could be persons. Apart from chimpanzees and gorillas who have been taught to use sign language, the other most likely group would be whales and dolphins, for there is some evidence that their buzzes and squeaks constitute a sophisticated form of communication which may, one day, be recognized as a language. With these few exceptions, however, the claim that language is necessary for reflective thought consigns the nonhuman animals to the level of conscious, but not self-aware, existence. But is this claim sound? I do not believe that it is. Hampshire's defence of it contains more assertion than argument, and in this respect he is representative of others who have advanced the same view.

There is nothing altogether inconceivable about a being possessing the capacity for conceptual thought without having a language and there are instances of animal behaviour which are difficult to explain except under the assumption that the animals are thinking conceptually. In one experiment, for instance, chimpanzees were trained to select the middle object from a row of objects. Even when the objects were not spaced regularly, the chimpanzees could pick out the middle object from a row of up to 11 objects. The most natural way to explain this is to say that the apes had grasped the concept of the 'middle object'. Many three- and four-year-old children, though accomplished language users, cannot perform this task.

Nor is it only in laboratory experiments that the behaviour of animals points to the conclusion that they possess both memory of the past and expectations about the future, and that their behaviour is intentional. Consider Jane Goodall's description of how a young wild chimpanzee she had named 'Figan' secured for itself one of the bananas which Goodall, to bring the animals closer to her observation post, had hidden in a tree:

One day, sometime after the group had been fed, Figan spotted a banana that had been overlooked – but Goliath [an adult male ranking above Figan in the group's hierarchy] was resting directly underneath it. After no more than a quick glance from the fruit to Goliath, Figan moved away and sat on the other side of the tent so that he could no longer see the fruit. Fifteen minutes later, when Goliath got up and left, Figan without a moment's hesitation went over and collected the banana. Quite obviously he had sized up the whole situation: if he had climbed for the fruit earlier, Goliath would almost certainly have snatched it away. If he had remained close to the banana, he would probably have looked at it from time to time. Chimps are very quick to notice and interpret the eye movements of their fellows, and Goliath would possibly, therefore, have seen the fruit himself. And so Figan had not only refrained from instantly gratifying his desire but had also gone away so that he could not 'give the game away' by looking at the banana.

Goodall's description of this episode does, of course, attribute to Figan a complex set of intentions, including the intention to avoid 'giving the game away' and the intention to obtain the banana after Goliath's departure. It also attributes to Figan an 'expectation of an order of events in the future', namely the expectation that Goliath would move away, that the banana would still be there, and that he, Figan, would then go and get it. Yet there seems nothing at all 'senseless' about these attributions, despite the fact that Figan cannot put his intentions or expectations into words. If an animal can devise a careful plan for obtaining a banana, not now but at some future time, and can take precautions against his own propensity to give away the object of the plan, that animal must be aware of itself as a distinct entity, existing over time.

Killing nonhuman persons

Some nonhuman animals are persons, as we have defined the term. To judge the significance of this we must set it in the context of our earlier discussion, in which I argued that the only defensible version of the doctrine of the sancitity of human life was what we might call the 'doctrine of the sanctity of personal life'. I suggested that if human life does have special value, it has it in so far as most human beings are persons. But if some nonhuman animals are persons too, there must be the same value in the lives of those animals. Whether we base the special value of the lives of human persons on preferential utilitarianism, a right to life deriving from their capacity to desire to go on living, or respect for autonomy, these arguments must apply to nonhuman persons as well. Only the indirect utilitarian reason for not killing persons – the fear that such acts are likely to arouse in other persons – applies less readily to nonhuman persons since nonhumans are less likely than humans to learn about killings that take place at a distance from them. But then, this reason does not apply to all killings of human persons either, since it is possible to kill in such a way that no one learns that a person has been killed.

Hence we should reject the doctrine that places the lives of members of our species above the lives of members of other species. Some members of other species are persons: some members of our own species are not. No objective assessment can give greater value to the lives of members of our species who are not persons than to the lives of members of other species who are. On the contrary, as we have seen there are strong arguments for placing the lives of persons above the lives of nonpersons. So it seems that killing, say, a chimpanzee is worse than the killing of a gravely defective human who is not a person.

At present the killing of a chimpanzee is not regarded as a serious matter. Large numbers of chimpanzees are used in scientific research. Because chimpanzees are difficult to breed in captivity, the corporations which supply these animals capture

them in African jungles. The standard method is to shoot a
female with an infant by her side. The infant is then captured
and shipped to Europe and the United States. Jane Goodall has
estimated that for every infant that reaches its destination alive,
six chimpanzees die.

Chimpanzees may be the clearest case of nonhuman persons,
but there are almost certainly others. Systematic observation of
whales and dolphins is only just beginning, but it is quite
possible that these large-brained mammals will turn out to be
rational and self-conscious. Today the whaling industry slaughters tens of thousands of whales annually, despite the avail-
ability of substitutes for every whale product. Will this industry
come to be thought of in the way we now think of the slave trade?
The same question may be asked of tuna fishermen who drown
hundreds of thousands of dolphins in their nets because they
prefer to net tuna by a method which does not allow dolphins in
the area to escape. Closer to home, many of those who live with
dogs and cats are convinced that these animals are self-
conscious and rational. Such observations may be 'unscientific',
but in the absence of better studies they should not be ignored.
An estimated 500,000 dogs and 200,000 cats die each year in
laboratories in the United States, and smaller but still sizeable
numbers in every 'developed' nation. And if dogs and cats
qualify as persons, the mammals we use for food cannot be far
behind. We think of dogs as being more like people than pigs;
but pigs are highly intelligent animals and if we kept pigs as pets
and reared dogs for food, we would probably reverse our order
of preference. Are we turning persons into bacon?

Admittedly, all this is speculative. It is notoriously difficult to
establish when another being is self-conscious. But if it is wrong
to kill a person when we can avoid doing so, and there is real
doubt about whether a being we are thinking of killing is a
person, we should give that being the benefit of the doubt.
The rule here is the same as that among deer hunters which
says: if you see something moving in the bushes and are not
sure if it is a deer or a hunter, don't shoot! (We may think the
hunters shouldn't shoot in either case, but the rule is a sound

one within the ethical framework hunters use.) On these grounds, a great deal of the killing of nonhuman animals must be condemned.

Killing other animals

Arguments against killing based on the capacity of a being to see itself as an individual existing over time apply to some nonhuman animals, but there are others which, though presumably conscious, cannot plausibly be said to be persons. Fish and reptiles would be in this category; perhaps also birds, including the much consumed chicken. The rightness or wrongness of killing these animals seems to rest on classical utilitarian considerations.

Before we discuss the utilitarian approach to killing itself, we should remind ourselves that a wide variety of indirect reasons will figure in the utilitarian's calculations. Many modes of killing used on animals do not inflict an instantaneous death, so there is pain in the process of dying. There is also the effect of the death of one animal on its mate or other members of its social group. There are many species of birds in which the bond between male and female lasts for a lifetime. The death of one member of this pair probably causes a sense of loss and sorrow for the survivor. The mother–child relationship may also be a source of misery if either is killed. In some species the death of one animal may be felt by a larger group – as the behaviour of wolves and elephants suggests. All these factors would lead the utilitarian to oppose a lot of killing. They would not, however, be reasons for opposing killing when it is painless and no other animals are affected.

The utilitarian verdict on killing which is painless and causes no loss to others is more complicated, because it depends on how we choose between the two versions of utilitarianism outlined in the previous chapter. If we take what I called the 'prior existence' view, we shall hold that it is wrong to kill any being whose life is likely to contain, or can be brought to contain, more pleasure than pain. This view implies that it is normally wrong to kill animals for food, since usually we could bring it about

that these animals had a few pleasant months or even years
before they died – and the brief pleasure we get from eating them
would not outweigh this.

The other version of utilitarianism – the 'total' view – on the
other hand, can lead to a different outcome which has been used
to justify meat-eating.

Leslie Stephen once wrote:

Of all the arguments for Vegetarianism none is so weak as the argument from humanity. The pig has a stronger interest than anyone in the
demand for bacon. If all the world were Jewish, there would be no pigs
at all.

Stephen views animals as if they were replaceable, and with this
those who accept the total view must agree. The total version of
utilitarianism regards sentient beings as valuable only in so far
as they make possible the existence of intrinsically valuable
experiences like pleasure. It is as if sentient beings are receptacles of something valuable and it does not matter if a receptacle
gets broken, so long as there is another receptacle to which the
contents can be transferred without any getting spilt. Although
meat-eaters are responsible for the death of the animal they eat
and for the loss of pleasure experienced by that animal, they are
also responsible for the creation of more animals, since if no one
ate meat there would be no more animals bred for fattening. The
loss meat-eaters inflict on one animal is thus balanced, on the
total view, by the benefit they confer on the next. We may call
this 'the replaceability argument'.

The first point to note about the replaceability argument is
that even if it is valid when the animals in question have a
pleasant life it would not justify eating the flesh of animals
reared in modern 'factory farms', where the animals are so
crowded together and restricted in their movements that their
lives seem to be more of a burden than a benefit to them.

A second point is that if it is good to create life, then presumably it is good for there to be as many people on our planet as it
can possibly hold. With the possible exception of arid areas
suitable only for pasture, the surface of our globe can support
more people if we grow plant foods than if we raise animals.

These two points greatly weaken the replaceability argument as a defence of meat-eating, but they do not go to the heart of the matter. Are sentient beings really replaceable?

Henry Salt, a nineteenth-century English vegetarian and author of a book called *Animals' Rights* thought that the argument rested on a simple philosophical error:

> The fallacy lies in the confusion of thought which attempts to compare existence with non-existence. A person who is already in existence may feel that he would rather have lived than not, but he must first have the *terra firma* of existence to argue from: the moment he begins to argue as if from the abyss of the non-existent, he talks nonsense, by predicating good or evil, happiness or unhappiness, of that of which we can predicate nothing.

When I wrote *Animal Liberation* I accepted Salt's view. I thought that it was absurd to talk as if one conferred a favour on a being by bringing it into existence, since at the time one confers this favour, there is no being at all. But now I am less confident. After all, as we saw in the preceding chapter, we do seem to do something bad if we knowingly bring a miserable being into existence, and if this is so, it is difficult to explain why we do not do something good when we knowingly bring a happy being into existence.

If we think of a living creature – human or nonhuman – as a self-conscious individual, leading its own life and with a desire to go on living, the replaceability argument holds little appeal. It is possible that Salt is thinking of such beings, for he concludes his essay by claiming that Lucretius long ago refuted Stephen's 'vulgar sophism' in the following passage of *De Rerum Natura*:

> What loss were ours, if we had known not birth?
> Let living men to longer life aspire,
> While fond affection binds their hearts to earth:
> But who never hath tasted life's desire,
> Unborn, impersonal, can feel no dearth.

This passage supports the claim that there is a difference between killing living beings who 'to longer life aspire' and failing to create a being which, being unborn and impersonal, can feel no loss of life. But what of a being which, though alive, cannot aspire to longer life, because it lacks the conception of itself as a living being with a future? This kind of being is, in a sense, 'impersonal'. Perhaps, therefore, in killing it, one does it no personal wrong, although one does reduce the quantity of happiness in the universe. But this wrong, if it is wrong, can be counter-balanced by bringing into existence a similar being which will lead an equally happy life.

The conclusion this points to harmonizes with the distinction already made between killing those who are rational and self-conscious beings, and those who are not. Rational, self-conscious beings are individuals, leading lives of their own, not mere receptacles for containing a certain quantity of happiness. Beings that are conscious, but not self-conscious, on the other hand, can properly be regarded as receptacles for experiences of pleasure and pain, rather than as individuals leading lives of their own.

The test of universalizability supports this view. If I imagine myself in turn as a self-conscious being and a conscious but not self-conscious being, it is only in the former case that I could have a desire to live in addition to a desire for pleasurable experiences. Hence it is only in the former case that my death is not adequately compensated for by the creation of a being with similar prospects of pleasurable experiences.

To take the view that non-self-conscious beings are replace-able is not to say that their interests do not count. I hope that the third chapter of this book makes it clear that their interests do count. As long as a sentient being is conscious, it has an interest in experiencing as much pleasure and as little pain as possible. Sentience suffices to place a being within the sphere of equal consideration of interests; but it does not mean that the being has a personal interest in continuing to live. For a non-self-conscious being, death is the cessation of experiences, in much the same way that birth is the beginning of experiences. Death cannot be contrary to an interest in continued life, any more than birth could be in accordance with an interest in commenc-ing life. To this extent, with non-self-conscious life, birth and death cancel each other out; whereas with self-conscious beings the fact that once self-conscious one may desire to continue living means that death inflicts a loss for which the birth of another is insufficient compensation.

This suggests a possible compromise between the two versions of utilitarianism discussed in the preceding chapter. We might grant that the total view applies when we are dealing with beings that do not exist as individuals living their own lives. Here it is appropriate to consider only the maximization of happiness. When we switch our attention to self-conscious beings, however, there is more at stake than impersonal quantities of happiness, and we are justified in concerning ourselves first and foremost with the quality of life of people who exist now or, independently of our decisions, will exist at some future time, rather than with the creation of possible extra people.

Conclusions

If the arguments in this chapter are correct, there is no single answer to the question: 'Is it normally wrong to take the life of an animal?' The term 'animal' – even in the restricted sense of 'nonhuman animal' – covers too diverse a range of lives for one principle to apply to all of them.

Some nonhuman animals appear to be rational and self-conscious beings, conceiving themselves as distinct beings with a past and a future. When this is so, or to the best of our knowledge may be so, the case against killing is strong, as strong as the case against killing permanently defective human beings at a similar mental level. (I have in mind here the *direct* reasons against killing; the effects on relatives of the defective human will sometimes – but not always – constitute additional indirect reasons against killing the human.)

This strong case against killing can be invoked against the slaughter of apes, whales and dolphins. It might also apply to monkeys, dogs and cats, pigs, seals and bears. This list is not intended to be exhaustive; it selects species with well-developed mental faculties which we kill in very large numbers, for scientific research, for oil, for food, for fur and for sport. Our discussion has raised a very large question mark over the justifiability of these forms of killing, even if it is possible (as it usually is not) to kill painlessly and without causing suffering to other members of the animal community.

When we come to animals who, as far as we can tell, are not rational and self-conscious beings, the case against killing is weaker. When we are not dealing with beings aware of themselves as distinct entities, the wrongness of killing amounts to no more than the reduction of pleasure it involves. Where the life taken would not, on balance, have been pleasant, no direct wrong is done. Even when the animal killed would have lived pleasantly, it is at least arguable that no wrong is done if the animal killed will, as a result of the killing, be replaced by another animal living an equally pleasant life. Taking this view involves holding that a wrong done to an existing being can be made up for by a benefit conferred on an as yet non-existent being. Thus it is possible to regard non-self-conscious animals as interchangeable with each other in a way that self-conscious beings are not. This means that in some circumstances – when animals lead pleasant lives, are killed painlessly, their deaths do not cause suffering to other animals, and the killing of one animal makes possible its replacement by another who would not otherwise have lived – the killing of non-self-conscious animals may not be wrong.

One possible case would be raising chickens for their meat, not in factory farm conditions but roaming freely around a farmyard. Let us make the questionable assumption that chickens are not self-conscious. Assume also that the birds can be killed painlessly, and the survivors do not appear to be affected by the death of one of their numbers. Assume, finally, that for economic reasons we could not rear the birds if we did not eat them. Then the replaceability argument will justify killing the birds, because depriving them of the pleasures of their existence can be offset against the pleasures of chickens who do not yet exist, and will exist only if existing chickens are killed.

It is important to realize how limited this point is in its

application. It cannot justify factory farming, where animals do not have pleasant lives. Nor does it normally justify the killing of wild animals. A duck shot by a hunter (making the shaky assumption that ducks are not self-conscious) has probably had a pleasant life, but the shooting of a duck does not lead to its replacement by another. Unless the duck population is at the maximum that can be sustained by the available food supply, the killing of a duck ends a pleasant life without starting another, and is for that reason wrong on straightforward utilitarian grounds. The only exception would be if there were overriding utilitarian reasons for the killing, if, for instance, killing was the only way to obtain food. So although there are situations in which it is not wrong to kill animals, these situations are special ones, and do not cover very many of the billions of premature deaths humans inflict, year after year, on nonhumans.

6

Taking life: abortion

The problem

Few ethical issues are as bitterly fought over today as abortion, and, while the pendulum has swung back and forth, neither side has had much success in altering the opinions of its opponents. Until 1967, abortion was illegal almost everywhere except in Sweden and Denmark. Then Britain changed its law to allow abortion on broad social grounds, and this was followed in 1970 by a New York State law which amounted to virtual abortion on demand. The crest of the pro-abortion wave was reached in the 1973 decision of the United States Supreme Court which held that women have a constitutional right to an abortion in the first six months of pregnancy. But those opposed to abortion have not given up, and in the United States they gained a Congressional ruling restricting the use of Federal funds to pay for abortions. 'Right to Life' movements in Britain, Australia and other countries have been demanding similar restrictions on the use of public funds.

Abortion poses a difficult ethical issue because the development of the human being is a gradual process. If we take the fertilized egg, or zygote, immediately after conception, it is hard to get upset about its death. The zygote is a tiny sphere of cells. It could not possibly feel pain, or be aware of anything. Many zygotes fail to implant in the lining of the uterus and are flushed out of the womb without the woman noticing anything amiss. Why then should the deliberate removal of an unwanted zygote arouse concern? At the other extreme is the adult human being. To kill a human adult is murder, and is unhesitatingly and universally condemned. Yet there is no obvious sharp line which marks the zygote from the adult. Hence the problem.

I shall begin by stating the position of those opposed to abortion, which I shall refer to as the conservative position. I shall then examine some of the standard liberal responses, and show why they are inadequate. Finally I shall use our earlier discussion of the value of life to approach the issue from a broader perspective, a perspective from which many of the difficulties can be resolved.

The conservative position

The central argument against abortion, put as a formal argument, would go something like this:

First premise: It is wrong to kill an innocent human being.
Second premise: A human fetus is an innocent human being.
Conclusion: Therefore it is wrong to kill a human fetus.

The usual liberal response is to deny the second premise of this argument. So it is on whether the fetus is a human being that the issue is joined, and the dispute about abortion is often taken to be a dispute about when a human life begins.

On this issue the conservative position is difficult to shake. The conservative points to the continuum between zygote and child, and challenges the liberal to point to any stage in this gradual process which marks a morally significant dividing line. Unless there is such a line, the conservative says, we must either upgrade the status of the zygote to that of the child, or downgrade the status of the child to that of the zygote; but no one wants to allow children to be dispatched on the request of their parents, and so the only tenable position is to grant the fetus the protection we now grant the child.

Is it true that there is no morally significant dividing line between zygote and child? Those commonly suggested are: birth, viability and quickening. Let us consider these in turn.

Birth

Birth is the most visible possible dividing line, and the one that would suit liberals best. It coincides to some extent with our sympathies – we are less disturbed at the construction of a fetus we have never seen that at the death of a being we can all see, hear and cuddle. But is this enough to make birth the line which decides whether a being may or may not be killed? The conservative can plausibly reply that the fetus/baby is the same entity, whether inside or outside the womb, with the same human features (whether we can see them or not) and the same degree of awareness and capacity for feeling pain. A prematurely born infant may well be *less* developed in these respects than a fetus nearing the end of its normal term. It seems peculiar to hold that we may not kill the premature infant, but may kill the more developed fetus. The location of a being – inside or outside the womb – should not make that much difference to the wrongness of killing it.

Viability

If birth does not mark a crucial moral distinction, should we push the line back to the time at which the fetus could survive outside the womb? This overcomes one objection to taking birth as the decisive point, for it treats the viable fetus on a par with the infant, born prematurely, at the same stage of development. Viability is where the United States Supreme Court drew the line in its historic 1973 decision, *Roe v. Wade*. The Court held that the state has a legitimate interest in protecting potential life, and this interest becomes 'compelling' at viability 'because the fetus then presumably has the capability of meaningful life outside the mother's womb'. Therefore statutes prohibiting abortion after viability (except where the life or health of the mother is at stake) woud not, the Court said, be unconstitutional. But the judges who wrote the majority decision gave no indication why, for a fetus at say, six months, life outside the womb should be more 'meaningful' than life inside the womb, or why the mere capacity to exist outside the womb should make such a difference to the state's interest in protecting potential life. After all, if we talk, as the Court does, of *potential* human life, then the nonviable fetus is as much a *potential* adult human as the viable fetus. (I shall return to this issue of potentiality shortly; but it is a different issue from the conservative argument we are now discussing, which claims that the fetus *is* a human being, and not just a potential human being.)

There is another important objection to making viability the cut-off point. The point at which the fetus can survive outside the mother's body varies according to the state of medical technology. Twenty years ago it was generally accepted that a baby born more than two months premature could not survive. Now a six-month fetus – three months premature – can often be pulled through, thanks to sophisticated medical techniques. So do we say that a six-month-old fetus should not be aborted now, but could have been aborted without wrongdoing twenty years ago? The same comparison can also be made, not between the present and the past, but between different places. A six-month-old fetus might have a fair chance of survival if born in a city, like London or New York, where the latest medical techniques are used, but no chance at all if born in a remote village in Chad or New Guinea. Suppose that for some reason a woman, six months pregnant, was to fly from New York to a New Guinea village and that, once she had arrived in the village, there was no way she could return quickly to a city with modern medical facilities. Are we to say that it would have been wrong for her to have an abortion before she left New York, but now that she is in the village she may go ahead? But the trip does not change the nature of the fetus, so why should it remove its claim to life?

The liberal might reply that the fact that the fetus is totally dependent on the mother for its survival means that it has no right to life independent of her wishes. In other cases, however, we do not hold that total dependence on another person means that that person may decide whether one lives or dies. A newborn baby is totally dependent on its mother, if it happens to be born in an isolated area in which there is no other lactating female, nor the means for bottle feeding. An elderly woman may

be totally dependent on her son looking after her, and a hiker
who breaks her leg five days' walk from the nearest road may die
if her companion does not bring help. We do not think that in
these situations the mother may take the life of her baby, the son
of his aged mother, or the hiker of her injured companion. So it is
not plausible to suggest that the dependence of the nonviable
fetus on its mother gives her the right to kill it; and if dependence
does not justify making viability the dividing line, it is hard to
see what does.

Quickening

If neither birth nor viability marks a morally significant distinction, there is less still to be said for a third candidate, quickening. Quickening is the time when the mother first feels the fetus
move, and in traditional Catholic theology, this was thought to
be the moment at which the fetus gained its soul. If we accepted
that view, we might think quickening important, since the soul
is, on the Christian view, what marks humans off from animals.
But the idea that the soul enters the fetus at quickening is an
outmoded piece of superstition, discarded now even by Catholic
theologians. Putting aside these religious doctrines make quickening insignificant. It is no more than the time when the fetus is
first felt to move of its own accord; but it cannot be denied that
the fetus is alive before this moment, and we do not regard the
lack of a capacity for physical motion as negating the claims of
paralysed people to go on living.

I conclude that the liberal search for a morally significant
dividing line between the newborn baby and the fetus fails. The
conservative is right to insist that the development from zygote
to infant is a thoroughly gradual process.

Some liberal arguments

Some liberals do not challenge the conservative claim that the
fetus is an innocent human being, but argue that abortion is
nonetheless permissible. I shall consider three arguments for
this view.

The consequences of restrictive laws

The first argument is that laws prohibiting abortion do not stop abortions, but merely drive them underground. Women who want to have abortions are often desperate. They will go to backyard abortionists or try folk remedies. Abortion performed by a qualified medical practitioner is as safe as any medical operation, but attempts to procure abortions by unqualified people often result in serious medical complications and sometimes death. Thus the effect of prohibiting abortion is not so much to reduce the number of abortions performed as to increase the difficulties and dangers for women with unwanted pregnancies.

This argument has been influential in gaining support for more liberal abortion laws. It was accepted by the Canadian Royal Commission on the Status of Women, which concluded that: 'A law that has more bad effects than good ones is a bad law ... As long as it exists in its present form thousands of women will break it.'

The main point to note about this argument is that it is an argument against laws prohibiting abortion, and not an argument against the view that abortion is wrong. This is an important distinction, often overlooked in the abortion debate. The present argument well illustrates the distinction, because one could quite consistently accept it and advocate that the law should allow abortion on request, while at the same time deciding oneself – if one were pregnant – or counselling another who was pregnant, that it would be wrong to have an abortion. It is a mistake to assume that the law should always enforce morality. It may be that, as alleged in the case of abortion, attempts to enforce right conduct lead to consequences no one wants, and no decrease in wrong-doing; or it may be that, as is proposed by the next argument we shall consider, there is an area of private ethics with which the law ought not to interfere.

So this first argument is an argument about abortion law, not about the ethics of abortion. Even within those limits, however, it is open to challenge, for it fails to meet the conservative claim that abortion is the deliberate killing of an innocent human being, and in the same ethical category as murder. Those who take this view of abortion will not rest content with the assertion that restrictive abortion laws do no more than drive women to backyard abortionists. They will insist that this situation can be changed, and the law properly enforced. They may also suggest measures to make pregnancy easier to accept for those women who become pregnant against their wishes. This is a perfectly reasonable response, given the initial ethical judgment against abortion, and for this reason the first argument does not succeed in avoiding the ethical issue.

Not the law's business?

The second argument is again an argument about abortion laws rather than the ethics of abortion. It uses the view that, as the report of a British government committee inquiring into laws about homosexuality and prostitution put it: 'There must remain a realm of private morality and immorality that is, in brief and crude terms, not the law's business.' This view is widely accepted among liberal thinkers, and can be traced back to John Stuart Mill's *On Liberty*. The 'one very simple principle' of this work is, in Mill's words:

That the only purpose for which power can be rightfully exercised over any member of a civilised community, against his will, is to prevent harm to others ... He cannot rightfully be compelled to do or forbear because it will be better for him to do so, because it will make him happier, because in the opinions of others, to do so would be wise or even right.

Mill's view is often and properly quoted in support of the repeal of laws that create 'victimless crimes' – like the laws prohibiting homosexual relations between consenting adults, the use of marijuana and other drugs, prostitution, gambling and so on. Abortion is often included in this list, for example by the criminologist Edwin Schur in his influential book *Crimes Without Victims*. Those who consider abortion a victimless crime say that, while everyone is entitled to hold and act on her own view about the morality of abortion, no section of the community should try to force others to adhere to its own particular view. In a pluralist society, we should tolerate others with different moral views and leave the decision to have an abortion up to the woman concerned.

The fallacy involved in numbering abortion among the victimless crimes should be obvious. The dispute about abortion is, largely, a dispute about whether or not abortion does have a 'victim'. Opponents of abortion maintain that the victim of abortion is the fetus. Those not opposed to abortion may deny that the fetus counts as a victim in any serious way. They might, for instance, say that a being cannot be a victim unless it has interests which are violated, and the fetus has no interests. But however this dispute may go, one cannot simply ignore it on the grounds that people should not attempt to force others to follow their own moral views. My view that what Hitler did to the Jews is wrong is a moral view, and if there were any prospect of a revival of Nazism I would certainly do my best to force others not to act contrary to this view. Mill's principle is defensible only if it is restricted, as Mill restricted it, to acts which do not harm others. To use the principle as a means of avoiding the difficulties of resolving the ethical dispute over abortion is to take it for granted that abortion does not harm an 'other' – which is precisely the point that needs to be proven before we can legitimately apply the principle to the case of abortion.

A feminist argument

The last of the three arguments which seek to justify abortion without denying that the fetus is an innocent human being is that a woman has a right to choose what happens to her own body. This is a relatively novel argument. It became prominent with the rise of the women's liberation movement and has been elaborated by American philosophers sympathetic to feminism, most notably Judith Jarvis Thomson. Thomson presents her case by means of an ingenious analogy. Imagine, she says, that you wake up one morning and find yourself in a hospital bed, somehow connected to an unconscious man in an adjacent bed. You are told that this man is a famous violinist with kidney disease. The only way he can survive is for his circulatory system to be plugged into the system of someone else with the same blood type, and you are the only person whose blood is suitable. So a society of music lovers kidnapped you, had the connecting operation performed, and there you are. Since you are now in a reputable hospital you could, if you choose, order a doctor to disconnect you from the violinist; but the violinist will then certainly die. On the other hand, if you remain connected for only (only?) nine months, the violinist will have recovered and you can be unplugged without endangering him.

Thompson believes that if you found yourself in this unexpected predicament you would not be morally required to allow the violinist to use your kidneys for nine months. It might be generous or kind of you to do so, but to say this is, Thomson claims, quite different from saying that you would be doing wrong if you did not do it.

Note that Thomson's conclusion does not depend on denying that the violinist is an innocent human being, with the same right to life as other innocent human beings. On the contrary, Thomson affirms that the violinist does have a right to life – but to have a right to life does not, she says, entail a right to the use of another's body, even if without that use one will die.

The parallel with pregnancy, especially pregnancy due to rape should be obvious. A woman pregnant through rape finds herself, through no choice of her own, linked to a fetus in much the same way as the person is linked to the violinist. True, a pregnant woman does not normally have to spend nine months in bed, but opponents of abortion would not regard this as a sufficient justification for abortion. Giving up a newborn baby for adoption might be more difficult, psychologically, than parting from the violinist at the end of his illness; but this in itself does not seem a sufficient reason for killing the fetus. Accepting for the sake of the argument that the fetus does count as a fully-fledged human being, having an abortion has the same moral significance as unplugging oneself from the violinist. So if we agree with Thomson that it would not be wrong to unplug oneself from the violinist, we must also accept that, whatever the status of the fetus, abortion is not wrong – at least not when the pregnancy results from rape.

Thomson's argument can probably be extended beyond the cases of rape. Suppose that you found yourself connected to the violinist, not because you were kidnapped by music lovers, but because you had intended to enter the hospital to visit a sick friend, and when you got into the elevator, you carelessly pressed the wrong button, and ended up in a section of the hospital normally visited only by those who have volunteered to be connected to patients who would not otherwise survive. A team of doctors, waiting for the next volunteer, assumed you were it, jabbed you with an anaesthetic, and connected you. If Thomson's argument was sound in the kidnap case it is probably sound here too, since nine months unwillingly supporting another is a high price to pay for ignorance or carelessness. In this way the argument might apply beyond rape cases to the much larger number of women who become pregnant through ignorance, carelessness, or contraceptive failure.

But is the argument sound? The short answer is: it is sound if the particular theory of rights that lies behind it is sound; and it is unsound if that theory of rights is unsound.

The theory of rights in question can be illustrated by another of Thomson's fanciful examples: suppose I am desperately ill and the only thing that can save my life is the touch of Henry Fonda's cool hand on my fevered brow. Well, Thomson says, even though I have a right to life, this does not mean that I have a right to force Henry Fonda to come to me, or that he is under any moral obligation to fly over and save me – although it would be frightfully nice of him to do so. Thus Thomson does not accept that we are always obliged to take the best course of action, all things considered, or to do what has the best consequences. She accepts, instead, a system of rights and obligations which allows us to justify our actions independently of their consequences.

I shall say more about this conception of rights in Chapter 8. At this stage it is enough to notice that a utilitarian would reject this theory of rights, and would reject Thomson's judgment in the case of the violinist. The utilitarian would hold that, however outraged I may be at having been kidnapped, if the consequences of disconnecting myself from the violinist are, on balance, and taking into account the interests of everyone affected, worse than the consequences of remaining connected, I ought to remain connected. This does not necessarily mean that utilitarians would regard a woman who disconnected herself as wicked or deserving of blame. They might recognize that she has been placed in an extraordinarily difficult situation, one in which to do what is right involves a considerable sacrifice. They might even grant that most people in this situation would follow self-interest rather than do the right thing. Nevertheless, they would hold that to disconnect oneself is wrong.

In rejecting Thomson's theory of rights, and with it her judgment in the case of the violinist, the utilitarian would also be rejecting her argument for abortion. Thomson claimed that her argument justified abortion even if we allowed the life of the fetus to count as heavily as the life of a normal person. The utilitarian would say that it would be wrong to refuse to sustain a person's life for nine months, if that was the only way the person could survive. Therefore if the life of the fetus is given the same weight as the life of a normal person, the utilitarian would say that it would be wrong to refuse to carry the fetus for the natural term of the pregnancy.

This concludes our discussion of the usual liberal replies to the conservative argument against abortion. We have seen that liberals have failed to establish a morally significant dividing line between the newborn baby and the fetus, and – with the possible exception of Thomson's argument if her theory of rights can be defended – to justify abortion in ways which do not challenge the conservative claim that the fetus is an innocent human being. Nevertheless, it would be premature for conservatives to assume that their case against abortion is sound. It is now time to bring into this debate some more general conclusions about the value of life.

The value of fetal life

Let us go back to the beginning. The central argument against abortion from which we started was:

First premise: It is wrong to kill an innocent human being.
Second premise: A human fetus is an innocent human being.
Conclusion: Therefore it is wrong to kill a human fetus.

The first set of replies we considered accepted the first premise of this argument but objected to the second. The second set of replies rejected neither premise, but objected to drawing the conclusion from these premises (or objected to the further conclusion that abortion should be prohibited by law). None of the replies questioned the first premise of the argument. Given the widespread acceptance of the doctrine of the sanctity of human life, this is not surprising; but our critique of this doctrine in the preceding chapters indicates that this premise should be questioned.

The weakness of the first premise of the conservative argument is that it relies on our acceptance of the special status of *human* life. We have seen that 'human' is a term which straddles two distinct notions, being a member of the species *homo sapiens*, and being a person. Once the term is dissected in this way, the weakness of the conservative's first premise becomes apparent. If 'human' is taken as equivalent to 'person', the second premise of the argument, which asserts that the fetus is a human being, is clearly false; for one cannot plausibly argue that a fetus is either rational or self-conscious. If, on the other hand, 'human' is taken to mean no more than 'member of the species *homo sapiens*', then the conservative defence of the life of the fetus is based on a characteristic lacking moral significance and so the first premise is false. The point should by now be familiar: whether a being is or is not a member of our species is, in itself no more relevant to the wrongness of killing it than whether it is or is not a member of our race. The belief that mere membership of our species, irrespective of other characteristics, makes a great difference to the wrongness of killing a being is a legacy of religious doctrines which even those opposed to abortion hesitate to bring into the debate.

Recognizing this simple point transforms the abortion issue. We can now look at the fetus for what it is – the actual characteristics it possesses – and can value its life on the same scale as the lives of beings with similar characteristics who are not members of our species. It now becomes apparent that the 'Right to Life' movement is misnamed. Far from having concern for all life, or a scale of concern impartially based on the nature of the life in question, those who protest against abortion but dine regularly on the bodies of chickens, pigs and calves, show only a biased concern for the lives of members of our own species. For on any fair comparison of morally relevant characteristics, like rationality, self-consciousness, awareness, autonomy, pleasure and pain, and so on, the calf, the pig and the much derided chicken come out well ahead of the fetus at any stage of pregnancy – while if we make the comparison with a fetus of less than three months, a fish, or even a prawn would show more signs of consciousness.

My suggestion, then, is that we accord the life of a fetus no greater value than the life of a nonhuman animal at a similar level of rationality, self-consciousness, awareness, capacity to feel, etc. Since no fetus is a person, no fetus has the same claim to life as a person. Moreover it is very unlikely that fetuses of less than 18 weeks are capable of feeling anything at all, since their nervous system appears to be insufficiently developed to·function. If this is so, an abortion up to this point terminates an existence that is of no intrinsic value at all. In between 18 weeks and birth, when the fetus may be conscious, though not self-conscious, abortion does end a life of some intrinsic value, and so should not be taken lightly. But a woman's serious interests would normally override the rudimentary interests of the fetus. Indeed, even an abortion late in pregnancy for the most trivial reasons is hard to condemn in a society that slaughters far more developed forms of life for the taste of their flesh.

The comparison between the fetus and other animals leads us to one more point. Where the balance of conflicting interests does make it necessary to kill a sentient creature, it is important that the killing be done as painlessly as possible. In the case of nonhuman animals the importance of humane killing is widely accepted; oddly, in the case of abortion little attention is paid to it. This is not because abortion is known to kill the fetus swiftly and humanely. Late abortions – which are the very ones in which the fetus may be able to suffer – are often performed by injecting a salt solution into the amniotic sac which surrounds the fetus. It has been claimed that the effect of this is to cause the fetus to have convulsions and die between one and three hours later. Afterwards the dead fetus is expelled from the womb. There is still much to be learnt about the development of the capacity to feel pain in the fetus and about the effects of different methods of abortion; but if there are grounds for thinking that a method of abortion causes the fetus to suffer, that method should be avoided.

The fetus as potential life

One likely objection to the argument I have offered in the preceding section is that it takes into account only the actual characteristics of the fetus, and not its potential characteristics. On the basis of its actual characteristics, some opponents of abortion will admit, the fetus compares unfavourably with many nonhuman animals; it is when we consider its potential as a mature human being that membership of the species *homo sapiens* becomes important, and the fetus far surpasses any chicken, pig or calf.

I have not raised the question of the potential of the fetus until now in order to concentrate on the central argument against abortion; but it is true that a different argument, based on the potential of the fetus, can be mounted. Now is the time to look at this other argument. We can state it as follows:

First premise: It is wrong to kill a potential human being.
Second premise: A human fetus is a potential human being.
Conclusion: Therefore it is wrong to kill a human fetus.

The second premise of this argument is stronger than the second premise of the preceding argument. Whereas it is problematic whether a fetus actually *is* a human being – it depends on what we mean by the term – it cannot be denied that the fetus is a potential human being. This is true whether by 'human being' we mean 'member of the species *homo sapiens*' or a rational and self-conscious being, a person. The strong second premise of the new argument is, however, purchased at the cost of a weaker first premise, for the wrongness of killing a potential human being – even a potential person – is more open to challenge than the wrongness of killing an actual human being.

It is of course true that the potential rationality, self-consciousness and so on of a fetal *homo sapiens* surpasses that of a cow or pig; but it does not follow that the fetus has a stronger claim to life. In general, a potential X does not have all the rights of an X. Prince Charles is a potential King of England, but he does not now have the rights of a king. Why should a potential person have the rights of a person? This question becomes especially pertinent if we recall the grounds on which, in the previous chapter, it was suggested that the life of a person merits greater protection than the life of a being who is not a person. These reasons, from the indirect classical utilitarian concern with not arousing in others the fear that they may be next, the weight given by the preference utilitarian to a person's desires, Tooley's link between a right to life and the capacity to desire that one continue to live, and the principle of respect for autonomy – are all based on the fact that persons see themselves as distinct entities with a past and future. They do not apply to those who are not now and never have been capable of seeing themselves in this way. If these are the grounds for not killing persons, the mere potential for becoming a person does not count against killing.

It might be said that this reply misunderstands the relevance of the potential of the human fetus, and that this potential is important, not because it creates in the fetus a right or claim to life, but because anyone who kills a human fetus deprives the world of a future rational and self-conscious being. If rational and self-conscious beings are intrinsically valuable, to kill a human fetus is to deprive the world of something intrinsically valuable, and so wrong.

The chief problem with this as an argument against abortion – apart from the difficulty of establishing that rational and self-conscious beings are of intrinsic value – is that it does not stand up as a reason for objecting to all abortions, or even to all abortions where the health of the mother is not at stake; and it leads us to condemn practices other than abortion which most anti-abortionists accept. It is not a reason for objecting to all abortions because not all abortions deprive the world of a rational and self-conscious being. Suppose a woman has been planning to join a mountain-climbing expedition in June, and in January she learns that she is two months pregnant. She has no children at present, and firmly intends to have a child within a year. The pregnancy is unwanted only because it is inconveniently timed. Opponents of abortion would presumably think an abortion in these circumstances particularly outrageous, for neither the life nor the health of the mother is at stake – only the enjoyment she gets from climbing mountains. Yet if abortion is wrong only because it deprives the world of a future person, this abortion is not wrong; it does no more than delay the entry of a person into the world.

Practices which this argument against abortion does lead us to condemn are those which reduce the future human population: contraception, whether by 'artificial' or 'natural' means, and also celibacy. This argument has, in fact, all the difficulties of the 'total' form of utilitarianism, discussed in Chapter 4, and it does not provide any reason for thinking abortion worse than any other means of population control. If the world is already overpopulated, the argument provides no reason at all against abortion.

Is there any other significance in the fact that the fetus is a potential person? If there is I have no idea what it could be. In writings against abortion we often find reference to the fact that each human fetus is unique. Paul Ramsey, Professor of Religion at Princeton University, has said that modern genetics, by teaching us that the first fusion of sperm and ovum creates a 'never-to-be-repeated' informational speck, seems to lead us to the conclusion that 'all destruction of fetal life should be classified as murder'. But why should this fact lead us to this conclusion? A canine fetus is also, no doubt, genetically unique. Does this mean that it is as wrong to abort a dog as a human? When identical twins are conceived, the genetic information is repeated. Would Ramsey therefore think it permissible to abort one of a pair of identical twins? The children that my wife and I would produce if we did not use contraceptives would be genetically unique. Does the fact that it is still indeterminate precisely what genetically unique character those children would have make the use of contraceptives less evil than abortion? Why should it? And if it does could the looming prospect of successful cloning – a technique in which the cells of one individual are used to reproduce a fetus which is a genetic carbon copy of the original – diminish the seriousness of abortion? Suppose the woman who wants to go mountain climbing were able to have her abortion, take a cell from the aborted fetus and then reimplant that cell in her womb so that an exact genetic replica of the aborted fetus would develop – the only difference being that the pregnancy would now come to term six months later, and thus she could still join the expedition. Would that make the abortion acceptable? I doubt that many opponents of abortion would think so.

Abortion and infanticide

There remains one major objection to the argument I have advanced in favour of abortion. We have already seen that the strength of the conservative position lies in the difficulty liberals have in pointing to a morally significant distinction between a fetus and a newborn baby. The standard liberal position needs to be able to point to some such distinction, because liberals standardly hold that it is permissible to kill a fetus but not a baby. I have argued that the life of a fetus is of no greater value than the life of a nonhuman animal at a similar level of rationality, self-consciousness, awareness, capacity to feel, etc., and that since no fetus is a person no fetus has the same claim to life as a person. Now it must be admitted that these arguments apply to the newborn baby as much as to the fetus. A week-old baby is not a rational and self-conscious being, and there are many nonhuman animals whose rationality, self-consciousness, awareness, capacity to feel, and so on, exceed that of a human baby a week, a month, or even a year old. If the fetus does not have the same claim to life as a person, it appears that the newborn baby does not either, and the life of a newborn baby is of less value than the life of a pig, a dog, or a chimpanzee. Thus while my position on the value of fetal life may be acceptable to many, the implications of this position for the value of newborn life are at odds with the virtually unchallenged assumption that the life of a newborn baby is as sacrosanct as that of an adult. Indeed, some people seem to think that the life of a baby is *more* precious than that of an adult. Lurid tales of German soldiers bayoneting Belgian babies figured prominently in the wave of anti-German propaganda that accompanied Britain's entry into the First World War, and it seemed to be tacitly understood that this was a greater atrocity than the murder of adults would be.

I do not regard the conflict between the position I have taken and widely accepted views about the sanctity of infant life as a ground for abandoning my position. I think these widely accepted views need to be challenged. It is true that infants appeal to us because they are small and helpless, and there are no doubt very good evolutionary reasons why we should instinctively feel protective towards them. It is also true that infants cannot be combatants in wartime, and killing infants in wartime is the clearest possible case of killing civilians, which is prohibited by international convention. In general, since infants are harmless and morally incapable of committing a crime, those who kill them lack the excuses often offered for the killing of adults. None of this shows, however, that the killing of an infant is as bad as the killing of an (innocent) adult.

In thinking about this matter we should put aside feelings based on the small, helpless and – sometimes – cute appearance of human infants. To think that the lives of infants are of special value because infants are small and cute is on a par with thinking that a baby seal, with its soft white fur coat and large round eyes deserves greater protection than a whale, which lacks these attributes. Nor can the helplessness or the innocence of the infant *homo sapiens* be a ground for preferring it to the equally helpless and innocent fetal *homo sapiens*, or, for that matter, to laboratory rats who are 'innocent' in exactly the same sense as the human infant, and, in view of the experimenters' power over them, almost as helpless.

If we can put aside these emotionally moving but strictly irrelevant aspects of the killing of a baby we can see that the grounds for not killing persons do not apply to newborn infants. The indirect, classical utilitarian reason does not apply, because no one capable of understanding what is happening when a newborn baby is killed could feel threatened by a policy which gave less protection to the newborn than to adults. In this respect Bentham was right to describe infanticide as 'of a nature not to give the slightest inquietude to the most timid imagination'. Once we are old enough to comprehend the policy, we are too old to be threatened by it.

Similarly, the preference utilitarian reason for respecting the life of a person cannot apply to a newborn baby. A newborn baby cannot see itself as a being which might or might not have a future, and so cannot have a desire to continue living. For the same reason, if a right to life must be based on the capacity to want to go on living, a newborn baby cannot have a right to life. Finally, a newborn baby is not an autonomous being, capable of making choices, and so to kill it cannot violate the principle of respect for autonomy. In all this the newborn baby is on the same footing as the fetus, and hence fewer reasons exist against killing both babies and fetuses than exist against killing those who are capable of seeing themselves as distinct entities, existing over time.

It would, of course, be difficult to say at what age a child begins to see itself as a distinct entity existing over time. Even when we talk with two and three year old children it is usually very difficult to elicit any coherent conception of death, or of the possibility that someone – let alone the child itself – might cease to exist. No doubt children vary greatly in the age at which they begin to understand these matters, as they do in most things. But a difficulty in drawing the line is not a reason for drawing it in a place that is obviously wrong, any more than the notorious difficulty in saying how much hair a man has to have lost before we can call him 'bald' is a reason for saying that someone whose pate is as smooth as a billiard ball is not bald. Of course, where rights are at risk, we should err on the side of safety. If there were to be legislation on this matter, it probably should deny a full legal right to life to babies only for a short period after birth – perhaps a month. But this is a matter for the next chapter.

If these conclusions seem too shocking to take seriously, it may be worth remembering that our present absolute protection of the lives of infants is a distinctively Judaeo-Christian attitude rather than a universal ethical value. Infanticide has been practised in societies ranging geographically from Tahiti to Greenland and varying in culture from the nomadic Australian aborigines to the sophisticated urbanites of ancient Greece or mandarin China. In some of these societies infanticide was not merely permitted but, in certain circumstances, deemed morally obligatory. Not to kill a deformed or sickly infant was often regarded as wrong, and infanticide was probably the first, and in several societies the only, form of population control.

We might think that we are just more 'civilized' than these 'primitive' peoples. But it is not easy to feel confident that we are more civilized than the best Greek and Roman moralists. As we have seen it was not just the Spartans who exposed their infants on hillsides: both Plato and Aristotle recommended that the state command the killing of deformed infants. Romans like Seneca, whose compassionate moral sense strikes the modern reader (or me, anyway) as superior to the early and mediaeval Christian writers, also thought infanticide the natural and humane solution to the problem posed by sick and deformed babies. The change in Western attitudes to infanticide since Roman times is, like the doctrine of the sanctity of human life of which it is a part, a product of Christianity. Perhaps it is now possible to think about these issues without assuming the Christian moral framework which has, for so long, prevented any fundamental reassessment.

None of this is meant to suggest that someone who goes around randomly killing babies is no worse than a woman who has an abortion, or a man who thinks it fine sport to shoot ducks. We should certainly put very strict conditions on permissible infanticide; but these restrictions might owe more to the effects of infanticide on others than to the intrinsic wrongness of killing an infant. Obviously, in most cases, to kill an infant is to inflict a terrible loss on those who love and cherish it. Our comparison of abortion and infanticide was prompted by the objection that the position I have taken on abortion also justifies infanticide. I have admitted this charge – without regarding the admission as fatal to my position – to the extent that the *intrinsic* wrongness of killing the late fetus and the *intrinsic* wrongness of killing the newborn infant are not markedly different. In cases of abortion, however, we assume that the people most affected – the parents-to-be, or at least the mother-to-be – want to have the abortion. Thus infanticide can only be equated with abortion when those closest to the child do not want it to live. As an infant can be adopted by others in a way that a pre-viable fetus cannot be, such cases will be rare. (Some of them are discussed in the following chapter.) Killing an infant whose parents do not want it dead is, of course, an utterly different matter.

Taking life: euthanasia

In dealing with an objection to the view of abortion presented in the preceding chapter, we have already looked beyond abortion to infanticide. In so doing we will have confirmed the suspicion of supporters of the sanctity of human life that once abortion is accepted, euthanasia lurks around the next corner – and for them, euthanasia is an unequivocal evil. It has, they point out, been rejected by doctors since the fifth century B.C., when physicians first took the Oath of Hippocrates and swore 'to give no deadly medicine to anyone if asked, nor suggest any such counsel'. Moreover, they argue, the Nazi extermination programme is a recent and terrible example of what can happen once we give the state the power to kill innocent human beings.

I do not deny that if one accepts abortion on the grounds provided in the preceding chapter, the case for euthanasia, in certain circumstances, is strong. As I shall try to show in this chapter, however, euthanasia is not something to be regarded with horror, and the use of the Nazi analogy is misleading. On the contrary, once we abandon those doctrines about the sanctity of human life which – as we saw in Chapter 4 – collapse as soon as they are questioned, it is the refusal to accept euthanasia which, in some cases, is horrific.

'Euthanasia' means, according to the dictionary, 'a gentle and easy death', but it is now used to refer to the killing of those who are incurably ill and in great pain or distress in order to spare them further suffering. Within this definition, however,

there are three different types of euthanasia and it will help our
discussion if we begin by setting out this threefold distinction,
and then deal with each type separately.

Types of euthanasia

Voluntary euthanasia

Most of the groups currently campaigning for changes in the
law to allow euthanasia are campaigning for voluntary
euthanasia – that is, euthanasia carried out at the request of the
person killed.

Sometimes voluntary euthanasia is scarcely distinguishable
from assisted suicide. In *Jean's Way*, Derek Humphry has told
how his wife Jean, when dying of cancer, asked him to provide
her with the means to end her life swiftly and without pain. They
had seen the situation coming and discussed it beforehand.
Derek obtained some tablets and gave them to Jean, who took
them and died soon afterwards.

In other cases, people wanting to die may be unable to kill
themselves. In 1973 George Zygmaniak was injured in a motor-
cycle accident near his home in New Jersey. He was taken to
hospital, where he was found to be totally paralysed from the
neck down. He was also in considerable pain. He told his doctor
and his brother, Lester, that he did not want to live in this
condition. He begged them both to kill him. Lester questioned
the doctor and hospital staff about George's prospects of recovery: he was told that they were nil. He then smuggled a gun into
the hospital, and said to his brother: 'I am here to end your pain,
George. Is it all right with you?' George, who was now unable to
speak because of an operation to assist his breathing, nodded
affirmatively. Lester shot him through the temple.

The Zygmaniak case appears to be a clear instance of voluntary euthanasia, although without some of the procedural
safeguards that advocates of the legalization of voluntary
euthanasia propose. For instance, medical opinions about the
patient's prospects of recovery were obtained only in an infor-
mal manner. Nor was there a careful attempt to establish, before
independent witnesses, that George's desire for death was of a

fixed and rational kind, based on the best available information about his situation. The killing was not carried out by a doctor. An injection would have been less distressing to others than shooting. But these choices were not open to Lester Zygmaniak, for the law in New Jersey, as in most other places, regards mercy killing as murder, and if he had made his plans known, he would not have been able to carry them out.

Euthanasia can be voluntary even if a person is not able, as Jean Humphry and George Zygmaniak were able, to indicate the wish to die right up to the moment the tablets are swallowed or the trigger pulled. A person may, while in good health, make a written request for euthanasia if, through accident or illness, she should come to be incapable of making or expressing a decision to die, in pain, or without the use of her mental faculties, and there is no reasonable hope of recovery. In killing a person who has made such a request, has re-affirmed it from time to time, and is now in one of the states described, one could truly claim to be acting with her consent.

Involuntary euthanasia

I shall regard euthanasia as involuntary when the person killed is capable of consenting to her own death, but does not do so, either because she is not asked, or because she is asked and chooses to go on living. Admittedly this definition lumps two different cases under one heading. There is a significant difference between killing someone who chooses to go on living, and killing someone who has not consented to being killed, but if asked, would have consented. In practice, though, it is hard to imagine cases in which a person is capable of consenting, and would have consented if asked, but was not asked. For why not ask? Only in the most bizarre situations could one conceive of a reason for not obtaining the consent of a person both able and willing to consent.

Killing someone who has not consented to being killed can be regarded as euthanasia only when the motive for killing is the desire to prevent suffering on the part of the person killed. It is, of course, odd that anyone acting from this motive should

disregard the wishes of the person for whose sake the action is
done. Genuine cases of involuntary euthanasia appear to be
rare.

Nonvoluntary euthanasia

These two definitions leave room for a third kind of euthanasia.
If a human being is not capable of understanding the choice
between life and death, euthanasia would be neither voluntary
nor involuntary, but nonvoluntary. Those in this situation
include gravely deformed or severely retarded infants, and
people who through accident, illness or old age have permanently lost the capacity to understand the issue involved, without having previously requested or rejected euthanasia in these
circumstances.

Several cases of nonvoluntary euthanasia have reached the
courts and the popular press. Here is one example. Louis
Repouille had a son who was described as 'incurably imbecile',
had been bed-ridden since infancy and blind for five years.
According to Repouille: 'He was just like dead all the time ...
He couldn't walk, he couldn't talk, he couldn't do anything.' In
the end Repouille killed his son with chloroform.

Obviously, this kind of case raises different issues from those
raised by voluntary euthanasia. Since it is the kind of case most
nearly akin to our previous discussions of the status of animals
and the human fetus, we shall consider it first.

Justifying nonvoluntary euthanasia

As we have seen, euthanasia is nonvoluntary when the subject
has never had the capacity to choose to live or die. This is the
situation of the deformed infant or the older human being who
has been severely mentally retarded since birth. Euthanasia is
also nonvoluntary when the subject is not now but once was
capable of making the crucial choice, and did not then express
any preference relevant to her present condition.

The case of someone who has never been capable of choosing
to live or die is a little more straightforward than that of a person
who had, but has now lost, the capacity to make such a decision.

We shall, once again, separate the two cases and take the more straightforward one first. For simplicity, I shall concentrate on infants, although everything I say about them would apply to older children or adults whose mental age remains that of an infant.

Euthanasia for defective infants

If we were to approach the issue of life or death for a seriously defective human infant without any prior discussion of the ethics of killing in general, we might be unable to resolve the conflict between the sanctity of human life and the goal of reducing suffering. Some say that such decisions are 'subjective', or that life and death questions must be left to God and Nature. Our discussions have, however, prepared the ground, and the principles established and applied in the preceding three chapters make the issue much less baffling than most take it to be.

In Chapter 4 we saw that the fact that a being is a human being, in the sense of a member of the species *homo sapiens*, is not relevant to the wrongness of killing it; it is, rather, characteristics like rationality, autonomy and self-consciousness that make a difference. Defective infants lack these characteristics. Killing them, therefore, cannot be equated with killing normal human beings, or any other self-conscious beings. This conclusion is not limited to infants who, because of irreversible mental retardation will never be rational, self-conscious beings. We saw in our discussion of abortion that the potential of a fetus to become a rational, self-conscious being, cannot count against killing it at a stage when it lacks these characteristics – not, that is, unless we are also prepared to count the value of rational self-conscious life as a reason against contraception and celibacy. No infant – defective or not – has as strong a claim to life as beings capable of seeing themselves as distinct entities, existing over time.

The difference between killing defective and normal infants lies not in any supposed right to life which the latter has and the former lacks, but in other considerations about killing. Most obviously there is the difference which often exists in the attitudes of the parents. The birth of a child is usually a happy event for the parents. They have, nowadays, often planned for the child. The mother has carried it for nine months. From birth, a natural affection begins to bind the parents to it. So one important reason why it is normally a terrible thing to kill an infant is the effect the killing will have on its parents.

It is different when the infant turns out to be defective. Defects vary, of course. Some are trivial, and have little effect on the happiness of the child or its parents; but other defects turn the normally joyful event of birth into a threat to the happiness of the parents, and any other children they may have.

Parents may, with good reason, regret that a defective child was ever born. In that event the effect that the death of the child will have on its parents can be a reason for, rather than against killing it. Of course, some parents want even the most gravely defective infant to live as long as possible, and this desire would then be a reason against killing the infant. But if this is not the case? In the discussion that follows I shall assume that the parents do not want the defective child to live. I shall also assume that the defect is so serious that – again in contrast to the situation of an unwanted but normal child today – there are no other couples keen to adopt the infant.

Taking the infant in itself, what we have is a sentient being that is neither rational nor self-conscious. Since its species is not relevant to its moral status, the principles that govern the wrongness of killing nonhuman animals who are sentient but not rational or self-conscious must apply here too. These principles are utilitarian. Hence the quality of life that the infant can be expected to have is important.

One common birth defect (affecting about one in every five hundred live births) is a faulty development of the spine known as spina bifida. In the more severe cases, the child will be permanently paralysed from the waist down and lack control of bowels or bladder. Often excess fluid accumulates in the brain, a condition known as hydrocephalus which results in mental retardation. Though some forms of treatment exist, if the child is badly affected at birth, the paralysis, incontinence and mental retardation cannot be overcome.

Some doctors closely connected with children suffering from severe spina bifida believe that the lives of some of these children are so miserable that it is wrong to resort to surgery to keep them alive. This implies that their lives are not worth living. Published descriptions of the lives of these children support this judgment. If this is correct, utilitarian principles suggest that it is right to kill such children.

When the life of an infant will be so miserable as not to be worth living, both the 'prior existence' and the 'total' version of utilitarianism entail that, if there are no 'extrinsic' reasons for keeping the infant alive – like the feelings of the parents – it is better to kill it. A more difficult problem arises – and the convergence between the two views ends – when we consider defects which make the child's life prospects significantly less happy than those of a normal child, but not so unhappy as to make the life one not worth living. Haemophilia is probably in this category. The haemophiliac lacks the element in normal blood which makes it clot, and thus risks prolonged bleeding, especially internal bleeding, from the slightest injury. If allowed to continue, this bleeding leads to permanent crippling and eventually death. The bleeding is very painful and although improved treatments have eliminated the need for constant blood transfusions, haemophiliacs still have to spend a lot of time in hospital. They are unable to play most sports, and live constantly on the edge of crisis. Nevertheless, haemophiliacs do not appear to spend their time wondering whether to end it all; most find life definitely worth living, despite the difficulties they face.

Given these facts, suppose that a newborn baby is diagnosed as a haemophiliac. The parents, daunted by the prospect of bringing up a child with this condition, are not anxious for him to live. Could euthanasia be defended here? Our first reaction may well be a firm 'no', for the infant can be expected to have a life that is worth living, even if not quite as good as that of a normal baby. The 'prior existence' version of utilitarianism supports this judgment. The infant exists. His life can be expected to contain a positive balance of happiness over misery. To kill him would deprive him of this positive balance of happiness. Therefore it would be wrong.

On the 'total' version of utilitarianism, on the other hand, we cannot reach a decision on the basis of this information alone. The total view makes it necessary to ask whether the death of the haemophiliac infant would lead to the creation of another being who would not otherwise have existed. In other words, if the haemophiliac child is killed, will his parents have another child whom they would not have if the haemophiliac child lives? If they would is the second child likely to have a better life than the one killed?

Often it will be possible to answer both these questions affirmatively. A woman may plan to have two children. If one dies while she is of child-bearing age, she may conceive another in its place. Suppose a woman planning to have two children has one normal child, and then gives birth to a haemophiliac child. The burden of caring for that child may make it impossible for her to cope with a third child; but if the defective child were to die, she would have another. It is also plausible to suppose that the prospects of a happy life are better for a normal child than for a haemophiliac.

When the death of a defective infant will lead to the birth of another infant with better prospects of a happy life, the total amount of happiness will be greater if the defective infant is killed. The loss of happy life for the first infant is outweighed by the gain of a happier life for the second. Therefore, if killing the haemophiliac infant has no adverse effect on others, it would, according to the total view, be right to kill him.

The total view treats infants as replaceable, in much the same way as non-self-conscious animals were treated in Chapter 5. Many will think that the replaceability argument cannot be applied to human infants. The direct killing of even the most hopelessly defective infants is still officially regarded as murder; how then could the killing of infants with relatively minor defects, like haemophilia, be accepted? Yet on further reflection, the implications of the replaceability argument do not seem so bizarre. For there are defective members of our species whom we now deal with exactly as the argument suggests we should. These cases closely resemble the ones we have been discussing. There is only one difference, and that is a difference of timing – the timing of the discovery of the defect, and the consequent killing of the defective being.

A medical technique known as amniocentesis has recently been developed. It enables us to learn a good deal about the fetus during the early months of pregnancy. Using it we can, for instance, discover the sex of the fetus. This is important in the case of sex-linked genetic defects. Only males suffer from haemophilia; females can carry the gene and pass it on to their male offspring without themselves being affected. So a woman who knows that she carries the gene for haemophilia can avoid giving birth to a haemophiliac child by undergoing amniocentesis. If the fetus turns out to be female, all is well; if not, the woman can have an abortion, and try again, until she does conceive a female.

Amniocentesis cannot – yet – directly show whether or not the fetus is a haemophiliac. It can only show that the fetus is male. Not all the sons of women who carry the gene that causes haemophilia actually inherit the disease. There are some other defects which it can detect more positively. Down's syndrome, more popularly known as mongolism, is one of these. Children with this condition are severely retarded and can never become normal adults, although their lives may be pleasant enough, as the lives of children are. The risk of having a Down's syndrome child increases sharply with the age of the mother, and for this reason amniocentesis is commonly advised for pregnant women over 35. Again, undergoing the procedure implies that if the test for Down's syndrome is positive, the woman will consider aborting the fetus and, if she still wishes to have another child, will start another pregnancy which has a good chance of being normal.

Amniocentesis, followed by abortion in selected cases, is common practice in countries with liberal abortion laws and

advanced medical techniques. I think this is as it should be. As
the arguments of the last chapter indicate, I believe that abortion can be justified. Note, however, that neither haemophilia
nor Down's syndrome is so crippling as to make life not worth
living. To abort a fetus with one of these defects, intending to
have another child that will not be defective, is to treat fetuses as
interchangeable or replaceable. If the mother has previously
decided to have a certain number of children, say two, then
what she is doing, in effect, is rejecting one potential child in
favour of another. She could, in defence of her actions, say: the
loss of life of the aborted fetus is outweighed by the gain of a
better life for the normal child that will be conceived only if the
defective one dies.

When death occurs before birth, replaceability does not conflict with generally accepted moral convictions. That a fetus is
known to be defective is widely accepted as a ground for abortion. Only those who believe in the sanctity of human life from
conception would think it wrong for a woman to abort a fetus
she knew to be seriously defective. Yet in discussing abortion,
we saw that birth does not mark a morally significant dividing
line. I cannot see how one could defend the view that fetuses
may be 'replaced' before birth, but newborn infants may not be.
Nor is there any other point, such as viability, which does a
better job of dividing the fetus from the infant. Self-
consciousness, which could provide a basis for holding that
it is wrong to kill one being and replace it with another, is not
to be found in either the fetus or the newborn infant. Neither
the fetus nor the newborn infant is an individual capable of
regarding itself as a distinct entity with a life of its own to
lead.

Regarding newborn infants as replaceable, as we now regard
fetuses, would have considerable advantages over amniocentesis followed by abortion. Amniocentesis can detect only a few
abnormalities, not necessarily the worst. At present parents can
choose to keep or destroy their defective offspring only if the
defect happens to be detected during pregnancy. There is no
logical basis for restricting parents' choice to these particular

defects. If defective newborn infants were not regarded as having a right to life until, say, a week or a month after birth it would allow us to choose on the basis of far greater knowledge of the infant's condition than is possible before birth.

Actual inspection of the baby has one advantage over amniocentesis that could make supporters of the sanctity of life pause before they condemn the killing of defective newborns. We have seen that there are some defects which amniocentesis cannot detect, but which can be avoided because they afflict only one sex, and the sex of the fetus can be determined. Haemophilia is an example. But while haemophilia affects only males, it does not affect all the male offspring of a female carrier of the gene. Some of her sons may inherit from their father a sound version of the gene needed for blood to clot. Statistically, half of the sons of female carriers are perfectly normal. They are neither haemophiliacs, nor carriers. So if we know that a pregnant woman is a carrier and amniocentesis tells us that the fetus is male, all we know is that the fetus has a 50% chance of being a haemophiliac. Many women, supported by their doctors, think it better not to run this risk. They prefer to abort the fetus and try again, in the hope of having a daughter who will not be a haemophiliac. This means that for every hundred fetuses aborted in these circumstances, fifty are perfectly normal. The problem is that we cannot know, before the abortions, which the normal ones are. This problem would be eliminated if the woman could wait until after birth before making the decision for or against the life of her child. Altering the time of the decision would immediately halve the number of lives that had to be taken. It would also make it possible for carriers of the haemophilia gene to have male children without risk.

All these remarks have been concerned with the wrongness of ending the life of the infant, considered in itself rather than for its effects on others. When we take effects on others into account, the picture may alter. Obviously, to go through the whole of pregnancy and labour, only to give birth to a child that one decides should not live, would be a difficult, perhaps heartbreaking, experience. For this reason many women would prefer amniocentesis and abortion rather than live birth with the possibility of infanticide; but if the latter is not morally worse than the former, this would seem to be a choice that the woman herself should be allowed to make.

Another factor to take into account is the possibility of adoption. When there are more couples wishing to adopt than normal children available for adoption, it could be that a child-less couple would be prepared to adopt a haemophiliac. This would relieve the mother of the burden of bringing up a haemophiliac child, and enable her to have another child, if she wished. Then the replaceability argument could not justify infanticide, for bringing the other child into existence would not be dependent on the death of the haemophiliac. The death of the haemophiliac would then be a straightforward loss of a worth-while life, not outweighed by the creation of another, more worthwhile life.

So the issue of euthanasia for defective newborn infants is not without complications, which we do not have the space to discuss adequately. Nevertheless the main point is clear: killing a defective infant is not morally equivalent to killing a person. Very often it is not wrong at all.

Other cases of nonvoluntary euthanasia

In the preceding section we discussed euthanasia for beings who have never been capable of choosing to live or die. Nonvoluntary euthanasia may also be considered in the case of those who were once persons capable of choosing to live or die, but now, through accident or old age, have permanently lost this capacity, and did not, prior to losing it, express any views about euthanasia in such circumstances. These cases are not rare. Many hospitals care for motor accident victims whose brains have been damaged beyond all possible recovery. They may survive, in a coma, or perhaps barely conscious, for several years.

In most respects, these beings do not differ importantly from defective infants. They are not self-conscious, rational or autonomous, and so the intrinsic value of their lives consists only in any pleasant experiences they may have. If they have no experiences at all, their lives have no intrinsic value. They are, in effect, dead. (If this verdict seems harsh, ask yourself whether there is anything to choose between the following options: (a) instant death or (b) instant coma, followed by death, without recovery, in ten years time. I can see no advantage in survival in a comatose state, if death without recovery is certain.) The lives of those who are not in a coma, and are conscious but not self-conscious, have value if they experience more pleasure than pain; but it is difficult to see the point of keeping such beings alive if their life is, on the whole, miserable.

There is one respect in which these cases differ from defective infants. In discussing infanticide in the final section of Chapter 6, I cited Bentham's comment that infanticide need not 'give the slightest inquietude to the most timid imagination'. This is because those old enough to be aware of the killing of defective infants are necessarily outside the scope of the policy. This cannot be said of euthanasia applied to those who once were rational and self-conscious. So a possible objection to this form of euthanasia would be that it will lead to insecurity and fear among those who are not now, but might come to be, within its scope. For instance, elderly people, knowing that nonvoluntary euthanasia is sometimes applied to senile elderly patients, bed-ridden, suffering and lacking the capacity to accept or reject death, might fear that every injection or tablet will be lethal. This fear might be quite irrational, but it would be difficult to convince people of this; particularly if old age really had affected their memory or powers of reasoning.

This objection might be met by a procedure allowing those who do not wish to be subjected to nonvoluntary euthanasia under any circumstances to register their refusal. Perhaps this would suffice; but perhaps it would not provide enough re-assurance. If not, nonvoluntary euthanasia would be justifiable only for those never capable of choosing to live or die.

Justifying voluntary euthanasia

Under existing laws people suffering unrelievable pain or distress from an incurable illness who ask their doctors to end their lives are asking their doctors to become murderers. Although juries are extremely reluctant to convict in cases of this kind the law is clear that neither the request, nor the degree of suffering, nor the incurable condition of the person killed, is a defence to a charge of murder. Advocates of voluntary euthanasia propose that this law be changed so that a doctor could legally act on a patient's desire to die without further suffering.

The case for voluntary euthanasia has some common ground with the case for nonvoluntary euthanasia, in that the reason for killing is to end suffering. The two kinds of euthanasia differ, however, in that voluntary euthanasia involves the killing of a person, a rational and self-conscious being and not a merely conscious being. (To be strictly accurate it must be said that this is not always so, because although only rational and self-conscious beings can consent to their own deaths, they may not be rational and self-conscious at the time euthanasia is contemplated – the doctor may, for instance, be acting on a prior written request for euthanasia if, through accident or illness, one's rational faculties should be irretrievably lost. For simplicity we shall, henceforth, disregard this complication.)

We have seen that it is possible to justify nonvoluntary euthanasia, when the being killed lacks the capacity to consent. We must now ask in what way the ethical issues are different when the being is capable of consenting, and does in fact consent.

Let us return to the general principles about killing proposed in Chapter 4. I argued there that the wrongness of killing a conscious being which is not self-conscious, rational or autonomous, depends on utilitarian considerations. It is on this basis that I have defended nonvoluntary euthanasia. On the other hand it is, as we saw, plausible to hold that killing a self-conscious being is a more serious matter than killing a merely conscious being. We found four distinct grounds on which this could be argued:

i. The classical utilitarian claim that since self-conscious beings are capable of fearing their own death, killing them has worse effects on others.

ii. The preference utilitarian calculation which counts the thwarting of the victim's desire to go on living as an important reason against killing.

iii. A theory of rights according to which to have a right one must have the ability to desire that to which one has a right, so that to have a right to life one must be able to desire one's own continued existence.

iv. Respect for the autonomous decisions of rational agents.

Now suppose we have a situation in which a person suffering from a painful and incurable disease wishes to die. If the individual were not a person – not rational or self-conscious – euthanasia would, as I have said, be justifiable. Do any of the four grounds for holding that it is normally worse to kill a person provide reasons against killing when the individual is a person?

The classical utilitarian objection does not apply to killing that takes place only with the genuine consent of the person killed. That people are killed under these conditions would have no tendency to spread fear or insecurity, since we have no cause to be fearful of being killed with our own genuine consent. If we do not wish to be killed, we simply do not consent. In fact, the argument from fear points in favour of voluntary euthanasia, for if voluntary euthanasia is not permitted we may, with good cause, be fearful that our deaths will be unnecessarily drawn-out and distressing.

Preference utilitarianism also points in favour of, not against, voluntary euthanasia. Just as preference utilitarianism must count a desire to go on living as a reason against killing, so it must count a desire to die as a reason for killing.

Next, according to the theory of rights we have considered, it is an essential feature of a right that one can waive one's rights if one so chooses. I may have a right to privacy; but I can, if I wish, film every detail of my daily life and invite the neighbours to my home movies. Neighbours sufficiently intrigued to accept my invitation could do so without violating my right to privacy, since the right has on this occasion been waived. Similarly, to say that I have a right to life is not to say that it would be wrong for my doctor to end my life, if she does so at my request. In making this request I waive my right to life.

Lastly, the principle of respect for autonomy tells us to allow rational agents to live their own lives according to their own autonomous decisions, free from coercion or interference; but if rational agents should autonomously choose to die, then respect for autonomy will lead us to assist them to do as they choose.

So, although there are reasons for thinking that killing a self-conscious being is normally worse than killing any other kind of being, in the special case of voluntary euthanasia most of these reasons count for euthanasia rather than against. Surprising as this result might at first seem, it really does no more than reflect the fact that what is special about self-conscious beings is that they can know that they exist over time and will, unless they die, continue to exist. Normally this continued existence is fervently desired; when the foreseeable continued existence is dreaded rather than desired however, the desire to die may take the place of the normal desire to live, reversing the reasons against killing based on the desire to live. Thus the case for voluntary euthanasia is arguably much stronger than the case for nonvoluntary euthanasia.

Some opponents of the legalization of voluntary euthanasia might concede that all this follows, if we have a genuinely free and rational decision to die: but, they add, we can never be sure that a request to be killed is the result of a free and rational decision. Will not the sick and elderly be pressured by their relatives to end their lives quickly? Will it not be possible to commit outright murder by pretending that a person has requested euthanasia? And even if there is no pressure of falsification, can anyone who is ill, suffering pain, and very probably in a drugged and confused state of mind, make a rational decision about whether to live or die?

These questions raise technical difficulties for the legalization of voluntary euthanasia, rather than objections to the underlying ethical principles; but they are serious difficulties nonetheless. Voluntary euthanasia societies in Britain and elsewhere have sought to meet them by proposing that euthanasia should be legal only for a person who:

i. is diagnosed by two doctors as suffering from an incurable illness expected to cause severe distress or the loss of rational faculties;

and

ii. has, at least 30 days before the proposed act of euthanasia, and in the presence of two independent witnesses, made a written request for euthanasia in the event of the situation described in (i) occurring.

Only a doctor could administer euthanasia, and if the patient was at the time still capable of consenting, the doctor would have to make sure that the patient still wished the declaration to be acted upon. A declaration could be revoked at any time.

These provisions, though in some respects cumbersome, appear to meet most of the technical objections to legalization. Murder in the guise of euthanasia would be far-fetched. Two independent witnesses to the declaration, the 30 day waiting period, and – in the case of a mentally competent person – the doctor's final investigation of the patient's wishes would together do a great deal to reduce the danger of doctors acting on requests which did not reflect the free and rational decisions of their patients.

It is often said, in debates about euthanasia, that doctors can be mistaken. Certainly some patients diagnosed by competent doctors as suffering from an incurable condition have survived. Possibly the legalization of voluntary euthanasia would, over the years, mean the deaths of one or two people who would otherwise have recovered. This is not, however, the knockdown argument against euthanasia that some imagine it to be. Against a very small number of unnecessary deaths that might occur if euthanasia is legalized we must place the very large amount of pain and distress that will be suffered by patients who really are terminally ill if euthanasia is not legalized. Longer life is not such a supreme good that it outweighs all other considerations. (If it were, there would be many more effective ways of saving life – such as a ban on smoking, or on cars that can drive faster than 10 m.p.h. – than prohibiting voluntary euthanasia.) The possibility that two doctors may make a mistake means that the person who opts for euthanasia is deciding on the balance of probabilities, and giving up a very slight chance of survival in order to avoid suffering that will almost certainly end in death. This may be a perfectly rational choice. Probability is, as Bishop Butler said, the guide of life, and we must follow its guidance right to the end. Against this, some will reply that improved care for the terminally ill has eliminated pain and made voluntary euthanasia unnecessary. Elisabeth Kübler-Ross, whose *On Death and Dying* is perhaps the best-known book on care for the dying, has claimed that none of her patients request euthanasia. Given personal attention and the right medication, she says, people come to accept their deaths and die peacefully without pain.

Kübler-Ross may be right. It may be possible, now, to eliminate pain. It may even be possible to do it in a way which leaves patients in possession of their rational faculties and free from vomiting, nausea, or other distressing side-effects. Unfortunately only a minority of dying patients now receive this kind of care. Nor is physical pain the only problem. There can also be other distressing conditions, like bones so fragile they fracture at sudden movements, slow starvation due to a cancerous growth, inability to control one's bowels or bladder, difficulty in breathing and so on.

Take the case of Jean Humphry, as described in *Jean's Way*. This is not a case from the period before effective painkillers: Jean Humphry died in 1975. Nor is it the case of someone unable to get good medical care: she was treated at an Oxford hospital and if there were anything else that could have been done for her, her husband, a well-connected Fleet St journalist, would have been better placed than most to obtain it. Yet Derek Humphry writes:

when the request for help in dying meant relief from relentless suffering and pain and I had seen the extent of this agony, the option simply could not be denied... And certainly Jean deserved the dignity of selecting her own ending. She must die soon – as we both now realized – but together we would decide when this would be.

Perhaps one day it will be possible to treat all terminally ill patients in such a way that no one requests euthanasia and the subject becomes a non-issue; but this still distant prospect is no reason to deny euthanasia to those who die in less comfortable conditions. It is, in any case, highly paternalistic to tell dying patients that they are now so well looked after they need not be offered the option of euthanasia. It would be more in keeping with respect for individual freedom and autonomy to legalize euthanasia and let patients decide whether their situation is bearable – let them, as Derek Humphry puts it, have the dignity of selecting their own endings. Better that voluntary euthanasia be an unexercised legal right than a prohibited act which, for all we know, some might desperately desire.

Finally, do these arguments for voluntary euthanasia perhaps give too much weight to individual freedom and autonomy? After all, we do not allow people free choices on matters like, for instance, the taking of heroin. This is a restriction of freedom but, in the view of many, one that can be justified on paternalistic grounds. If preventing people becoming heroin addicts is justifiable paternalism, why isn't preventing people having themselves killed?

The question is a reasonable one, because respect for individual freedom can be carried too far. John Stuart Mill thought that the state should never interfere with the individual except to prevent harm to others. The individual's own good, Mill thought, is not a proper reason for state intervention. But Mill may have had too high an opinion of the rationality of a human being. It may occasionally be right to prevent people making choices which are obviously not rationally based and which we can be sure they will later regret. The prohibition of voluntary euthanasia cannot be justified on paternalistic grounds, however, for voluntary euthanasia is, by definition, an act for which good reasons exist. Voluntary euthanasia occurs only when, to the best of medical knowledge, a person is suffering from an incurable and painful or distressing condition. In these circumstances one cannot say that to choose to die quickly is obviously irrational. The strength of the case for voluntary euthanasia lies in this combination of respect for the preferences, or autonomy, of those who decide for euthanasia; and the clear rational basis of the decision itself.

Not justifying involuntary euthanasia

Involuntary euthanasia resembles voluntary euthanasia in that it involves the killing of those capable of consenting to their own death. It differs in that they do not consent. This difference is crucial, as the argument of the preceding section shows. All the four reasons against killing self-conscious beings apply when the person killed does not choose to die.

Would it ever be possible to justify involuntary euthanasia on paternalistic grounds, to save someone extreme agony? It might be possible to imagine a case in which the agony was so great, and so certain, that the weight of utilitarian considerations favouring euthanasia override all four reasons against killing self-conscious beings. Yet to make this decision one would have to be confident that one can judge when a person's life is so bad as to be not worth living, better than that person can judge herself. It is not clear that we are ever justified in having much confidence in our judgments about whether the life of another person is, to that person, worth living. That the other person wishes to go on living is good evidence that her life is worth living. What better evidence could there be?

The only kind of case in which the paternalistic argument is at all plausible is one in which the person to be killed does not realize what agony she will suffer in future, and if she is not killed now she will have to live through to the very end. On these grounds one might kill a person who has – though she does not yet realize it – fallen into the hands of homicidal sadists who will torture her to death. These cases are, fortunately, more commonly encountered in fiction than reality.

If in real life we are unlikely ever to encounter a case of justifiable involuntary euthanasia, then it may be best to dismiss from our minds the fanciful cases in which one might imagine defending it, and treat the rule against involuntary euthanasia as, for all practical purposes, absolute. We can then say that euthanasia is only justifiable if those killed either:

i. lack the ability to consent to death, because they lack the capacity to understand the choice between their own continued existence or non-existence; or
ii. have the capacity to choose between their own continued life or death and make an informed, voluntary and settled decision to die.

Active and passive euthanasia

The conclusions we have reached in this chapter will shock a large number of readers, for they violate one of the most fundamental tenets of Western ethics – the wrongness of killing innocent human beings. I have already made one attempt to show that our conclusions are, at least in the area of defective infants, a less radical departure from existing practice than one might suppose. I pointed out that we are prepared to kill a fetus at a late stage of pregnancy if we believe that there is a significant risk of it being defective; and since the line between a developed fetus and a newborn infant is not a crucial moral divide, it is difficult to see why it is worse to kill a newborn infant known to be defective. In this section I shall argue that there is another area of accepted medical practice that is not intrinsically different from the practices that the arguments of this chapter would allow.

I have referred to the birth defect known as spina bifida, in which the infant is born with an opening in the back, exposing the spinal cord. Until 1957, most of these infants died young, but in that year doctors began using a new device, known as a Holter valve, to drain off the excess fluid that otherwise accumulates in the head with this condition. In some hospitals it then became standard practice to make vigorous efforts to save every spina bifida infant. The result was that few spina bifida infants died – but of those that survived, many were severely handicapped, with gross paralysis, multiple deformities of the legs and spine, and no control of bowel or bladder. More than half were mentally retarded. Keeping the valve working properly and free from infection required repeated operations. In short, the existence of these children caused great difficulty for their families, strained the available medical resources, and was often a misery for the children themselves.

After studying the results of this policy of active treatment a British doctor, John Lorber, proposed that instead of treating all cases of spina bifida, only those who have the defect in a mild form should be selected for treatment. (In fact he proposed that the final decision should be up to the parents, but parents nearly always accept the recommendations of the doctors.) This principle of selective treatment has now been widely accepted, and in Britain has been recognized as legitimate by the Department of Health and Social Security. The result is that fewer spina bifida children survive beyond infancy, but those that do are, by and large, the ones whose physical and mental handicaps are relatively minor.

The policy of selection, then, appears to be a desirable one: but what happens to those defective infants not selected for treatment? Lorber does not disguise the fact that in these cases the hope is that the infant will die soon and without suffering. It is to achieve this objective that surgical operations and other forms of active treatment are not undertaken, although pain and discomfort are as far as possible relieved. If the infant happens to get an infection, the kind of infection which in a normal infant would be swiftly cleared up with antibiotics, no antibiotics are given. Since the survival of the infant is not desired, no steps are taken to prevent a condition, easily curable by ordinary medical techniques, proving fatal.

All this is, as I have said, accepted medical practice. In articles in medical journals, doctors have described cases in which they have allowed infants to die. These cases are not limited to spina bifida, but include, for instance, babies born with Down's syndrome (mongolism). According to testimony given to a United States Senate sub-committee in 1974, several thousand mentally and physically defective children are allowed to die each year.

The question is: if it is right to allow infants to die, why is it wrong to kill them?

This question has not escaped the notice of the doctors involved. Frequently they answer it by a pious reference to the nineteenth-century poet, Arthur Clough, who wrote:

> Thou shalt not kill; but need'st not strive
> Officiously to keep alive.

Unfortunately for those who appeal to Clough's immortal lines as an authoritative ethical pronouncement, they come from a piece of verse – 'The Latest Decalogue' – the intent of which is satirical. The opening lines, for example, are:

> Thou shalt have one god only; who
> Would be at the expense of two.
>
> No graven images may be
> Worshipped except the currency.

So Clough cannot be numbered on the side of those who think it wrong to kill, but right not to try too hard to keep alive. Is there, nonetheless, something to be said for this idea? The view that there is something to be said for it is often termed 'the acts and omissions doctrine'. It holds that there is an important moral distinction between performing an act that has certain consequences – say, the death of a defective child – and omitting to do something that has the same consequences. If this doctrine is correct, the doctor who gives the child a lethal injection does wrong; the doctor who omits to give the child antibiotics, knowing full well that without antibiotics the child will die, does not.

What grounds are there for accepting the acts and omissions doctrine? Few champion the doctrine for its own sake, as an important ethical first principle. It is, rather, an implication of one view of ethics, of a view which holds that so long as we do not violate specified moral rules which place determinate moral obligations upon us, we do all that morality demands of us. These rules are of the kind made familiar by the Ten Commandments and similar moral codes: Do not kill, Do not lie, Do not steal, and so on. Characteristically they are formulated in the negative, so that to obey them it is necessary only to abstain from the actions they prohibit. Hence obedience can be demanded of every member of the community.

An ethic consisting of specific duties, prescribed by moral rules which everyone can be expected to obey, must make a sharp moral distinction between acts and omissions. Take, for example, the rule 'Do not kill.' If this rule is interpreted, as it has been in the Judaeo-Christian tradition, as prohibiting only the taking of innocent human life, it is not too difficult to avoid overt acts in violation of it. Few of us are murderers. It is not so easy to avoid letting innocent humans die. Many people die because of insufficient food, or poor medical facilities. If we could assist some of them, but do not do so, we are letting them die. Taking the rule against killing to apply to omissions would make living in accordance with it a mark of saintliness or moral heroism, rather than a minimum required of every morally decent person.

An ethic which judges acts according to whether they do or do not violate specific moral rules must, therefore, place moral weight on the distinction between acts and omissions. An ethic which judges acts by their consequences will not do so, for the consequences of an act and an omission will often be, in all significant respects, indistinguishable. For instance, omitting to give antibiotics to a child with pneumonia may have consequences no less fatal than giving the child a lethal injection.

Which approach is right? I have argued for a consequentialist approach to ethics. The acts/omissions issue poses the choice between these two basic approaches in an unusually clear and direct way. What we need to do is imagine two parallel situations differing only in that in one a person performs an act resulting in the death of another human being, while in the other she omits to do something, with the same result. Suppose that a road accident victim has been in a coma for several months.

Large parts of her brain have been destroyed and there is no prospect of recovery; only a respirator and intravenous feeding are keeping her alive. The parents of the victim visit her daily, and it is obvious that the long ordeal is placing a great strain on them. Knowing all this, the victim's doctor notices one day that the plug of the respirator has worked loose. Unless she replaces it the victim will die. After thinking about the situation she decides not to replace it.

The second case is exactly like the first, except that the respirator has a tight-fitting plug and so the situation will go on indefinitely unless the doctor does something. After thinking about the situation, the doctor gives the patient a lethal injection.

Comparing these two cases, is it reasonable to hold that the doctor who gives the injection does wrong, while the doctor who decides not to replace the plug acts rightly? I do not think it is. In both cases, the outcome is the swift and painless death of the comatose patient. In both cases, the doctor knows that this will be the result, and decides what she will do on the basis of this knowledge, because she judges this result to be better than the alternative. In both cases the doctor must take responsibility for her decision – it would not be correct for her to say, in the first case, that she was not responsible for the patient's death because she did nothing. Doing nothing, in this situation, is itself a deliberate choice and one cannot escape responsibility for its consequences.

One might say, of course, that in the first case the doctor does not kill the patient, she merely allows the patient to die; but one must then answer the further question why killing is wrong, and letting die is not. The answer that most advocates of the distinction give is simply that there is a moral rule against killing (innocent human beings, that is) and none against allowing to die. This answer treats a conventionally accepted moral rule as if it were beyond questioning; it does not go on to ask whether we should have a moral rule against killing (but not against allowing to die). But we have already seen that the conventionally accepted principle of the sanctity of human life is untenable.

The moral rule against killing cannot be taken for granted either.

I suggest that reflecting on these cases leads us to the conclusion that there is no *intrinsic* moral difference between killing and allowing to die. That is, there is no difference which depends solely on the distinction between an act and an omission. (This does not mean that all cases of allowing to die are morally equivalent to killing. Other factors – extrinsic factors – will sometimes be relevant. This will be discussed further in the next chapter.) Allowing to die – 'passive euthanasia' – is already accepted as a humane and proper course of action in certain cases. If there is no intrinsic moral difference between killing and allowing to die, active euthanasia should also be accepted as humane and proper in certain circumstances.

Indeed, because of extrinsic differences – especially differences in the time it takes for death to occur – active euthanasia may even be the *only* humane and morally proper course. Passive euthanasia can be a slow process. In an article in the *British Medical Journal*, John Lorber has charted the fate of 25 infants born with spina bifida on whom it had been decided, in view of the poor prospects for a worthwhile life, not to operate. It will be recalled that Lorber freely grants that the object of not treating infants is that they should die soon and painlessly. Yet of the 25 untreated infants, 14 were still alive after one month, and 7 after three months. In Lorber's sample, all the infants died within nine months, but this cannot be guaranteed. An Australian clinic following Lorber's approach to spina bifida found that of 79 untreated infants, 5 survived for more than 2 years. For both the infants, and their families, this must be a long-drawn out ordeal; nor should the burden on the hospital staff and facilities be disregarded.

Or consider those infants born with Down's syndrome, better known as mongolism. Most mongoloid infants are reasonably healthy, and will live for many years. A few, however, are born with a blockage between the stomach and the intestine which, if not removed, will prevent anything taken into the stomach from being digested, and hence bring about death. These become candidates for passive euthanasia. Yet the blockage is easy to remove and has nothing to do with the degree of mental retardation the child will have. Moreover, the death resulting from passive euthanasia in these circumstances is, though sure, neither swift nor painless. The infant dies from dehydration or hunger. It may take two weeks for death to come.

It is interesting, in this context, to think again of our earlier argument that the fact that a being is a member of the species *homo sapiens* does not entitle it to better treatment than a being at a similar mental level who is a member of a different species. We could also have said – except that it seemed too obvious to need saying – that the fact that a being is a member of the species *homo sapiens* is not a reason for giving it *worse* treatment than a member of a different species. Yet in respect of euthanasia, this needs to be said. We do not doubt that it is right to shoot a badly injured or sick animal, if it is in pain and its chances of recovery are negligible. To 'allow nature to take its course', withholding treatment but refusing to kill, would obviously be wrong. It is only our misplaced respect for the doctrine of the sanctity of human life that prevents us from seeing that what it is obviously wrong to do to a horse it is equally wrong to do to a defective infant.

To summarize: passive euthanasia often results in a drawn-out death. It introduces irrelevant factors (a blockage in the intestine, or an easily curable infection) into the selection of those who shall die. If we are able to admit that our objective is a swift and painless death we should not leave it up to chance to determine whether this objective is achieved. Having chosen death we should ensure that it comes in the best possible way.

The slippery slope: from euthanasia to genocide?

Before we leave this topic we must consider an objection which looms so large in the anti-euthanasia literature that it merits a section to itself. It is, for instance, the reason why John Lorber rejects active euthanasia. Lorber has written:

I wholly disagree with euthanasia. Though it is fully logical, and in expert and conscientious hands it could be the most humane way of dealing with such a situation, legalizing euthanasia would be a most dangerous weapon in the hands of the State or ignorant or unscrupulous individuals. One does not have to go far back in history to know what crimes can be committed if euthanasia were legalized.

Would euthanasia be the first step on to a slippery slope? In the absence of prominent moral footholds to check our descent, would we slide all the way down into the abyss of state terror and mass murder? The experience of Nazism, to which Lorber no doubt is referring, has often been used as an illustration of what could follow acceptance of euthanasia. Here is a more specific example, from an article by another doctor, Leo Alexander:

Whatever proportions [Nazi] crimes finally assumed, it became evident to all who investigated them that they had started from small beginnings. The beginnings at first were merely a subtle shift in emphasis in the basic attitude of the physicians. It started with the acceptance of the attitude, basic in the euthanasia movement, that there is such a thing as life not worthy to be lived. This attitude in its early stages concerned itself merely with the severely and chronically sick. Gradually the sphere of those to be included in the category was enlarged to encompass the socially unproductive, the ideologically unwanted, the racially unwanted and finally all non-Germans. But it is important to realize that the infinitely small wedged-in lever from which this entire trend of mind received its impetus was the attitude toward the nonrehabilitable sick.

In discussing the lessons to be learnt from Nazism it is essential, first of all, to avoid one obvious fallacy. The Nazis committed horrendous crimes; but this does not mean that *everything* the Nazis did was horrendous. We cannot condemn euthanasia just because the Nazis did it, any more than we can condemn the building of new roads for this reason. If euthanasia somehow leads to the Nazi atrocities that would be a reason for condemning euthanasia. But is euthanasia – rather than, for example, racism – to be blamed for the mass murders the Nazis carried out?

Alexander singles out euthanasia because it implies 'that there is such a thing as life not worthy to be lived'. Lorber could hardly agree with Alexander on this, since his recommended procedure of not treating selected infants is based on exactly this judgment. Although people sometimes talk as if we should never judge a life to be not worth living (presumably 'life of a member of the species homo sapiens' is what they have in mind, although the species bias would need to be justified), there are times when such a judgment is obviously correct. A life of physical suffering, unredeemed by any form of pleasure or by a minimal level of self-consciousness, is not worth living. If we can set criteria for deciding who is to be allowed to die and who is to be given treatment, then we can set criteria, perhaps the same criteria, for deciding who should be killed.

So it is not the attitude that some lives are not worth living that marks out the Nazis from normal people who do not commit mass murder. What then is it? Is it that they went beyond passive euthanasia, and practised active euthanasia? Many, like Lorber, worry about the power that a programme of active euthanasia could place in the hands of an unscrupulous government. This worry is not negligible, but should not be exaggerated. Unscrupulous governments already have within their power more plausible means of getting rid of their opponents than euthanasia administered by doctors on medical grounds. 'Suicides' can be arranged. 'Accidents' can occur. If necessary, assassins can be hired. Our best defence against such possibilities is to do everything possible to keep our government democratic, open, and in the hands of people who would not seriously wish to kill their opponents. Once the wish is serious enough, governments will find a way, whether euthanasia is legal or not.

In the case of Nazism, it was the racist attitude towards 'non-Aryans' – the attitude that they are sub-human and a danger to the purity of the *Volk* – that made the holocaust possible. Nor was the so-called 'euthanasia' programme anything like the kind of euthanasia that could be defended on ethical grounds – as can be seen from the fact that the Nazis kept their operations completely secret, deceived relatives about the cause of death of those killed, and exempted from the programme certain privileged classes, such as veterans of the armed services, or relatives of the euthanasia staff. Nazi was never voluntary, and often involuntary rather than euthanasia was never voluntary, and often involuntary rather than nonvoluntary. 'Doing away with useless mouths' – a phrase used by those in charge – gives a better idea of the objectives of the programme than 'mercy-killing'. Both racial origin and ability to work were among the factors considered in the selection of patients to be killed. There is no analogy between this and the proposals of those seeking to legalize euthanasia today.

The absence of any real parallel between Nazi 'euthanasia' and modern proposals may be granted, but the slippery slope argument could still be defended as a way of suggesting that the present strict rule against the direct killing of innocent human beings serves a useful purpose. However arbitrary and unjustifiable the distinctions between human and non-human, fetus and infant, killing and allowing to die, may be, the rule against direct killing of innocent humans at least marks a work-able line. The distinction between an infant whose life may be worth living, and one whose life definitely is not, is much more difficult to draw. Perhaps people who see that certain kinds of human beings are killed in certain circumstances may go on to conclude that it is not wrong to kill others not very different from the first kind. So will the boundary of acceptable killing be pushed gradually back? In the absence of any logical stopping place, will the outcome be the loss of all respect for human life?

If our laws were altered so that anyone could carry out an act of euthanasia, the absence of a clear line between those who might justifiably be killed and those who might not would pose a real danger; but that is not what advocates of euthanasia propose. If acts of euthanasia could only be carried out by a member of the medical profession, with the concurrence of a second doctor, it is not likely that the propensity to kill would spread unchecked throughout the community. Doctors already have a good deal of power over life and death, through their ability to withhold treatment. There has been no suggestion that doctors who begin by allowing grossly defective infants to die from pneumonia will move on to withhold antibiotics from racial minorities or political extremists. In fact legalizing euthanasia might well act as a check on the power of doctors since it would bring into the open and under the scrutiny of another doctor what some doctors now do on their own initiative and in secret.

There is, anyway, little historical evidence to suggest that a permissive attitude towards the killing of one category of human beings leads to a breakdown of restrictions against killing other humans. Ancient Greeks regularly killed or exposed infants, but appear to have been at least as scrupulous about taking the lives of their fellow-citizens as medieval Christians or modern Americans. In traditional Eskimo societies it was the custom for a man to kill his elderly parents, but the murder of a normal healthy adult was almost unheard of. If these societies could separate human beings into different categories without transferring their attitudes from one group to another, we with our more sophisticated legal systems and greater medical knowledge should be able to do the same.

All of this is not to deny that departing from the traditional sanctity of life ethic carries with it some risk of unwanted consequences. Against this risk we must balance the tangible harm to which the traditional ethic gives rise – harm to those whose misery is needlessly prolonged. We must also ask if the widespread acceptance of abortion and passive euthanasia has not already revealed flaws in the traditional ethic which make it a weak defence against those who lack respect for individual lives. A sounder, if less clear-cut, ethic may in the long run provide a firmer ground for resisting unjustifiable killing.

8

Rich and poor

Some facts

The last four chapters dealt with issues associated with killing. In the last of these, in the context of euthanasia, we questioned the distinction between killing and allowing to die, concluding that the distinction is of no intrinsic ethical significance. This conclusion has implications which go far beyond euthanasia.

Consider these facts: by the most cautious estimates, 400 million people lack the calories, protein, vitamins and minerals needed for a normally healthy life. Millions are constantly hungry; others suffer from deficiency diseases and from infections they would be able to resist on a better diet. Children are worst affected. According to one estimate, 15 million children under five die every year from the combined effects of malnutrition and infection. In some areas, half the children born can be expected to die before their fifth birthday.

Nor is lack of food the only hardship of the poor. To give a broader picture, Robert McNamara, President of the World Bank, has suggested the term 'absolute poverty'. The poverty we are familiar with in industrialized nations is relative poverty – meaning that some citizens are poor, relative to the wealth enjoyed by their neighbours. People living in relative poverty in Australia might be quite comfortably off by comparison with old-age pensioners in Britain, and British old-age pensioners are not poor in comparison with the poverty that exists in Mali or Ethiopia. Absolute poverty, on the other hand, is poverty by any standard. In McNamara's words:

Poverty at the absolute level . . . is life at the very margin of existence.

The absolute poor are severely deprived human beings struggling to survive in a set of squalid and degraded circumstances almost beyond the power of our sophisticated imaginations and privileged circumstances to conceive.

Compared to those fortunate enough to live in developed countries, individuals in the poorest nations have:

An infant mortality rate eight times higher

A life expectancy one-third lower

An adult literacy rate 60% less

A nutritional level, for one out of every two in the population, below acceptable standards; and for millions of infants, less protein than is sufficient to permit optimum development of the brain.

And McNamara has summed up absolute poverty as:

a condition of life so characterized by malnutrition, illiteracy, disease, squalid surroundings, high infant mortality and low life expectancy as to be beneath any reasonable definition of human decency.

Absolute poverty is, as McNamara has said, responsible for the loss of countless lives, especially among infants and young children. When absolute poverty does not cause death it still causes misery of a kind not often seen in the affluent nations. Malnutrition in young children stunts both physical and mental development. It has been estimated that the health, growth and learning capacity of nearly half the young children in developing countries are affected by malnutrition. Millions of people on poor diets suffer from deficiency diseases, like goitre, or blindness caused by a lack of vitamin A. The food value of what the poor eat is further reduced by parasites such as hookworm and ringworm, which are endemic in conditions of poor sanitation and health education.

Death and disease apart, absolute poverty remains a miserable condition of life, with inadequate food, shelter, clothing, sanitation, health services and education. According to World Bank estimates which define absolute poverty in terms of income levels insufficient to provide adequate nutrition, something like 800 million people – almost 40% of the people of developing countries – live in absolute poverty. Absolute poverty is probably the principal cause of human misery today.

This is the background situation, the situation that prevails on our planet all the time. It does not make headlines. People died from malnutrition and related diseases yesterday, and more will die tomorrow. The occasional droughts, cyclones, earthquakes and floods that take the lives of tens of thousands in one place and at one time are more newsworthy. They add greatly to the total amount of human suffering; but it is wrong to assume that when there are no major calamities reported, all is well.

The problem is not that the world cannot produce enough to feed and shelter its people. People in the poor countries consume, on average, 400 lbs of grain a year, while North Americans average more than 2000 lbs. The difference is caused by the fact that in the rich countries we feed most of our grain to animals, converting it into meat, milk and eggs. Because this is an inefficient process, wasting up to 95% of the food value of the animal feed, people in rich countries are responsible for the consumption of far more food than those in poor countries who eat few animal products. If we stopped feeding animals on grains, soybeans and fishmeal the amount of food saved would – if distributed to those who need it – be more than enough to end hunger throughout the world.

These facts about animal food do not mean that we can easily solve the world food problem by cutting down on animal products, but they show that the problem is essentially one of distribution rather than production. The world does produce enough food. Moreover the poorer nations themselves could produce far more if they made more use of improved agricultural techniques.

So why are people hungry? Poor people cannot afford to buy grain grown by American farmers. Poor farmers cannot afford to buy improved seeds, or fertilizers, or the machinery needed for drilling wells and pumping water. Only by transferring some of the wealth of the developed nations to the poor of the undeveloped nations can the situation be changed.

That this wealth exists is clear. Against the picture of absolute poverty that McNamara has painted, one might pose a picture of 'absolute affluence'. Those who are absolutely affluent are not necessarily affluent by comparison with their neighbours, but they are affluent by any reasonable definition of human needs. This means that they have more income than they need to provide themselves adequately with all the basic necessities of life. After buying food, shelter, clothing, necessary health services and education, the absolutely affluent are still able to spend money on luxuries. The absolutely affluent choose their food for the pleasures of the palate, not to stop hunger; they buy new clothes to look fashionable, not to keep warm; they move house to be in a better neighbourhood or have a play room for the children, not to keep out the rain; and after all this there is still money to spend on books and records, colour television, and overseas holidays.

At this stage I am making no ethical judgments about absolute affluence, merely pointing out that it exists. Its defining characteristic is a significant amount of income above the level necessary to provide for the basic human needs of oneself and one's dependents. By this standard Western Europe, North America, Japan, Australia, New Zealand and the oil-rich Middle Eastern states are all absolutely affluent, and so are many, if not all, of their citizens. The USSR and Eastern Europe might also be included on this list. To quote McNamara once more:

The average citizen of a developed country enjoys wealth beyond the wildest dreams of the one billion people in countries with per capita incomes under $200...

These, therefore, are the countries – and individuals – who have wealth which they could, without threatening their own basic welfare, transfer to the absolutely poor.

At present, very little is being transferred. Members of the Organization of Petroleum Exporting Countries lead the way, giving an average of 2.1% of their Gross National Product. Apart from them, only Sweden, The Netherlands and Norway have reached the modest UN target of 0.7% of GNP. Britain gives 0.38% of its GNP in official development assistance and a small additional amount in unofficial aid from voluntary organizations. The total comes to less than £1 per month per person, and compares with 5.5% of GNP spent on alcohol, and 3% on tobacco. Other, even wealthier nations, give still less: Germany gives 0.27%, the United States 0.22% and Japan 0.21%.

The moral equivalent of murder?

If these are the facts, we cannot avoid concluding that by not giving more than we do, people in rich countries are allowing those in poor countries to suffer from absolute poverty, with consequent malnutrition, ill health and death. This is not a conclusion which applies only to governments. It applies to each absolutely affluent individual, for each of us has the opportunity to do something about the situation; for instance, to give our time or money to voluntary organizations like Oxfam, War on Want, Freedom From Hunger, and so on. If, then, allowing someone to die is not intrinsically different from killing someone, it would seem that we are all murderers.

Is this verdict too harsh? Many will reject it as self-evidently absurd. They would sooner take it as showing that allowing to die cannot be equivalent to killing than as showing that living in an affluent style without contributing to Oxfam is ethically equivalent to going over to India and shooting a few peasants. And no doubt, put as bluntly as that, the verdict *is* too harsh.

There are several significant differences between spending money on luxuries instead of using it to save lives, and deliberately shooting people.

First, the motivation will normally be different. Those who deliberately shoot others go out of their way to kill; they presumably want their victims dead, from malice, sadism, or some equally unpleasant motive. A person who buys a colour television set presumably wants to watch television in colour – not in itself a terrible thing. At worst, spending money on luxuries instead of giving it away indicates selfishness and indifference to the sufferings of others, characteristics which may be undesirable but are not comparable with actual malice or similar motives.

Second, it is not difficult for most of us to act in accordance with a rule against killing people: it is, on the other hand, very difficult to obey a rule which commands us to save all the lives we can. To live a comfortable, or even luxurious life it is not necessary to kill anyone; but it is necessary to allow some to die whom we might have saved, for the money that we need to live comfortably could have been given away. Thus the duty to avoid killing is much easier to discharge completely than the duty to save. Saving every life we could would mean cutting our standard of living down to the bare essentials needed to keep us alive.* To discharge this duty completely would require a degree of moral heroism utterly different from what is required by mere avoidance of killing.

A third difference is the greater certainty of the outcome of shooting when compared with not giving aid. If I point a loaded gun at someone and pull the trigger, it is virtually certain that the person will be injured, if not killed; whereas the money that I could give might be spent on a project that turns out to be unsuccessful and helps no one.

Fourth, when people are shot there are identifiable individuals who have been harmed. We can point to them and to their grieving families. When I buy my colour television, I cannot know who my money would have saved if I had given it away. In a time of famine I may see dead bodies and grieving families on my new television, and I might not doubt that my money would have saved some of them; even then it is imposs-ible to point to a body and say that had I not bought the set, that person would have survived.

Fifth, it might be said that the plight of the hungry is not my doing, and so I cannot be held responsible for it. The starving would have been starving if I had never existed. If I kill,

* Strictly, we would need to cut down to the minimum level compatible with earning the income which, after providing for our needs, left us most to give away. Thus if my present position earns me, say, £10,000 a year, but requires me to spend £1,000 a year on dressing respectably and maintaining a car, I cannot save more people by giving away the car and clothes if that will mean taking a job which, although it does not involve me in these expenses, earns me only £5,000.

however, I am responsible for my victims' deaths, for those people would not have died if I had not killed them.

These differences need not shake our previous conclusion that there is no intrinsic difference between killing and allowing to die. They are extrinsic differences, that is, differences normally but not necessarily associated with the distinction between killing and allowing to die. We can imagine cases in which someone allows another to die for malicious or sadistic reasons; we can imagine a world in which there are so few people needing assistance, and they are so easy to assist, that our duty not to allow people to die is as easily discharged as our duty not to kill; we can imagine situations in which the outcome of not helping is as sure as shooting; we can imagine cases in which we can identify the person we allow to die. We can even imagine a case of allowing to die in which, if I had not existed, the person would not have died – for instance, a case in which if I had not been in a position to help (though I don't help) someone else would have been in my position and would have helped.

Our previous discussion of euthanasia illustrates the extrinsic nature of these differences, for they do not provide a basis for distinguishing active from passive euthanasia. If a doctor decides, in consultation with the parents, not to operate on – and thus to allow to die – a mongoloid infant with an intestinal blockage, his motivation will be similar to that of a doctor who gives a lethal injection rather than allow the infant to die. No extraordinary sacrifice or moral heroism will be required in either case. Not operating will just as certainly end in death as administering the injection. Allowing to die does have an identifiable victim. Finally, it may well be that the doctor is personally responsible for the death of the infant he decides not to operate upon, since he may know that if he had not taken this case, other doctors in the hospital would have operated.

Nevertheless, euthanasia is a special case, and very different from allowing people to starve to death. (The major difference being that when euthanasia is justifiable, death is a good thing.) The extrinsic differences which *normally* mark off killing and allowing to die do explain why we *normally* regard killing as much worse than allowing to die.

To explain our conventional ethical attitudes is not to justify them. Do the five differences not only explain, but also justify, our attitudes? Let us consider them one by one:

(1) Take the lack of an identifiable victim first. Suppose that I am a travelling salesman, selling tinned food, and I learn that a batch of tins contains a contaminant, the known effect of which when consumed is to double the risk that the consumer will die from stomach cancer. Suppose I continue to sell the tins. My decision may have no identifiable victims. Some of those who eat the food will die from cancer. The proportion of consumers dying in this way will be twice that of the community at large, but which among the consumers died because they ate what I sold, and which would have contracted the disease anyway? It is impossible to tell; but surely this impossibility makes my decision no less reprehensible than it would have been had the contaminant had more readily detectable, though equally fatal, effects.

(2) The lack of certainty that by giving money I could save a life does reduce the wrongness of not giving, by comparison with deliberate killing; but it is insufficient to show that not giving is acceptable conduct. The motorist who speeds through pedestrian crossings, heedless of anyone who might be on them, is not a murderer. She may never actually hit a pedestrian; yet what she does is very wrong indeed.

(3) The notion of responsibility for acts rather than omissions is more puzzling. On the one hand we feel ourselves to be under a greater obligation to help those whose misfortunes we have caused. (It is for this reason that advocates of overseas aid often argue that Western nations have created the poverty of Third World nations, through forms of economic exploitation which go back to the colonial system.) On the other hand any consequentialist would insist that we are responsible for all the consequences of our actions, and if a consequence of my spending money on a luxury item is that someone dies, I am responsible for that death. It is true that the person would have died even if I

had never existed, but what is the relevance of that? The fact is that I do exist, and the consequentialist will say that our responsibilities derive from the world as it is, not as it might have been.

One way of making sense of the non-consequentialist view of responsibility is by basing it on a theory of rights of the kind proposed by John Locke or, more recently, Robert Nozick. If everyone has a right to life, and this right is a right *against* others who might threaten my life, but not a right *to* assistance from others when my life is in danger, then we can understand the feeling that we are responsible for acting to kill but not for omitting to save. The former violates the rights of others, the latter does not.

Should we accept such a theory of rights? If we build up our theory of rights by imagining, as Locke and Nozick do, individuals living independently from each other in a 'state of nature', it may seem natural to adopt a conception of rights in which as long as each leaves the other alone, no rights are violated. I might, on this view, quite properly have maintained my independent existence if I had wished to do so. So if I do not make you any worse off than you would have been if I had had nothing at all to do with you, how can I have violated your rights? But why start from such an unhistorical, abstract and ultimately inexplicable idea as an independent individual? We now know that our ancestors were social beings long before they were human beings, and could not have developed the abilities and capacities of human beings if they had not been social beings first. In any case we are not, now, isolated individuals. If we consider people living together in a community, it is less easy to assume that rights must be restricted to rights against interference. We might, instead, adopt the view that taking rights to life seriously is incompatible with standing by and watching people die when one could easily save them.

(4) What of the difference in motivation? That a person does not positively wish for the death of another lessens the severity of the blame she deserves; but not by as much as our present attitudes to giving aid suggest. The behaviour of the speeding motorist is again comparable, for such motorists usually have

no desire at all to kill anyone. They merely enjoy speeding and are indifferent to the consequences. Despite their lack of malice, those who kill with cars deserve not only blame but also severe punishment.

(5) Finally, the fact that to avoid killing people is normally not difficult, whereas to save all one possibly could save is heroic, must make an important difference to our attitude to failure to do what the respective principles demand. Not to kill is a minimum standard of acceptable conduct we can require of everyone; to save all one possibly could is not something that can realistically be required, especially not in societies accustomed to giving as little as ours do. Given the generally accepted standards, people who give, say, £100 a year to Oxfam are more aptly praised for above average generosity than blamed for giving less than they might. The appropriateness of praise and blame is, however, a separate issue from the rightness or wrongness of actions. The former evaluates the agent: the latter evaluates the action. Perhaps people who give £100 really ought to give at least £1,000, but to blame them for not giving more could be counterproductive. It might make them feel that what is required is too demanding, and if one is going to be blamed anyway, one might as well not give anything at all.

(That an ethic which put saving all one possibly can on the same footing as not killing would be an ethic for saints or heroes should not lead us to assume that the alternative must be an ethic which makes it obligatory not to kill, but puts us under no obligation to save anyone. There are positions in between these extremes, as we shall soon see.)

To summarize our discussion of the five differences which normally exist between killing and allowing to die, in the context of absolute poverty and overseas aid. The lack of an identifiable victim is of no moral significance, though it may play an important role in explaining our attitudes. The idea that we are directly responsible for those we kill, but not for those we do not help, depends on a questionable notion of responsibility, and may need to be based on a controversial theory of rights. Differences in certainty and motivation are ethically significant, and show that not aiding the poor is not to be condemned as murdering them; it could, however, be on a par with killing someone as a result of reckless driving, which is serious enough. Finally the difficulty of completely discharging the duty of saving all one possibly can makes it inappropriate to blame those who fall short of this target as we blame those who kill; but this does not show that the act itself is less serious. Nor does it indicate anything about those who, far from saving all they possibly can, make no effort to save anyone.

These conclusions suggest a new approach. Instead of attempting to deal with the contrast between affluence and poverty by comparing not saving with deliberate killing, let us consider afresh whether we have an obligation to assist those whose lives are in danger, and if so, how this obligation applies to the present world situation.

The obligation to assist

The argument for an obligation to assist

The path from the library at my university to the Humanities lecture theatre passes a shallow ornamental pond. Suppose that on my way to give a lecture I notice that a small child has fallen in and is in danger of drowning. Would anyone deny that I ought to wade in and pull the child out? This will mean getting my clothes muddy, and either cancelling my lecture or delaying it until I can find something dry to change into; but compared with the avoidable death of a child this is insignificant.

A plausible principle that would support the judgment that I ought to pull the child out is this: if it is in our power to prevent something very bad happening, without thereby sacrificing anything of comparable moral significance, we ought to do it. This principle seems uncontroversial. It will obviously win the assent of consequentialists; but non-consequentialists should accept it too, because the injunction to prevent what is bad applies only when nothing comparably significant is at stake. Thus the principle cannot lead to the kinds of actions of which non-consequentialists strongly disapprove – serious violations of individual rights, injustice, broken promises, and so on. If a non-consequentialist regards any of these as comparable in moral significance to the bad thing that is to be prevented, he will automatically regard the principle as not applying in those cases in which the bad thing can only be prevented by violating rights, doing injustice, breaking promises, or whatever else is at stake. Most non-consequentialists hold that we ought to prevent what is bad and promote what is good. Their dispute with consequentialists lies in their insistence that this is not the sole ultimate ethical principle: that it is *an* ethical principle is not denied by any plausible ethical theory.

Nevertheless the uncontroversial appearance of the principle that we ought to prevent what is bad when we can do so without sacrificing anything of comparable moral significance is deceptive. If it were taken seriously and acted upon, our lives and our world would be fundamentally changed. For the principle applies, not just to rare situations in which one can save a child from a pond, but to the everyday situation in which we can assist those living in absolute poverty. In saying this I assume that absolute poverty, with its hunger and malnutrition, lack of shelter, illiteracy, disease, high infant mortality and low life expectancy, is a bad thing. And I assume that it is within the power of the affluent to reduce absolute poverty, without sacrificing anything of comparable moral significance. If these two assumptions and the principle we have been discussing are correct, we have an obligation to help those in absolute poverty which is no less strong than our obligation to rescue a drowning child from a pond. Not to help would be wrong, whether or not it is intrinsically equivalent to killing. Helping is not, as conventionally thought, a charitable act which it is praiseworthy to do, but not wrong to omit; it is something that everyone ought to do.

This is the argument for an obligation to assist. Set out more formally, it would look like this.

First premise: If we can prevent something bad without sacrificing anything of comparable significance, we ought to do it.

Second premise: Absolute poverty is bad.

Third premise: There is some absolute poverty we can pre-
                  vent without sacrificing anything of compar-
                  able moral significance.
Conclusion: We ought to prevent some absolute poverty.

The first premise is the substantive moral premise on which
the argument rests, and I have tried to show that it can be
accepted by people who hold a variety of ethical positions.

The second premise is unlikely to be challenged. Absolute
poverty is, as McNamara put it, 'beneath any reasonable
definition of human decency' and it would be hard to find a
plausible ethical view which did not regard it as a bad thing.

The third premise is more controversial, even though it is
cautiously framed. It claims only that some absolute poverty
can be prevented without the sacrifice of anything of comparable moral significance. It thus avoids the objection that any aid
I can give is just 'drops in the ocean' for the point is not whether
my personal contribution will make any noticeable impression
on world poverty as a whole (of course it won't) but whether it
will prevent some poverty. This is all the argument needs to
sustain its conclusion, since the second premise says that any
absolute poverty is bad, and not merely the total amount of
absolute poverty. If without sacrificing anything of comparable
moral significance we can provide just one family with the
means to raise itself out of absolute poverty, the third premise is
vindicated.

I have left the notion of moral significance unexamined in
order to show that the argument does not depend on any specific
values or ethical principles. I think the third premise is true for
most people living in industrialized nations, on any defensible
view of what is morally significant. Our affluence means that we
have income we can dispose of without giving up the basic
necessities of life, and we can use this income to reduce absolute
poverty. Just how much we will think ourselves obliged to give
up will depend on what we consider to be of comparable moral
significance to the poverty we could prevent: colour television,
stylish clothes, expensive dinners, a sophisticated stereo system,

overseas holidays, a (second?) car, a larger house, private schools for our children ... For a utilitarian, none of these is likely to be of comparable significance to the reduction of absolute poverty; and those who are not utilitarians surely must, if they subscribe to the principle of universalizability, accept that at least *some* of these things are of far less moral significance than the absolute poverty that could be prevented by the money they cost. So the third premise seems to be true on any plausible ethical view – although the precise amount of absolute poverty that can be prevented before anything of moral significance is sacrificed will vary according to the ethical view one accepts.

Objections to the argument

Taking care of our own Anyone who has worked to increase overseas aid will have come across the argument that we should look after those near us, our families and then the poor in our own country, before we think about poverty in distant places.

No doubt we do instinctively prefer to help those who are close to us. Few could stand by and watch a child drown; many can ignore a famine in Africa. But the question is not what we usually do, but what we ought to do, and it is difficult to see any sound moral justification for the view that distance, or community membership, makes a crucial difference to our obligations.

Consider, for instance, racial affinities. Should whites help poor whites before helping poor blacks? Most of us would reject such a suggestion out of hand, and our discussion of the principle of equal consideration of interests in Chapter 2 has shown why we should reject it: people's need for food has nothing to do with their race, and if blacks need food more than whites, it would be a violation of the principle of equal consideration to give preference to whites.

The same point applies to citizenship or nationhood. Every affluent nation has some relatively poor citizens, but absolute poverty is limited largely to the poor nations. Those living on the streets of Calcutta, or in a drought-stricken region of the

Sahel, are experiencing poverty unknown in the West. Under these circumstances it would be wrong to decide that only those fortunate enough to be citizens of our own community will share our abundance.

We feel obligations of kinship more strongly than those of citizenship. Which parents could give away their last bowl of rice if their own children were starving? To do so would seem unnatural, contrary to our nature as biologically evolved beings – although whether it would be wrong is another question altogether. In any case, we are not faced with that situation, but with one in which our own children are well-fed, well-clothed, well-educated, and would now like new bikes, a stereo set, or their own car. In these circumstances any special obligations we might have to our children have been fulfilled, and the needs of strangers make a stronger claim upon us.

The element of truth in the view that we should first take care of our own, lies in the advantage of a recognized system of responsibilities. When families and local communities look after their own poorer members, ties of affection and personal relationships achieve ends that would otherwise require a large, impersonal bureaucracy. Hence it would be absurd to propose that from now on we all regard ourselves as equally responsible for the welfare of everyone in the world; but the argument for an obligation to assist does not propose that. It applies only when some are in absolute poverty, and others can help without sacrificing anything of comparable moral significance. To allow one's own kin to sink into absolute poverty would be to sacrifice something of comparable significance; and before that point had been reached, the breakdown of the system of family and community responsibility would be a factor to weigh the balance in favour of a small degree of preference for family and community. This small degree of preference is, however, decisively outweighed by existing discrepancies in wealth and property.

Property rights Do people have a right to private property, a right which contradicts the view that they are under an obligation to give some of their wealth away to those in absolute poverty? According to some theories of rights (for instance, Robert Nozick's) provided one has acquired one's property without the use of unjust means like force and fraud, one may be entitled to enormous wealth while others starve. This individualistic conception of rights is in contrast to other views, like the early Christian doctrine to be found in the works of Thomas Aquinas, which holds that since property exists for the satisfaction of human needs, 'whatever a man has in superabundance is owed, of natural right, to the poor for their sustenance'. A socialist would also, of course, see wealth as belonging to the community rather than the individual, while utilitarians, whether socialist or not, would be prepared to override property rights to prevent great evils.

Does the argument for an obligation to assist others therefore presuppose one of these other theories of property rights, and not an individualistic theory like Nozick's? Not necessarily. A theory of property rights can insist on our *right* to retain wealth without pronouncing on whether the rich *ought* to give to the poor. Nozick, for example, rejects the use of compulsory means like taxation to redistribute income, but suggests that we can achieve the ends we deem morally desirable by voluntary means. So Nozick would reject the claim that rich people have an 'obligation' to give to the poor, in so far as this implies that the poor have a right to our aid, but might accept that giving is something we ought to do and failing to give, though within one's rights, is wrong – for rights is not all there is to ethics.

The argument for an obligation to assist can survive, with only minor modifications, even if we accept an individualistic theory of property rights. In any case, however, I do not think we should accept such a theory. It leaves too much to chance to be an acceptable ethical view. For instance, those whose forefathers happened to inhabit some sandy wastes around the Persian Gulf are now fabulously wealthy, because oil lay under those sands; while those whose forefathers settled on better land south of the Sahara live in absolute poverty, because of drought and bad harvests. Can this distribution be acceptable from an impartial point of view? If we imagine ourselves about to begin life as a citizen of either Kuwait or Chad – but we do not know which – would we accept the principle that citizens of Kuwait are under no obligation to assist people living in Chad?

Population and the ethics of triage Perhaps the most serious objection to the argument that we have an obligation to assist is that since the major cause of absolute poverty is overpopulation, helping those now in poverty will only ensure that yet more people are born to live in poverty in the future.

In its most extreme form, this objection is taken to show that we should adopt a policy of 'triage'. The term comes from medical policies adopted in wartime. With too few doctors to cope with all the casualties, the wounded were divided into three categories: those who would probably survive without medical assistance, those who might survive if they received assistance, but otherwise probably would not, and those who even with medical assistance probably would not survive. Only those in the middle category were given medical assistance. The idea, of course, was to use limited medical resources as effectively as possible. For those in the first category, medical treatment was not strictly necessary; for those in the third category, it was likely to be useless. It has been suggested that we should apply the same policies to countries, according to their prospects of becoming self-sustaining. We would not aid countries which even without our help will soon be able to feed their populations. We would not aid countries which, even with our help, will not be able to limit their population to a level they can feed. We would aid those countries where our help might make the difference between success and failure in bringing food and population into balance.

Advocates of this theory are understandably reluctant to give a complete list of the countries they would place into the 'hopeless' category; but Bangladesh is often cited as an example. Adopting the policy of triage would, then, mean cutting off assistance to Bangladesh and allowing famine, disease and natural disasters to reduce the population of that country (now around 80 million) to the level at which it can provide adequately for all.

In support of this view Garrett Hardin has offered a metaphor: we in the rich nations are like the occupants of a crowded lifeboat adrift in a sea full of drowning people. If we try to save the drowning by bringing them aboard our boat will be overloaded and we shall all drown. Since it is better that some survive than none, we should leave the others to drown. In the world today, according to Hardin, 'lifeboat ethics' apply. The rich should leave the poor to starve, for otherwise the poor will drag the rich down with them.

Against this view, some writers have argued that over-population is a myth. The world produces ample food to feed its population, and could, according to some estimates, feed ten times as many. People are hungry not because there are too many but because of inequitable land distribution, the manipulation of Third World economies by the developed nations, wastage of food in the West, and so on.

Putting aside the controversial issue of the extent to which food production might one day be increased, it is true, as we have already seen, that the world now produces enough to feed its inhabitants – the amount lost by being fed to animals itself being enough to meet existing grain shortages. Nevertheless population growth cannot be ignored. Bangladesh could, with land reform and using better techniques, feed its present population of 80 million; but by the year 2000, according to World Bank estimates, its population will be 146 million. The enormous effort that will have to go into feeding an extra 66 million people, all added to the population within a quarter of a century, means that Bangladesh must develop at full speed to stay where she is. Other low income countries are in similar situations. By the end of the century, Ethiopia's population is expected to rise from 29 to 54 million; Somalia's from 3 to 7 million, India's from 620 to 958 million, Zaire's from 25 to 47 million. What will happen then? Population cannot grow indefinitely. It will be checked by a decline in birth rates or a rise in death rates. Those who advocate triage are proposing that we allow the population growth of some countries to be checked by a rise in death rates – that is, by increased malnutrition, and related diseases; by widespread famines; by increased infant mortality; and by epidemics of infectious diseases.

The consequences of triage on this scale are so horrible that we are inclined to reject it without further argument. How could we sit by our television sets, watching millions starve while we do nothing? Would not that (far more than the proposals for legalizing euthanasia discussed in the last chapter) be the end of all notions of human equality and respect for human life? Don't people have a right to our assistance, irrespective of the consequences?

Anyone whose initial reaction to triage was not one of repugnance would be an unpleasant sort of person. Yet initial reactions based on strong feelings are not always reliable guides. Advocates of triage are rightly concerned with the long-term consequences of our actions. They say that helping the poor and starving now merely ensures more poor and starving in the future. When our capacity to help is finally unable to cope – as one day it must be – the suffering will be greater than it would be if we stopped helping now. If this is correct, there is nothing we can do to prevent absolute starvation and poverty, in the long run, and so we have no obligation to assist. Nor does it seem reasonable to hold that under these circumstances people have a right to our assistance. If we do accept such a right, irrespective of the consequences, we are saying that, in Hardin's metaphor, we would continue to haul the drowning into our lifeboat until the boat sank and we all drowned.

If triage is to be rejected it must be tackled on its own ground, within the framework of consequentialist ethics. Here it is vulnerable. Any consequentialist ethics must take probability of outcome into account. A course of action that will certainly produce some benefit is to be preferred to an alternative course that may lead to a slightly larger benefit, but is equally likely to result in no benefit at all. Only if the greater magnitude of the uncertain benefit outweighs its uncertainty should we choose it. Better one certain unit of benefit than a 10% chance of 5 units;

but better a 50% chance of 3 units than a single certain unit. The same principle applies when we are trying to avoid evils.

The policy of triage involves a certain, very great evil: population control by famine and disease. Tens of millions would die slowly. Hundreds of millions would continue to live in absolute poverty, at the very margin of existence. Against this prospect, advocates of the policy place a possible evil which is greater still: the same process of famine and disease, taking place in, say, fifty years time, when the world's population may be three times its present level, and the number who will die from famine, or struggle on in absolute poverty, will be that much greater. The question is: how probable is this forecast that continued assistance now will lead to greater disasters in the future?

Forecasts of population growth are notoriously fallible, and theories about the factors which affect it remain speculative. One theory, at least as plausible as any other, is that countries pass through a 'demographic transition' as their standard of living rises. When people are very poor and have no access to modern medicine their fertility is high, but population is kept in check by high death rates. The introduction of sanitation, modern medical techniques and other improvements reduces the death rate, but initially has little effect on the birth rate. Then population grows rapidly. Most poor countries are now in this phase. If standards of living continue to rise, however, couples begin to realize that to have the same number of children surviving to maturity as in the past, they do not need to give birth to as many children as their parents did. The need for children to provide economic support in old age diminishes. Improved education and the emancipation and employment of women also reduce the birthrate, and so population growth begins to level off. Most rich nations have reached this stage, and their populations are growing only very slowly.

If this theory is right, there is an alternative to the disasters accepted as inevitable by supporters of triage. We can assist poor countries to raise the living standards of the poorest members of their population. We can encourage the governments of these countries to enact land reform measures, improve education, and liberate women from a purely child-bearing role. We can also help other countries to make contraception and sterilization widely available. There is a fair chance that these measures will hasten the onset of the demographic transition and bring population growth down to a manageable level. Success cannot be guaranteed; but the evidence that improved economic security and education reduce population growth is strong enough to make triage ethically unacceptable. We cannot allow millions to die from starvation and disease when there is a reasonable probability that population can be brought under control without such horrors.

Population growth is therefore not a reason against giving overseas aid, although it should make us think about the kind of aid to give. Instead of food handouts, it may be better to give aid that hastens the demographic transition. This may mean agricultural assistance for the rural poor, or assistance with education, or the provision of contraceptive services. Whatever kind of aid proves most effective in specific circumstances, the obligation to assist is not reduced.

One awkward question remains. What should we do about a poor and already overpopulated country which, for religious or nationalistic reasons, restricts the use of contraceptives and refuses to slow its population growth? Should we nevertheless offer development assistance? Or should we make our offer conditional on effective steps being taken to reduce the birth-rate? To the latter course, some would object that putting conditions on aid is an attempt to impose our own ideas on independent sovereign nations. So it is – but is this imposition unjustifiable? If the argument for an obligation to assist is sound, we have an obligation to reduce absolute poverty; but we have no obligation to make sacrifices that, to the best of our knowledge, have no prospect of reducing poverty in the long run. Hence we have no obligation to assist countries whose governments have policies which will make our aid ineffective. This could be very harsh on poor citizens of these countries – for they may have no say in the government's policies – but we will help more people in the long run by using our resources where they are most effective. (The same principles may apply, incidentally, to countries that refuse to take other steps that could make assistance effective – like refusing to reform systems of land holding that impose intolerable burdens on poor tenant farmers.)

Leaving it to the government We often hear that overseas aid should be a government responsibility, not left to privately-run charities. Giving privately, it is said, allows the government to escape its responsibilities.

Since increasing government aid is the surest way of making a significant increase to the total amount of aid given, I would agree that the governments of affluent nations should give much more genuine, no strings attached, aid than they give now. One quarter of one percent of GNP is a scandalously small amount for a nation as wealthy as the United States to give. Even the official UN target of 0.7% seems much less than affluent nations can and should give – though it is a target few have reached. But is this a reason against each of us giving what we can privately, through voluntary agencies? To believe that it is seems to assume that the more people there are who give through voluntary agencies, the less likely it is that the government will do its part. Is this plausible? The opposite view – that if no one gives voluntarily the government will assume that its citizens are not in favour of overseas aid, and will cut its programme accordingly – is more reasonable. In any case, unless there is a definite probability that by refusing to give we would be helping to bring about an increase in government assistance, refusing to give privately is wrong for the same reason that triage is wrong: it is a refusal to prevent a definite evil for the sake of a very uncertain gain. The onus of showing how a refusal to give privately will make the government give more is on those who refuse to give.

This is not to say that giving privately is enough. Certainly we should campaign for entirely new standards for both public and private overseas aid. We should also work for fairer trading arrangements between rich and poor countries, and less domination of the economies of poor countries by multinational corporations more concerned to produce profits for share-holders back home than food for the local poor. Perhaps it is more important to be politically active in the interests of the poor than to give to them oneself – but why not do both? Unfortunately many use the view that overseas aid is the government's responsibility as a reason against giving, but not as a reason for being politically active.

Too high a standard? The final objection to the argument for an obligation to assist is that it sets a standard so high that none but a saint could attain it. How many people can we really expect to give away everything not comparable in moral significance to the poverty their donation could relieve? For most of us, with commonsense views about what is of moral significance, this would mean a life of real austerity. Might it not be counter-productive to demand so much? Might not people say: 'As I can't do what is morally required anyway, I won't bother to give at all.' If, however, we were to set a more realistic standard, people might make a genuine effort to reach it. Thus setting a lower standard might actually result in more aid being given.

It is important to get the status of this objection clear. Its accuracy as a prediction of human behaviour is quite compatible with the argument that we are obliged to give to the point at which by giving more we sacrifice something of comparable moral significance. What would follow from the objection is that public advocacy of this standard of giving is undesirable. It would mean that in order to do the maximum to reduce absolute poverty, we should advocate a standard lower than the amount we think people really ought to give. Of course we ourselves – those of us who accept the original argument, with its higher standard – would know that we ought to do more than we publicly propose people ought to do, and we might actually give more than we urge others to give. There is no inconsistency here, since in both our private and our public behaviour we are trying to do what will most reduce absolute poverty.

For a consequentialist, this apparent conflict between public and private morality is always a possibility, and not in itself an indication that the underlying principle is wrong. The consequences of a principle are one thing, the consequences of publicly advocating it another.

Is it true that the standard set by our argument is so high as to be counterproductive? There is not much evidence to go by, but discussions of the argument, with students and others have led me to think it might be. On the other hand the conventionally accepted standard – a few coins in a collection tin when one is waved under your nose – is obviously far too low. What level should we advocate? Any figure will be arbitrary, but there may be something to be said for a round percentage of one's income like, say, 10% – more than a token donation, yet not so high as to be beyond all but saints. (This figure has the additional advantage of being reminiscent of the ancient tithe, or tenth, which was traditionally given to the church, whose responsibilities included care of the poor in one's local community. Perhaps the idea can be revived and applied to the global community.) Some families, of course, will find 10% a considerable strain on their finances. Others may be able to give more without difficulty. No figure should be advocated as a rigid minimum or maximum; but it seems safe to advocate that those earning average or above average incomes in affluent societies, unless they have an unusually large number of dependents or other special needs, ought to give a tenth of their income to reducing absolute poverty. By any reasonable ethical standards this is the minimum we ought to do, and we do wrong if we do less.

9

Ends and means

We have examined a number of ethical issues. We have seen that many accepted practices are open to serious objections. What ought we to do about it? This, too, is an ethical issue.

Take a particular example: there now exists, in Britain, an Animal Liberation Front. Members of the ALF are opposed to the exploitation of animals in factory farms, for furs, in laboratories and so on. Instead of protesting against these practices in the usual way, however, they have taken direct action, raiding fur farms, releasing the animals, damaging laboratories used for animal experiments, and holing boats about to be used for seal-hunting expeditions. Taking care to do no violence to any animals, human or nonhuman, they have done extensive damage to property. Some members have been caught and received jail sentences of up to three years.

It is right to object strongly to abuses of animals which, as we have seen, are tolerated only because we do not take the interests of members of other species as seriously as we take the interests of other *homo sapiens*. Is it also right to take direct illegal action against these abuses? Or do we have an overriding obligation to obey the law? If we agree with the goal of eliminating the abuse of animals, must we also accept the means?

The question cannot be dealt with by invoking the simplistic formula: 'the end never justifies the means'. For all but the strictest adherent of an ethic of rules, the end sometimes does justify the means. Most people think that lying is wrong, yet think it right to lie in order to avoid causing unnecessary offence or embarrassment – for instance, when a relative gives you a hideous vase for your birthday, and then asks if you really like it. If this relatively trivial end can justify lying, it is even more obvious that some important end – preventing a murder, or saving animals from unnecessary suffering – can justify lying. Thus the principle that the end cannot justify the means is easily breached. The difficult issue is not whether the end can ever justify the means, but which means are justified by which ends. In particular: do the ends argued for in previous chapters of this book – ends like equal consideration of interests irrespective of race, sex or species, liberal abortion laws, voluntary euthanasia, and the reduction of absolute poverty – justify the use of any means that may bring about the desired end?

Individual conscience and the law

The most obvious difference between the activities of the Animal Liberation Front and those of the Royal Society for the Prevention of Cruelty to Animals is that the ALF activities are illegal. No doubt some members of the RSPCA do not commit illegal acts because they do not wish to be fined or imprisoned; but others would be prepared to take the consequences of illegal acts and refrain only because they do not think it right to break the law. They will do everything possible, through legal channels, to end painful experimentation and factory farming; but they respect and obey the moral authority of the law.

Who is right in this ethical disagreement? Are we under any moral obligation to obey the law, if the law protects and sanctions things we hold utterly wrong? A clear-cut answer to this question was given by the nineteenth-century American radical, Henry Thoreau. In his essay entitled 'Civil Disobedience' – perhaps the first use of this now-familiar phrase – he wrote:

Must the citizen never for a moment, or in the least degree, resign his conscience to the legislator? Why has every man a conscience, then? I think we should be men first and subjects afterwards. It is not desirable to cultivate a respect for the law, so much as for the right. The only obligation which I have a right to assume, is to do at any time what I think right.

More recently the American philosopher Robert Paul Wolff has
written in similar vein:

The defining mark of the state is authority, the right to rule. The
primary obligation of man is autonomy, the refusal to be ruled. It
would seem, then, that there can be no resolution of the conflict
between the autonomy of the individual and the putative authority of
the state. Insofar as a man fulfills his obligation to make himself the
author of his decisions, he will resist the state's claim to have authority
over him.

Thoreau and Wolff resolve the conflict between individual and
society in favour of the individual. We should do as our conscience dictates, as we autonomously decide we ought to do: not
as the law directs. Anything else would be a denial of our
capacity for ethical choice.

So stated the issue looks straightforward and the
Thoreau–Wolff answer obviously right. But is it that simple?
There is a sense in which it is undeniable that, as Thoreau says,
we ought to do what we think right; or, as Wolff puts it, make
ourselves the author of our decisions. Faced with a choice
between doing what we think right and what we think wrong, of
course we ought to do what we think right. But this, though true,
is not much help. What we need to know is not whether we
should do what we decide to be right, but how we should decide
what is right.

Recall the difference of opinion between members of the
Animal Liberation Front and more law-abiding members of the
RSPCA: ALF members think inflicting unnecessary pain on
animals is wrong, and if the best way to stop it is by breaking the
law then breaking the law is right. RSPCA members think
inflicting unnecessary pain on animals is wrong, but think
breaking the law wrong too. Now suppose there are people
opposed to inflicting unnecessary pain on animals who are
uncertain whether they should join the militant lawbreakers or
the more orthodox animal welfare group. How does telling these
people to do what they think right, or to be the author of their
own decisions, resolve their uncertainty? The uncertainty is an
uncertainty about what is the right thing to do, not about
whether to do what one has decided to be right.

This point can be obscured by talk of 'following one's conscience' irrespective of what the law commands. Some who talk of 'following conscience' mean no more than doing what, on reflection, one thinks right – and this may, as in the case of our imagined RSPCA members, depend on what the law commands. Others mean by 'conscience' not something dependent on critical reflective judgment, but a kind of internal voice which tells us that something is wrong and may continue to tell us this despite our careful reflective decision, based on all the relevant ethical considerations, that the action is not wrong. In this sense of conscience an unmarried woman brought up as a strict Roman Catholic to believe that sex outside marriage is always wrong may abandon her religion and come to hold that there is no sound basis for restricting sex to marriage – yet continue to feel guilty when she has sex.

To say that we should follow our conscience is unobjectionable – and unhelpful – when 'following conscience' means doing what, on reflection, one thinks right. When 'following conscience' means doing as one's 'internal voice' prompts one to do, however, to follow one's conscience is to abdicate one's responsibility as a rational agent, to fail to take all the relevant factors into account and act on one's best judgment of the rights and wrongs of the situation. The 'internal voice' is more likely to be a product of one's upbringing and education than a source of genuine ethical insight.

Presumably neither Thoreau nor Wolff wish to suggest that we should always follow our conscience in the 'internal voice' sense. They must mean, if their views are to be at all plausible, that we should follow our judgment about what we ought to do. In this case the most that can be said for their recommendations is that they remind us that decisions about obeying the law are ethical decisions which the law itself cannot settle for us. We should not assume, without reflection, that if the law prohibits, say, releasing rabbits from cosmetic laboratories, it is wrong to release rabbits from cosmetic laboratories. Law and ethics are distinct. On the other hand this does not mean that the law carries no moral weight. It does not mean that any action which would have been right if it had been legal must be right although it is in fact illegal. That an action is illegal *may* be of ethical, as well as legal, significance. Whether it really is ethically significant is a separate question.

Law and order

If we think it wrong to test shampoos on the eyes of rabbits and have the courage and ability to disrupt this practice by breaking into laboratories and releasing rabbits, how could the illegality of this action provide an ethical reason against it? To answer a question as specific as this, we should first ask a more general one: why have laws at all?

Human beings are social in nature, but not so social that we do not need to protect ourselves against the risk of being assaulted or killed by our fellow humans. We might try to do this by forming vigilante organizations to prevent assaults and punish those who commit them; but the results would be haphazard and liable to grow into gang warfare. Thus it is desirable to have as John Locke said long ago, 'an established, settled, known law', interpreted by an authoritative judge and backed with sufficient power to carry out the judge's decisions.

If people voluntarily refrained from assaulting others, or acting in other ways inimical to a harmonious and happy social existence, we might manage without judges and sanctions. We would need law-like conventions about such matters as which side of the road one drives on. Even an anarchist utopia would have some settled principles of co-operation. So we would still have something rather like law. In reality, not everyone is going to voluntarily refrain from behaviour, like assaults, which others cannot tolerate. Nor is it only the danger of individual acts like assaults that make law necessary. In any society there will be disputes: about how much water farmers may take from the river to irrigate their crops, about the ownership of land, or the custody of a child, about the control of pollution and the level of taxation. Some settled decision-procedure is necessary for resolving such disputes economically and speedily, or else the parties to the dispute are likely to resort to force. Almost any established decision-procedure is better than a resort to force, for when force is used people get hurt. Moreover, most decision-procedures produce results at least as beneficial and just as a resort to force.

So laws and a settled decision-procedure to generate them are a good thing. This gives rise to one important reason for obeying the law. By obeying the law, I can contribute to the respect in which the established decision-procedure and the laws are held. By disobeying I set an example to others which may lead them to disobey too. The effect may multiply and contribute to a decline in law and order. In an extreme case it may lead to civil war.

A second reason for obedience follows immediately from this first. If law is to be effective – outside the anarchist's utopia – there must be some machinery for detecting and penalizing law-breakers. This machinery will cost something to maintain and operate, and the cost will have to be met by the community. If I break the law the community will be put to the expense of enforcement.

These two reasons for obeying the law are neither universally applicable nor conclusive. They are not, for instance, applicable to breaches of the law which remain secret. If, late at night when the streets are deserted, I cross the road against the red light, there is no one to be led into disobedience by my example, and no one to enforce the law against so crossing. But this is not the kind of illegality we are interested in.

Where they are applicable, these two reasons for obedience are not conclusive, because there are times when the reasons against obeying a particular law are more important than the risks of encouraging others to disobey or the costs to the community of enforcing the law. They are genuine reasons for obeying, and in the absence of reasons for disobeying, are sufficient to resolve the issue in favour of obedience; but where there are conflicting reasons, we must assess each case on its merits in order to see if the reasons for disobeying outweigh these reasons for obedience. If, for instance, illegal acts were the only way of preventing huge numbers of painful and unnecessary experiments, or of prodding governments into increasing overseas aid, the importance of the ends would justify running some risk of contributing to a general decline in obedience to law.

Democracy

At this point some will say: if the *only* means of ending the abuse of animals in unnecessary experiments were to damage laboratories and release the animals, perhaps these drastic acts would be justified; but in a democracy there are legal means of ending abuses. The existence of legal procedures for changing the law makes the use of illegal means unjustifiable.

It is true that in parliamentary democracies, of which the United Kingdom is an example, there are legal procedures which can be used by those seeking reforms; but this in itself does not show that the use of illegal means is wrong. Legal channels may exist, but the prospects of using them to bring about change may be very poor. An extremely remote possibility of legal change is not a strong reason against using means more likely to succeed. The most that can follow from the mere existence of legitimate channels is that, since we cannot know whether they will prove successful until we have tried them, their existence is a reason for postponing illegal acts until legal means have been tried and have failed.

Animal experimentation provides an illustration of how long and frustrating the attempt to secure reform by legal means can be. The law regulating animal experiments in Britain today dates back to 1876. After more than a century of unsuccessful attempts by legal means to have it strengthened, militant opponents of uncontrolled experimentation can plausibly claim that legal means have been tried and have failed. This is not to say that attempts to secure reform by legal means will never succeed and hence should be abandoned; only that they do not seem likely to bring about reform soon. The longer reform is delayed, the more animals suffer unnecessarily. (Compare opposition to the war in Vietnam: legal opposition might have eventually led to the withdrawal of American forces, but how many more would have died or been wounded before it did?) So pointing out that in democratic societies there are legal means of bringing about reform will not convince the militant animal liberationist who is more concerned about the practical matter of preventing suffering that is going on now than about reform in the far distant future.

Here the upholder of democratic laws can try another tack: if legal means fail to bring about reform, it shows that the proposed reform does not have the approval of the majority of the electorate; and to attempt to implement the reform by illegal means against the wishes of the majority would be a violation of the central principle of democracy, majority rule.

The militant can challenge this argument on two grounds, one factual and the other philosophical. The factual claim in the democrat's argument is that a reform which cannot be implemented by legal means lacks the approval of the majority of the electorate. Perhaps this would hold in a direct democracy, in which the whole electorate voted on each issue; but it is certainly not always true of modern representative democracies. There is no way of ensuring that on any given issue a majority of representatives will take the same view as a majority of their constituents. In choosing between representatives – or more realistically, in choosing between political parties – voters elect to take one 'package deal' in preference to other package deals on offer. It will often happen that in order to vote for policies they favour, voters must go along with other policies they are not keen on. It will also happen that policies voters favour are not offered by any major party.

Animal experimentation is again a case in point. Opinion polls in Britain have consistently shown overwhelming majorities against the use of animals in the testing of cosmetics, toiletries and weapons. Members of parliament reportedly receive more mail about animal welfare than any other issue. Yet the testing goes on. Special techniques are used to frustrate the democratic process. When it was proposed to amend the law on experiments to require that alternatives to live animals be used whenever possible,

Parliament spent so much time discussing the proposed amendment that it died without a vote being taken. The utmost delicacy was used in avoiding any stand on the bill ... The bill died, yet no one can be accused of voting against it. Therefore each member of Parliament is able to face the animal lobby in his home district.

This quotation comes, not from the publications of militant anti-vivisectionists, but from the *Bulletin* of the National Society for Medical Research, an American organization devoted to defending the freedom of researchers to use animals. (The article went on to congratulate British researchers on their resistance to the proposal.) In this light the link between major-ity approval and parliamentary action looks shaky.

What if the facts were otherwise? What if a majority did approve of testing cosmetics on animals? Would it then be wrong to use illegal means? Here we have the philosophical claim underlying the democratic argument for obedience, the claim that we ought to accept the majority decision.

The case for majority rule shculd not be overstated. No sensible democrat would claim that the majority is always right. If 49% of the population can be wrong, so can 51%. Animal Liberation Front members faced with an opinion poll showing that most people approved of testing cosmetics on animals would have no reason to abandon their goal of ending such testing.

Whether they should reconsider their means is another matter. With a majority behind them, they could claim to be acting with democratic principles on their side, using illegal means to ᴊvercome flaws in the democratic machinery. Without that majority, all the weight of democratic tradition is against them and it is they who appear as coercers, trying to force the majority into accepting something against its will. But how much moral weight should we give to democratic principles?

Thoreau, as we might expect, was not impressed by majority decision-making. 'All voting,' he wrote, 'is a sort of gaming, like checkers or backgammon, with a slight moral tinge to it, a playing with right and wrong, with moral questions.' In a sense Thoreau was right. If we reject, as we must, the doctrine that the majority is always right, to submit moral issues to the vote is to gamble that what we believe to be right will come out of the ballot with more votes behind it than what we believe to be wrong; and that is a gamble we will often lose.

Nevertheless we should not be too contemptuous about voting, or gambling either. Cowboys who agree to play poker to decide matters of honour do better than cowboys who continue to settle such matters in the traditional Western manner. A society which decides its controversial issues by ballots does better than one which uses bullets. To some extent this is a point we have already encountered, under the heading 'law and order'. It applies to any society with an established, peaceful method of resolving disputes; but in a democracy there is a subtle difference which gives added weight to the outcome of the decision-procedure. A method of settling disputes in which no one has greater ultimate power than anyone else is a method which can be recommended to all as a fair compromise between competing claims to power. Any other method must give greater power to some than to others and thereby invites opposition from those who have less. That, at least, is true in the egalitarian age in which we live. In a feudal society, where people accept their status, to rule or be ruled, as natural and proper, there is no challenge to the feudal lord and no compromise would be needed. (I am thinking of an ideal feudal system, as I am thinking of an ideal democracy.) Those times, however, seem to be gone forever. The breakdown of traditional authority created a need for political compromise. Among possible compromises, giving one vote to each person is uniquely acceptable to all. As such, in the absence of any agreed procedure for deciding on some other distribution of power, it offers, in principle, the firmest possible basis for a peaceful method of settling disputes.

To reject majority rule, therefore, is to reject the best possible basis for the peaceful ordering of society in an egalitarian age. Where else should one turn? To a meritocratic franchise, with extra votes for the more intelligent or better educated, as John Stuart Mill once proposed? But could we agree on who merits extra votes? To a benevolent despot? Many would accept that –

if they could choose the despot. In practice the likely outcome of abandoning majority rule is none of these: it is the rule of those who command the greatest armed force.

So the principle of majority rule does carry substantial moral weight. We should be reluctant to take any action which amounts to an attempt to coerce the majority, for such attempts imply the rejection of majority rule and there is no acceptable alternative to that. There may, of course, be cases where the majority decision is so appalling that coercion is justified, whatever the risk. The obligation to obey a genuine majority decision is not absolute. We show our respect for the principle not by blind obedience to the majority, but by regarding ourselves as justified in disobeying only in extreme circumstances.

Disobedience, civil or otherwise

If we draw together our conclusions on the use of illegal means to achieve laudable ends, we shall find that: (1) there are reasons why we should normally accept the verdict of an established peaceful method of settling disputes; (2) these reasons are particularly strong when the decision-procedure is democratic and the verdict represents a genuine majority view; but (3) there are still situations in which the use of illegal means can be justified. In this section we shall explore further the situations in which breaking the law is a legitimate means of obtaining an ethical end.

We have seen that there are two distinct ways in which one might try to justify the use of illegal means in a society which, like the United Kingdom, is nominally democratic. The first is on the grounds that the decision one is objecting to is not a genuine expression of majority opinion. The second is that although the decision is a genuine expression of the majority view, this view is so seriously wrong that action against the majority is justified.

It is disobedience on the first ground that best merits the name 'civil disobedience'. Here the use of illegal means can be regarded as an extension of the use of legal means to secure a genuinely democratic decision. The extension may be necessary because the normal channels for securing reform are not working properly. On some issues parliamentary representatives are overly influenced by skilled and well-paid special interests. On others the public is unaware of what is happening. Perhaps the abuse requires administrative, rather than legislative change, and the bureaucrats of the civil service have refused to be inconvenienced. Perhaps the legitimate interests of a minority are being ignored by prejudiced officials. In all these cases, the now-standard forms of civil disobedience – passive resistance, marches or sit-ins – are appropriate.

In these situations disobeying the law is not an attempt to coerce the majority. Instead disobedience attempts to inform the majority; or to persuade parliamentarians that large numbers of electors feel very strongly about the issue; or to draw national attention to an issue previously left to bureaucrats; or to appeal for reconsideration of a decision too hastily made. Civil disobedience is an appropriate means to these ends when legal means have failed, because, although it is illegal, it does not threaten the majority or attempt to coerce them. By not resisting the force of the law, by remaining non-violent and by accepting the legal penalty for their actions, civil disobedients make manifest both the sincerity of their protest and their respect for the rule of law and the fundamental principles of democracy.

So conceived, civil disobedience is not difficult to justify. The justification does not have to be strong enough to override the obligation to obey a democratic decision, since disobedience is an attempt to restore, rather than frustrate, the process of democratic decision making. Disobedience of this kind could be justified by, for instance, the aim of making the public aware of how animals are treated in the laboratories and factory farms which few people ever see.

The use of illegal means to prevent action undeniably in accordance with the majority view is harder – but not impossible – to justify. We may think it unlikely that a Nazi-style policy of genocide could ever be approved by a majority vote, but if that were to happen it would be carrying respect for majority rule to absurd lengths to regard oneself as bound to accept the majority decision. To oppose evils of that magnitude, we are justified in using virtually any means likely to be effective.

Genocide is an extreme case. To grant that it justifies the use of illegal means even against a majority concedes very little in terms of practical political action. Yet admitting even one exception to the obligation to abide by democratic decisions raises further questions: where is the line to be drawn between evils like genocide, where the obligation is clearly overriden, and less serious issues, where it is not? And who is to decide on which side of this imaginary line a particular issue falls?

The second question is the easier, though some will not find the answer satisfactory. We must decide for ourselves on which side of the line particular cases fall. There is no other way of deciding, since the society's method of settling issues has already made its decision. The majority cannot be judge in its own case. If we think the majority decision wrong, we must make up our own minds about how gravely it is wrong.

This does not mean that any decision we make on this issue is subjective or arbitrary. Here we come to the first, and more difficult, of the two questions. In making up our minds we have to balance the magnitude of the evil we are trying to stop against the possibility that our actions will lead to a drastic decline in respect for law and for democracy. We must also take into account the likelihood that our actions will fail in their objective and provoke a reaction which will reduce the chances of success by other means. (As, for instance, terrorist attacks on an oppressive regime provide the government with an ideal excuse to lock up its more moderate political opponents.)

One result of a consequentialist approach to this issue which may at first seem odd is that the more deeply ingrained the habit of obedience to democratic rule, the more easily disobedience can be defended. There is no paradox here, however, merely another instance of the homely truth that while young plants need to be cosseted, well-established specimens can take rougher treatment. Thus on a given issue disobedience might be justifiable in Britain or the United States but not in Spain or Portugal during the period when these countries seek to establish democratic systems of government.

These issues cannot be settled in general terms. Every case differs. When the evils to be stopped are neither utterly horrendous (like genocide) nor relatively harmless (like Concorde's noisy take-off) reasonable people will differ on the justifiability of attempting to thwart the implementation of a considered decision democratically reached. Where illegal means are used with this aim, an important step has been taken, for disobedience then ceases to be 'civil disobedience', if by that term is meant disobedience which is justified by an appeal to principles which the community itself accepts as the proper way of running its affairs. It may still be best for such obedience to be civil in the other sense of the term, which makes a contrast with the use of violence or the tactics of terrorism.

Violence

Civil disobedience is less common now than it was in the 'sixties, perhaps because the wrongs for which thousands willingly went to jail – civil rights for blacks, an end to the Vietnam war – have been righted. In newspaper headlines civil disobedience has been supplanted by terrorism. Few welcome the change. Civil disobedience was sympathetically regarded by a broad section of the community: terrorism is almost universally execrated. These disparate attitudes are broadly appropriate. Civil disobedience intended as a means of attracting publicity or persuading the majority to reconsider is much easier to justify than disobedience intended to coerce the majority. Violence is obviously harder still to defend. Some go so far as to say that the use of violence as a means, particularly violence against people, is never justified, no matter how good the end.

Opposition to the use of violence can be on the basis of an absolute rule, or an assessment of its consequences. Pacifists have usually regarded the use of violence as absolutely wrong, irrespective of its consequences. This, like other 'no matter what' prohibitions, assumes the validity of the distinction between acts and omissions. Without this distinction, pacifists who refuse to use violence when it is the only means of preventing greater violence would be responsible for the greater violence they fail to prevent.

Suppose we have an opportunity to assassinate a tyrant who is systematically murdering his opponents and anyone else he dislikes. We know that if the tyrant dies he will be replaced by a popular opposition leader, now in exile, who will restore the rule of law. If we say that violence is always wrong, and refuse to carry out the assassination, mustn't we bear some responsibility for the tyrant's future murders?

If the objections made to the acts and omissions distinction in Chapter 7 were sound, those who do not use violence to prevent greater violence have to take responsibility for the violence they could have prevented. Thus the rejection of the acts and omissions distinction makes a crucial difference to the discussion of violence, for it opens the door to a plausible argument in defence of violence.

Marxists have often used this argument to rebut attacks on their doctrine of the need for violent revolution. In his classic indictment of the social effects of nineteenth-century capitalism, *The Condition of the Working Class in England*, Engels wrote:

If one individual inflicts a bodily injury upon another which leads to the death of the person attacked we call it manslaughter; on the other hand, if the attacker knows beforehand that the blow will be fatal we call it murder. Murder has also been committed if society places hundreds of workers in such a position that they inevitably come to premature and unnatural ends. Their death is as violent as if they had been stabbed or shot ... Murder has been committed if thousands of workers have been deprived of the necessities of life or if they have been forced into a situation in which it is impossible for them to survive ... Murder has been committed if society knows perfectly well that thousands of workers cannot avoid being sacrificed so long as these conditions are allowed to continue. Murder of this sort is just as culpable as the murder committed by an individual. At first sight it does not appear to be murder at all because responsibility for the death of the victim cannot be pinned on any individual assailant. Everyone is responsible and yet no one is responsible, because it appears as if the victim has died from natural causes. If a worker dies no one places the responsibility for his death on society, though some would realize that society has failed to take steps to prevent the victim from dying. But it is murder all the same.

One might object to Engels' use of the term 'murder'. The objection would resemble the arguments discussed in Chapter 8, when we considered whether our failure to aid the starving makes us murderers. We saw that there is no intrinsic significance in the distinction between acts and omissions; but from the point of view of motivation and the appropriateness of blame, most cases of failing to prevent death are not equivalent to murder. The same would apply to the cases Engels describes. Engels tries to pin the blame on 'society', but 'society' is not a person or a moral agent, and cannot be held responsible in the way an individual can.

Still, this is nit-picking. Whether or not 'murder' is the right term, whether or not we are prepared to describe as 'violent' the deaths of malnourished workers in unhealthy and unsafe factories, Engels' fundamental point stands. These deaths are a wrong of the same order of magnitude as the deaths of hundreds of people in a terrorist bombing would be. It would be one-sided to say that violent revolution is always absolutely wrong, without taking account of the evils that the revolutionaries are trying to stop. If violent means had been the only way of changing the conditions Engels describes, those who opposed the use of violent means would have been responsible for the continuation of those conditions.

Some of the practices we have been discussing in this book are violent, either directly or by omission. In the case of nonhuman animals, our treatment is often violent by any description. In the case of humans, what are we to say of an avoidable situation in which some countries have infant mortality rates eight times higher than others, and a person born in one country can expect to live 20 years more than someone born in another country? Is this violence? Again, it doesn't really matter whether we call it violence or not. In its effects it is as terrible as violence.

Absolutist condemnations of violence stand or fall with the distinction between acts and omissions. Therefore they fall. There are, however, strong consequentialist objections to the use of violence. We have been premising our discussion on the assumption that violence might be the only means of changing things for the better. Absolutists have no interest in challenging this assumption because they reject violence whether the assumption is true or false. Consequentialists must ask whether violence ever is the only means to an important end, or, if not the only means, the swiftest means. They must also ask about the long-term effects of pursuing change by violent means.

Could one defend, on consequentialist grounds, a condemnation of violence that is in practice, if not in principle, as all-encompassing as that of the absolute pacifist? One might attempt to do so by emphasizing the hardening effect that the use of violence has, how committing one murder, no matter how 'necessary' or 'justified' it may seem, lessens the resistance to committing further murders. Is it likely that people who have become inured to acting violently will be able to create a better society? This is a question on which the historical record is relevant. The course taken by the Russian Revolution must shake the belief that a burning desire for social justice provides immunity to the corrupting effects of violence. There are, admittedly, other examples which may be read the other way; but it would take a considerable number of examples to outweigh the legacy of Lenin and Stalin.

The consequentialist pacifist can use another argument – the argument I urged against the suggestion that we should allow starvation to reduce the populations of the poorest nations to the level at which they could feed themselves. Like this policy, violence involves certain harm, said to be justified by the prospects of future benefits. But the future benefits can never be certain, and even in the few cases where violence does bring about desirable ends, we can rarely be sure that the ends could not have been achieved equally soon by non-violent means. What, for instance, has been achieved by the thousands of deaths and injuries caused by ten years of IRA bombings in Northern Ireland? What have the Palestinian terrorists gained? What have been the consequences of terrorism for Uruguay, and Argentina? One may sympathize with the ends some of these groups are fighting for, but the means they are using hold no promise of gaining their ends. Using these means therefore indicates callous disregard of the interests of their victims. These consequentialist arguments add up to a strong case against the use of violence as a means, particularly when the violence is indiscriminately directed against ordinary members of the public, as terrorist violence often is. In practical terms, that kind of violence would seem never justified.

There are other kinds of violence which cannot be ruled out so convincingly. There is, for instance, the assassination of a murderous tyrant. Here, provided the murderous policies are an expression of the tyrant's personality rather than part of the institutions he commands, the violence is strictly limited, the aim is the end of much greater violence, success from a single violent act may be highly probable, and there may be no other way of ending the tyrant's rule. It would be implausible for a consequentialist to maintain that committing violence in these circumstances would have a corrupting effect, or that more, rather than less, violence would result from the assassination.

Violence may be limited in a different way. The cases we have been considering have involved violence against people. These are the standard cases that come to mind when we discuss violence, but there are other kinds of violence. Animal Liberation Front members have damaged laboratories, cages, and other property used to confine, hurt or kill animals, but they avoid violent acts against any animal, human or nonhuman. There seems no risk that by their tactics they will harden themselves to the use of violence against people (or other animals).

Damage to property is not as serious a matter as injuring or killing; hence it may be justified on grounds which would not justify anything that caused harm to sentient beings. This does not mean that violence to property is of no significance. Property means a great deal to some people, and one would need to have strong reasons to justify destroying it. But such reasons *may* exist. The justification might not be anything so epoch-making as transforming society. It might be the specific and short-term goal of saving a number of animals from a painful and unnecessary experiment. Again, whether such an action would really be justifiable from a consequentialist point of view would depend on the details of the actual situation. Someone lacking expertise could easily be mistaken about the value of an experiment or the degree of suffering it involved. And will not the result of damaging equipment and liberating one lot of animals simply be that more equipment is bought and more animals are bred? What is to be done with the liberated animals? Will illegal acts mean that the government will resist moves to reform the law relating to animal experiments, arguing that it must not appear to be yielding to violence? All these questions would need to be answered satisfactorily before one could come to a decision in favour of, say, damaging a laboratory.

Violence is not easy to justify, even if it is violence against property rather than against sentient beings, or violence against a dictator rather than indiscriminate violence against the general public. Nevertheless the differences between kinds of violence are important, because only by observing them can we condemn one kind of violence – the terrorist kind – in virtually absolute terms. The differences are blurred by sweeping condemnations of everything that falls under the general heading 'violence'.

Why act morally?

Previous chapters of this book have discussed what we ought, morally, to do about several practical issues and what means we are justified in adopting to achieve our ethical goals. The nature of our conclusions about these issues – the demands they make upon us – raises a further, more fundamental question: why should we act morally?

Take our conclusions about the use of animals for food, or the aid the rich should give the poor. Some readers may accept these conclusions, become vegetarians, and do what they can to reduce absolute poverty. Others may disagree with our conclusions, maintaining that there is nothing wrong with eating animals and that they are under no moral obligation to do anything about reducing absolute poverty. There is also, however, likely to be a third group, consisting of readers who find no fault with the ethical arguments of these chapters, yet do not change their diets or their contributions to overseas aid. Of this third group, some will just be weak-willed, but others may want an answer to a further practical question. If the conclusions of ethics require so much of us, they may ask, should we bother about ethics at all?

Understanding the question

'Why should I act morally?' is a different type of question from those that we have been discussing up to now. Questions like 'Why should I treat blacks and whites equally?' or 'Why is abortion justifiable?' seek ethical reasons for acting in a certain way. These are questions within ethics. They presuppose the ethical point of view. 'Why should I act morally?' is on another level. It is not a question within ethics, but a question about ethics.

'Why should I act morally?' is therefore a question about something normally presupposed. Such questions are perplexing. Some philosophers have found this particular question so perplexing that they have rejected it as logically improper, as an attempt to ask something which cannot properly be asked.

One ground for this rejection is the claim that our ethical principles are, by definition, the principles we take as overridingly important. This means that whatever principles are overriding for a particular person are necessarily that person's ethical principles, and a person who accepts as an ethical principle that she ought to give her wealth to help the poor must, by definition, have actually decided to give away her wealth. On this definition of ethics once a person has made an ethical decision no further practical question can arise. Hence it is impossible to make sense of the question: 'Why should I act morally?'

It might be thought a good reason for accepting the definition of ethics as overriding that it allows us to dismiss as meaningless an otherwise troublesome question. Adopting this definition cannot solve real problems, however, for it leads to correspondingly greater difficulties in establishing any ethical conclusion. Take, for example, the conclusion that the rich ought to aid the poor. We were able to argue for this in Chapter 8 only because we assumed that, as suggested in the first two chapters of this book, the universalizability of ethical judgments requires us to go beyond thinking only about our own interests, and leads us to take a point of view from which we must give equal consideration to the interests of all affected by our actions. We cannot hold that ethical judgments must be universalizable and *at the same time* define a person's ethical principles as whatever principles that person takes as overridingly important – for what if I take as overridingly important some non-universalizable principle, like 'I ought to do whatever benefits me'? If we define ethical principles as whatever principles one takes as overriding, then anything whatever may count as an ethical principle, for one may take any principle whatever as overridingly important. Thus what we gain by being able to dismiss the question: 'Why should I act morally?' we lose by being unable to use the universalizability of ethical judgments – or any other feature of ethics – to argue for particular conclusions about what is morally right. Taking ethics as in some sense necessarily involving a universal point of view seems to me a more natural and less confusing way of discussing these issues.

Other philosophers have rejected 'Why should I act morally?' for a different reason. They think it must be rejected for the same reason that we must reject another question, 'Why should I be rational?' which, like 'Why should I act morally?' also questions something – in this case rationality – normally presupposed. 'Why should I be rational?' really is logically improper because in answering it we would be giving reasons for being rational. Thus we would presuppose rationality in our attempt to justify rationality. The resulting justification of rationality would be circular – which shows, not that rationality lacks a necessary justification, but that it needs no justification, because it cannot intelligibly be questioned unless it is already presupposed.

Is 'Why should I act morally?' like 'Why should I be rational?' in that it presupposes the very point of view it questions? It would be, if we interpreted the 'should' as a moral 'should'. Then the question would ask for moral reasons for being moral. This would be absurd. Once we have decided that an action is morally obligatory, there is no further *moral* question to ask. It is redundant to ask why I should, morally, do the action that I morally should do.

There is, however, no need to interpret the question as a request for an ethical justification of ethics. 'Should' need not mean 'should, morally'. It could simply be a way of asking for reasons for action, without any specification about the kind of reasons wanted. We sometimes want to ask a very general practical question, from no particular point of view. Faced with a difficult choice, we ask a close friend for advice. Morally, he says, we ought to do *A*, but *B* would be more in our interests, while etiquette demands *C* and *D* would contribute most to art and culture. This answer may not satisfy us. We want advice on which of these standpoints to adopt. If it is possible to ask such a question we must ask it from a position of neutrality between all these points of view, not of commitment to any one of them.

'Why should I act morally?' is this sort of question. If it is not possible to ask practical questions without presupposing a point of view, we are unable to say anything intelligible about the most ultimate practical choices. Whether to act according to considerations of ethics, self-interest, etiquette, or aesthetics would be a choice 'beyond reason' – in a sense, an arbitrary choice. Before we resign ourselves to this conclusion we should at least attempt to interpret the question so that the mere asking of it does not commit us to any particular point of view.

We can now formulate the question more precisely. It is a question about the ethical point of view, asked from a position outside it. But what is 'the ethical point of view'? I have suggested that a distinguishing feature of ethics is that ethical judgments are universalizable. Ethics requires us to go beyond our own personal point of view to a standpoint like that of the impartial spectator who takes a universal point of view.

Given this conception of ethics, 'Why should I act morally?' is a question which may properly be asked by anyone wondering whether to act only on grounds that would be acceptable from this universal point of view. It is, after all, possible to act – and some people do act – without thinking of anything except one's own interests. The question asks for reasons for going beyond this personal basis of action and acting only on judgments one is prepared to prescribe universally.

Reason and ethics

There is an ancient line of philosophical thought which attempts to demonstrate that to act rationally is to act ethically. The argument is today associated with Kant and is mainly found in the writings of modern Kantians, though it goes back as least as far as the Stoics. The form in which the argument is presented varies, but the common structure is as follows:

1. Some requirement of universalizability or impartiality is essential to ethics.

2. Reason is universally or objectively valid. If, for example, it follows from the premises 'All humans are mortal' and 'Socrates is human' that Socrates is mortal, then this inference must follow universally. It cannot be valid for me and invalid for you. This is a general point about reason, whether theoretical or practical.

Therefore:

3. Only a judgment which satisfies the requirement described in (1) as a necessary condition of an ethical judgment will be an objectively rational judgment in accordance with (2). For I cannot expect any other rational agents to accept as valid for them a judgment which I would not accept if I were in their place; and if two rational agents could not accept each other's judgments, they could not be rational judgments, for the reason given in (2). To say that I would accept the judgment I make, even if I were in someone else's position and they in mine is, however, simply to say that my judgment is one I can prescribe from a universal point of view. Ethics and reason both require us to rise above our own particular point of view and take a perspective from which our own personal identity – the role we happen to occupy – is unimportant. Thus reason requires us to act on universalizable judgments and, to that extent, to act ethically.

Is this argument valid? I have already indicated that I accept the first point, that ethics involves universalizability. The second point also seems undeniable. Reason must be universal. Does the conclusion therefore follow? Here is the flaw in the argument. The conclusion appears to follow directly from the premises; but this move involves a slide from the limited sense in which it is true that a rational judgment must be universally valid, to a stronger sense of 'universally valid' which is equivalent to universalizability.

The difference between these two senses can be seen by considering a non-universalizable imperative, like the purely egoistic: 'Let everyone do what is in *my* interests.' This differs from the imperative of universalizable egoism – 'Let everyone do what is in *her own* interests' – because it contains an ineliminable reference to a particular person. It therefore cannot be an ethical imperative. Does it also lack the universality required if it is to be a rational basis for action? Surely not. Every rational agent could accept that the purely egoistic activity of other rational agents is rationally justifiable. Pure egoism could be rationally adopted by everyone.

Let us look at this more closely. It must be conceded that there is a sense in which one purely egoistic rational agent – call him Jack – could not accept the practical judgments of another purely egoistic rational agent – call her Jill. Assuming Jill's interests differ from Jack's, Jill may be acting rationally in urging Jack to do *A*, while Jack is also acting rationally in deciding against doing *A*.

This disagreement is, however, compatible with all rational agents accepting pure egoism. Though they accept pure egoism, it points them in different directions because they start from different places. When Jack adopts pure egoism, it leads him to further his interests and when Jill adopts pure egoism it leads her to further her interests. Hence the disagreement over what to do. On the other hand – and this is the sense in which pure egoism could be accepted as valid by all rational agents – if we were to ask Jill (off the record and promising not to tell Jack) what she thinks it would be rational for Jack to do, she would, if truthful, have to reply that it would be rational for Jack to do what is in his own interests, rather than what is in her interests.

So when purely egoistic rational agents oppose each other's acts, it does not indicate disagreement over the rationality of pure egoism. Pure egoism, though not a universalizable principle, could be accepted as a rational basis of action by all rational agents. The sense in which rational judgments must be universally acceptable is weaker than the sense in which ethical judgments must be. That an action will benefit *me* rather than anyone else could be a valid reason for doing it, though it could not be an ethical reason for doing it.

A consequence of this conclusion is that rational agents may rationally try to prevent each other doing what they admit the other is rationally justified in doing. There is, unfortunately, nothing paradoxical about this. Two businessmen competing for an important sale will accept each other's conduct as rational, though each aims to thwart the other. The same holds of two soldiers meeting in battle, or two footballers vying for the ball.

Accordingly this attempted demonstration of a link between reason and ethics fails. There may be other ways of forging this link, but it is difficult to see any that hold greater promise of success. The chief obstacle to be overcome is the nature of practical reason. Long ago David Hume argued that reason in action applies only to means, not to ends. The ends must be given by our wants and desires. Hume unflinchingly drew out the implications of this view:

'Tis not contrary to reason to prefer the destruction of the whole world to the scratching of my finger. 'Tis not contrary to reason for me to choose my total ruin, to prevent the least uneasiness of an Indian or person wholly unknown to me. 'Tis as little contrary to reason to prefer even my own acknowledged lesser good to my greater, and have a more ardent affection for the former than the latter.

Extreme as it is, Hume's view of practical reason has stood up to criticism remarkably well. His central claim – that in practical reasoning we start from something wanted – is difficult to refute; yet it must be refuted if any argument is to succeed in showing that it is rational for all of us to act ethically irrespective of what we want.

Nor is the refutation of Hume all that is needed for a demonstration of the rational necessity of acting ethically. In *The Possibility of Altruism*, Thomas Nagel has argued forcefully that not to take one's own future desires into account in one's practical deliberations – irrespective of whether one *now* happens to desire the satisfaction of those future desires – would indicate a failure to see oneself as a person existing over time, the present being merely one time among others in one's life. So it is my conception of myself as a person that makes it rational for me to consider my long-term interests. This holds true even if I have 'a more ardent affection' for something that I acknowledge is not really, all things considered, in my own interest.

Whether Nagel's argument succeeds in vindicating the

rationality of prudence is one question: whether a similar argument can also be used in favour of a form of altruism based on
taking the desires of *others* into account is another question
altogether. Nagel attempts this analogous argument. The role
occupied by 'seeing the present as merely one time among
others' is, in the argument for altruism, taken by 'seeing oneself
as merely one person among others'. But whereas it would be
extremely difficult for most of us to cease conceiving of ourselves
existing over time, with the present merely one time among
others that we will live through, the way we see ourselves as a
person among others is quite different. Henry Sidgwick's observation on this point seems to me exactly right:

It would be contrary to Common Sense to deny that the distinction
between any one individual and any other is real and fundamental, and
that consequently 'I' am concerned with the quality of my existence as
an individual in a sense, fundamentally important, in which I am not
concerned with the quality of the existence of other individuals: and
this being so, I do not see how it can be proved that this distinction is
not to be taken as fundamental in determining the ultimate end of
rational action for an individual.

So it is not only Hume's view of practical reason that stands in
the way of attempts to show that to act rationally is to act
ethically; we might succeed in overthrowing that barrier, only to
find our way blocked by the commonsense distinction between
self and others. Taken together, these are formidable obstacles
and I know of no way of overcoming them.

Ethics and self-interest

If practical reasoning begins with something wanted, to show
that it is rational to act morally would involve showing that in
acting morally we achieve something we want. If, agreeing with
Sidgwick rather than Hume, we hold that it is rational to act in
our long-term interests irrespective of what we happen to want
at the present moment, we could show that it is rational to act
morally by showing that it is in our long-term interests to do so.
There have been many attempts to argue along one or other of
these lines, ever since Plato, in *The Republic*, portrayed Socrates

as arguing that to be virtuous is to have the different elements of one's personality ordered in a harmonious manner, and this is necessary for happiness. We shall look at these arguments shortly; but first it is necessary to assess an objection to this whole approach to 'Why should I act morally?'

People often say that to defend morality by appealing to self-interest is to misunderstand what ethics is all about. F. H. Bradley stated this eloquently:

What answer can we give when the question Why should I be Moral?, in the sense of What will it advantage Me?, is put to us? Here we shall do well, I think, to avoid all praises of the pleasantness of virtue. We may believe that it transcends all possible delights of vice, but it would be well to remember that we desert a moral point of view, that we degrade and prostitute virtue, when to those who do not love her for herself we bring ourselves to recommend her for the sake of her pleasures.

In other words, we can never get people to act morally by providing reasons of self-interest, because if they accept what we say and act on the reasons given, they will only be acting self-interestedly, not morally.

One reply to this objection would be that the substance of the action, what is actually done, is more important than the motive. People might give money to famine relief because their friends will think better of them, or they might give the same amount because they think it their duty. Those saved from starvation by the gift will benefit to the same extent either way.

This is true but crude. It can be made more sophisticated if it is combined with an appropriate account of the nature and function of ethics. Ethics, though not consciously created, is a product of social life which has the function of promoting values common to the members of the society. Ethical judgments do this by praising and encouraging actions in accordance with these values. Ethical judgments are concerned with motives because this is a good indication of the tendency of an action to promote good or evil, but also because it is here that praise and blame may be effective in altering the tendency of a person's actions. Conscientiousness (that is, acting for the sake of doing what is right) is a particularly useful motive, from the community's point of view. People who are conscientious will, if they accept the values of their society (and if most people did not accept these values they would not be the values of the society) always tend to promote what the society values. They may have no generous or sympathetic inclinations, but if they think it their duty to give famine relief, they will do so. Moreover, those motivated by the desire to do what is right can be relied upon to act as they think right in all circumstances, whereas those who act from some other motive, like self-interest, will only do what they think right when they believe it will also be in their interest. Conscientiousness is thus a kind of multi-purpose gap-filler that can be used to motivate people towards whatever is valued, even if the natural virtues normally associated with action in accordance with those values (generosity, sympathy, honesty, tolerance, humility, etc.) are lacking. (This needs some qualification: a conscientious mother may provide as well for her children as a mother who loves them, but she cannot love them because it is the right thing to do. Sometimes conscientiousness is a poor substitute for the real thing.)

On this view of ethics it is still results, not motives, that really matter. Conscientiousness is of value because of its consequences. Yet, unlike, say, benevolence, conscientiousness can be praised and encouraged only for its own sake. To praise a conscientious act for its consequences would be to praise not conscientiousness, but something else altogether. If we appeal to sympathy or self-interest as a reason for doing one's duty, then we are not encouraging people to do their duty for its own sake. If conscientiousness is to be encouraged, it must be thought of as good for its own sake.

It is different in the case of an act done from a motive that people act upon irrespective of praise and encouragement. The use of ethical language is then inappropriate. We do not normally say that people ought to do, or that it is their duty to do, whatever gives them the greatest pleasure, for most people are sufficiently motivated to do this anyway. So, whereas we praise good acts done for the sake of doing what is right, we withhold our praise when we believe the act was done from some motive like self-interest.

This emphasis on motives and on the moral worth of doing right for its own sake is now embedded in our notion of ethics. To the extent that it is so embedded, we will feel that to provide considerations of self-interest for doing what is right is to empty the action of its moral worth.

My suggestion is that our notion of ethics has become misleading to the extent that moral worth is attributed only to action done because it is right, without any ulterior motive. It is understandable, and from the point of view of society desirable, that this attitude should prevail; nevertheless, those who accept this view of ethics, and are led by it to do what is right because it is right, without asking for any further reason, are falling victim to a kind of confidence trick – though not, of course, a consciously perpetrated one.

That this view of ethics is unjustifiable has already been indicated by the failure of the argument discussed earlier in this chapter for a rational justification of ethics. In the history of Western philosophy, no one has urged more strongly than Kant that our ordinary moral consciousness finds moral worth only when duty is done for duty's sake. Yet Kant himself saw that without a rational justification this common conception of ethics would be 'a mere phantom of the brain'. And this is indeed the case. If we reject – as in general terms we have done – the Kantian justification of the rationality of ethics, but try to retain the Kantian conception of ethics, ethics is left hanging without support. It becomes a closed system, a system that cannot be questioned because its first premise – that only action done because it is right has any moral worth – rules out any possible justification for accepting this very premise. Morality is, on this view, no more rational an end than any other allegedly self-justifying practice, like etiquette or the kind of religious faith that comes only to those who first set aside all sceptical doubts.

Taken as a view of ethics as a whole, we should abandon this Kantian notion of ethics. This does not mean, however, that we should never do what we see to be right simply because we see it to be right, without further reasons. Here we need to appeal to the distinction Hare has made between intuitive and critical thinking. When we stand back from our day-to-day ethical decisions and ask why we should act morally, we should not allow ourselves to be put off seeking reasons, even self-interested ones. If our search is successful, however, it may provide us with reasons for taking up the ethical point of view as a settled policy, a way of living. We would not then ask, in our day-to-day ethical decision making, whether each particular right action was in our interest. In all but the most extraordinary situations, we would assume that it was, and once we had decided what was right we would go ahead and do it, without thinking about further reasons for doing what is right. To deliberate over the ultimate reasons for doing what is right in each case would impossibly complicate our lives; it would also be inadvisable because in particular situations we might be too greatly influenced by strong but temporary desires and inclinations, and so make decisions we would later regret.

So a justification of ethics in terms of self-interest would not defeat its own aim, and we can now ask if such a justification exists. There is a daunting list of those who, following Plato's lead, have offered one: Aristotle, Aquinas, Spinoza, Butler, Hegel, even – for all his strictures against prostituting virtue – Bradley. Like Plato, these philosophers made broad claims about human nature and the conditions under which human beings can be happy. Some were also able to fall back on a belief that virtue will be rewarded and wickedness punished in a life after our bodily death. Philosophers cannot use this argument if they want to carry conviction nowadays; nor can they adopt sweeping psychological theories on the basis of their own general experience of their fellows, as philosophers used to do when psychology was a branch of philosophy.

It might be said that since philosophers are not empirical scientists, discussion of the connection between acting ethically and living a fulfilled and happy life should be left to psychologists, sociologists and other appropriate experts. The question is not, however, dealt with by any other single discipline and its relevance to practical ethics is reason enough for our looking into it.

What facts about human nature could show that ethics and self-interest coincide? One theory is that we all have benevolent or sympathetic inclinations which make us concerned about the welfare of others. Another relies on a natural conscience which gives rise to guilt feelings when we do what we know to be wrong. But how strong are these benevolent desires or feelings of guilt? Is it possible to suppress them? If so, isn't it possible that in a world in which humans and other animals are suffering in great numbers, suppressing one's conscience and sympathy for others is the surest way to happiness?

To meet this objection those who would link ethics and happiness must assert that we cannot be happy if these elements of our nature are suppressed. Benevolence and sympathy, they might argue, are tied up with the capacity to take part in friendly or loving relations with others, and there can be no real happiness without such relationships. For the same reason it is necessary to take at least some ethical standards seriously, and to be open and honest in living by them – for a life of deception and dishonesty is a furtive life, in which the possibility of discovery always clouds the horizon. Genuine acceptance of ethical standards is likely to mean that we feel some guilt – or at least that we are less pleased with ourselves than we otherwise would be – when we do not live up to them.

These claims about the connection between our character and our prospects of happiness are no more than hypotheses. Attempts to confirm them by detailed research are sparse and inadequate. A. H. Maslow, an American psychologist, asserts that human beings have a need for self-actualization, which involves growing towards courage, kindness, knowledge, love, honesty, and unselfishness. When we fulfil this need we feel serene, joyful, filled with zest, sometimes euphoric, and generally happy. When we act contrary to our need for self-actualization we experience anxiety, despair, boredom, shame, emptiness and are generally unable to enjoy ourselves. It would be nice if Maslow should turn out to be right; unfortunately the data Maslow produces in support of his theory consists of very limited studies of selected people. The theory must await confirmation or falsification from larger, more rigorous and more representative studies.

Human nature is so diverse that one may doubt if any generalization about the kind of character that leads to happiness could hold for all human beings. What, for instance, of those we call 'psychopaths'? Psychiatrists use this term as a label for a person who is asocial, impulsive, egocentric, unemotional, lacking in feelings of remorse, shame or guilt, and apparently unable to form deep and enduring personal relationships. Psychopaths are certainly abnormal, but whether it is proper to say that they are mentally ill is another matter. At least on the surface, they do not *suffer* from their condition, and it is not obvious that it is in their interest to be 'cured'. Hervey Cleckley, the author of a classic study of psychopathy entitled *The Mask of Sanity*, notes that since his book was first published he has received countless letters from people desperate for help – but they are from the parents, spouses and other relatives of psychopaths, almost never from the psychopaths themselves. This is not surprising, for while psychopaths are asocial and indifferent to the welfare of others, they seem to enjoy life. Psychopaths often appear to be charming, intelligent people, with no delusions or other signs of irrational thinking. When interviewed they say things like:

A lot has happened to me, a lot more will happen. But I enjoy living and I am always looking forward to each day. I like laughing and I've done a lot. I am essentially a clown at heart – but a happy one. I always take the bad with the good.

There is no effective therapy for psychopathy, which may be explained by the fact that psychopaths see nothing wrong with their behaviour and often find it extremely rewarding, at least in the short term. Of course their impulsive nature and lack of a sense of shame or guilt means that some psychopaths end up in prison, though it is hard to tell how many do not, since those who avoid prison are also more likely to avoid contact with psychiatrists. Studies have shown that a surprisingly large number of psychopaths are able to avoid prison despite grossly antisocial behaviour, probably because of their well-known ability to convince others that they are truly repentant, that it will never happen again, that they deserve another chance, etc., etc.

The existence of psychopathic people counts against the contention that benevolence, sympathy and feelings of guilt are present in everyone. It also appears to count against attempts to link happiness with the possession of these inclinations. But let us pause before we accept this latter conclusion. Must we accept psychopaths' own evaluations of their happiness? They are, after all, notoriously persuasive liars. Moreover even if they are telling the truth as they see it, are they qualified to say that they are really happy, when they seem unable to experience the emotional states that play such a large part in the happiness and fulfilment of more normal people? Admittedly, a psychopath could use the same argument against us: how can we say that we are truly happy when we have not experienced the excitement and freedom that comes from complete irresponsibility? Since we cannot enter into the subjective states of psychopathic people, nor they into ours, the dispute is not easy to resolve.

Cleckley suggests that the psychopaths' behaviour can be explained as a response to the meaninglessness of their lives. It is characteristic of psychopaths to work for a while at a job and then just when their ability and charm have taken them to the crest of success, commit some petty and easily detectable crime. A similar pattern occurs in their personal relationships. (There is support to be found here for Thomas Nagel's account of imprudence as rational only if one fails to see oneself as a person existing over time, with the present merely one among other times one will live through. Certainly psychopathic people live largely in the present and lack any coherent life plan.)

Cleckley explains this erratic and to us inadequately motivated behaviour by likening the psychopath's life to that of children forced to sit through a performance of *King Lear*. Children are restless and misbehave under these conditions because they cannot enjoy the play as adults do. They act to relieve boredom. Similarly, Cleckley says, psychopaths are bored because their emotional poverty means that they cannot take interest in, or gain satisfaction from, what for others are the most important things in life: love, family, success in business or professional life, etc. These things simply do not matter to them. Their unpredictable and anti-social behaviour is an attempt to relieve what would otherwise be a tedious existence.

These claims are speculative and Cleckley admits that they may not be possible to establish scientifically. They do suggest, however, an aspect of the psychopath's life that undermines the otherwise attractive nature of the psychopath's free-wheeling life. Most reflective people, at some time or other, want their life to have some kind of meaning. Few of us could deliberately choose a way of life which we regarded as utterly meaningless. For this reason most of us would not choose to live a psychopathic life, however enjoyable it might be.

Yet there is something paradoxical about criticizing the psychopath's life for its meaninglessness. Don't we have to accept, in the absence of religious belief, that life really is meaningless, not just for the psychopath but for all of us? And if this is so, why should we not choose – if it were in our power to choose our personality – the life of a psychopath? But is it true that, religion aside, life is meaningless? Now our pursuit of reasons for acting morally has led us to what is often regarded as the ultimate philosophical question.

Has life a meaning?

In what sense does rejection of belief in a god imply rejection of the view that life has any meaning? If this world had been created by some divine being with a particular goal in mind, it could be said to have a meaning, at least for that divine being. If we could know what the divine being's purpose in creating us was, we could then know what the meaning of our life was for our creator. If we accepted our creator's purpose (though why we should do that would need to be explained) we could claim to know the meaning of life.

When we reject belief in a god we must give up the idea that life on this planet has some preordained meaning. Life *as a whole* has no meaning. Life began, as the best available theories tell us, in a chance combination of gases; it then evolved through random mutations and natural selection. All this just happened; it did not happen for any overall purpose. Now that it has resulted in the existence of beings who prefer some states of affairs to others, however, it may be possible for particular lives to be meaningful. In this sense atheists can find meaning in life.

Let us return to the comparison between the life of a psychopath and that of a more normal person. Why should the psychopath's life not be meaningful? We have seen that psychopaths are egocentric to an extreme: neither other people, nor worldly success, nor anything else really matters to them. But why is their own enjoyment of life not sufficient to give meaning to their lives?

Most of us would not be able to find happiness by deliberately setting out to enjoy ourselves without caring about anyone or anything else. The pleasures we obtained in that way would seem empty, and soon pall. We seek a meaning for our lives beyond our own pleasures, and find fulfilment and happiness in doing what we see to be meaningful. If our life has no meaning other than our own happiness, we are likely to find that when we have obtained what we think we need to be happy, happiness itself still eludes us.

That those who aim at happiness for happiness's sake often fail to find it, while others find happiness in pursuing altogether different goals, has been called 'the paradox of hedonism'. It is not, of course, a logical paradox but a claim about the way in which we come to be happy. Like other generalizations on this subject it lacks empirical confirmation. Yet it matches our everyday observations, and is consistent with our nature as evolved, purposive beings. Human beings survive and repro-duce themselves through purposive action. We obtain happi-ness and fulfilment by working towards and achieving our goals. In evolutionary terms we could say that happiness functions as an internal reward for our achievements. Subjectively, we regard achieving the goal (or progressing towards it) as a reason for happiness. Our own happiness, therefore, is a by-product of aiming at something else, and not to be obtained by setting our sights on happiness alone.

The psychopath's life can now be seen to be meaningless in a way that a normal life is not. It is meaningless because it looks inward to the pleasures of the present moment and not outward to anything more long-term or far-reaching. More normal lives have meaning because they are lived to some larger purpose.

All this is speculative. You may accept or reject it to the extent that it agrees with your own observation and introspection. My next – and final – suggestion is more speculative still. It is that to find an enduring meaning in our lives it is not enough to go beyond psychopaths who have no long-term commitments or life-plans; we must also go beyond more prudent egoists who have long-term plans concerned only with their own interests. The prudent egoists may find meaning in their lives for a time, for they have the purpose of furthering their own interests; but what, in the end, does that amount to? When everything in our interests has been achieved, do we just sit back and be happy? Could we be happy in this way? Or would we decide that we had still not quite reached our target, that there was something else we needed before we could sit back and enjoy it all? Most materially successful egoists take the latter route, thus escaping the necessity of admitting that they cannot find happiness in permanent holidaying. People who slaved to establish small businesses, telling themselves they would do it only until they had made enough to live comfortably, keep working long after they have passed their original target. Their material 'needs' expand just fast enough to keep ahead of their income. Retirement is a problem for many because they cannot enjoy themselves without a purpose in life. The recommended solution is, of course, to find a new purpose, whether it be stamp collecting or voluntary work for a charity.

Now we begin to see where ethics comes into the problem of living a meaningful life. If we are looking for a purpose broader than our own interests, something which will allow us to see our lives as possessing significance beyond the narrow confines of our own conscious states, one obvious solution is to take up the ethical point of view. The ethical point of view does, as we have seen, require us to go beyond a personal point of view to the standpoint of an impartial spectator. Thus looking at things ethically is a way of transcending our inward-looking concerns and identifying ourselves with the most objective point of view possible – with, as Sidgwick put it, 'the point of view of the universe'.

The point of view of the universe is a lofty standpoint. In the rarefied air that surrounds it we may get carried away into talking, as Kant does, of the moral point of view 'inevitably' humbling all who compare their own limited nature with it. I do not want to suggest anything as sweeping as this. Earlier in this chapter, in rejecting Thomas Nagel's argument for the rationality of altruism, I said that there is nothing irrational about being concerned with the quality of one's own existence in a way that one is not concerned with the quality of existence of other individuals. Without going back on this, I am now suggesting that rationality, in the broad sense which includes self-awareness and reflection on the nature and point of our own existence, may push us towards concerns broader than the quality of our own existence; but the process is not a necessary one and those who do not take part in it – or, in taking part, do not follow it all the way to the ethical point of view – are not irrational or in error. Psychopaths, for all I know, may simply be unable to obtain as much happiness through caring about others as they obtain by antisocial acts. Other people find collecting stamps an entirely adequate way of giving purpose to their lives. There is nothing irrational about that; but others again grow out of stamp collecting as they become more aware of their situation in the world and more reflective about their purposes. To this third group the ethical point of view offers a meaning and purpose in life that one does not grow out of.

(At least, one cannot grow out of the ethical point of view until all ethical tasks have been accomplished. If that utopia were ever achieved, our purposive nature might well leave us dissatisfied, much as the egoist is dissatisfied when he has everything he needs to be happy. There is nothing paradoxical about this, for we should not expect evolution to have equipped us, in advance, with the ability to enjoy a situation that has never previously occurred. Nor is this going to be a practical problem in the near future.)

'Why act morally?' cannot be given an answer that will provide everyone with overwhelming reasons for acting morally. Ethically indefensible behaviour is not always irrational. We will probably always need the sanctions of the law and social pressure to provide additional reasons against serious violations of ethical standards. On the other hand, those reflective enough to ask the question we have been discussing in this chapter are also those most likely to appreciate the reasons that can be offered for taking the ethical point of view.

NOTES, REFERENCES AND
FURTHER READING

Chapter 1: About ethics

The issues discussed in the first section – relativism, subjectivism and the alleged dependence of ethics on religion – are dealt with in several textbooks. R. B. Brandt's *Ethical Theory* (Englewood Cliffs, NJ, 1959) is more thorough than most. Bernard Williams' *Morality* (Cambridge 1976) is more recent and much briefer. Plato's argument against defining 'good' as 'what the gods approve' is in his *Euthyphro*. Engels' discussion of the Marxist view of morality, and his reference to a 'really human morality' is in his *Herr Eugen Dühring's Revolution in Science*, Ch. 9, the central passages of which are reprinted in L. Feuer (ed.), *Marx and Engels: Basic Writings on Philosophy and Politics* (New York, 1959) pp. 271–2. C. L. Stevenson's emotivist theory is most fully expounded in his *Ethics and Language* (New Haven, 1944). R. M. Hare's basic position is to be found in *The Language of Morals* (Oxford, 1952) and *Freedom and Reason* (Oxford, 1963). J. L. Mackie's *Ethics: Inventing Right and Wrong* (Harmondsworth, Middlesex, 1977) defends a version of subjectivism.

The more important formulations of the universalizability principle referred to in the section are in: I. Kant, *Groundwork of the Metaphysic of Morals*, Section II (various translations and editions); R. M. Hare, *Freedom and Reason* and 'Ethical Theory and Utilitarianism' in *Contemporary British Philosophy*, 4, ed. H. D. Lewis (London, 1976); R. Firth, 'Ethical Absolutism and the Ideal Observer', *Philosophy and Phenomenological Research*, vol. 12 (1951–2); J. J. C. Smart and B. Williams, *Utilitarianism, For and Against* (Cambridge, 1973); John Rawls, *A Theory of Justice* (Oxford, 1972); J. P. Sartre, 'Existentialism is a Humanism' in W. Kaufmann (ed.) *Existentialism from Dostoevsky to*

Sartre (New York, 2nd edition, 1975) and Jürgen Habermas, *Legitima-tion Crisis*, (tr. T. McCarthy, London 1976) Pt. III, Chs. 2–4.

The tentative argument for a utilitarianism based on interests or preferences owes most to Hare's 'Ethical Theory and Utilitarianism', although it does not go as far as the argument in that article.

Chapter 2: Equality and its implications

Rawls' argument that equality can be based on the natural characteris-tics of human beings is to be found in Sec. 77 of *A Theory of Justice*.

The major arguments in favour of a link between IQ and race can be found in A. R. Jensen, *Genetics and Education* (London, 1972) and *Educability and Group Differences* (London, 1973) and in H. J. Eysenck's *Race, Intelligence and Education* (London, 1971). A variety of objections are collected in K. Richardson and D. Spears (eds.), *Race, Culture and Intelligence* (Harmondsworth, Middlesex, 1972). See also N. J. Block and G. Dworkin, *The IQ Controversy* (New York, 1976). Thomas Jeffer-son's comment on the irrelevance of intelligence to the issue of rights was made in a letter to Henri Gregoire, 25 February 1809.

The debate over the nature and origin of psychological differences between the sexes is soberly and comprehensively surveyed in E. Maccoby and C. Jacklin, *The Psychology of Sex Differences* (Stanford, 1974). Corinne Hutt, in *Males and Females* (Harmondsworth, Middlesex, 1972) states the case for a biological basis for sex differ-ences. Steven Goldberg's *The Inevitability of Patriarchy* (New York, 1973) is a polemic against feminist views like those in Kate Millett's *Sexual Politics* (New York, 1971) or Juliet Mitchell's *Women's Estate* (Har-mondsworth, Middlesex, 1971).

For a typical defence of equality of opportunity as the only justifiable form of equality, see Danel Bell, 'A "Just" Equality', *Dialogue* (Washington, DC) vol. 8, no. 2 (1975). The quotation on pp. 38–9 is from Jeffrey Gray, 'Why Should Society Reward Intelligence?', *The Times*, September 8, 1972.

The leading United States case on reverse discrimination, *Regents of the University of California v Allan Bakke*, was decided by the US Supreme Court on 5 July 1978. For a summary account, see *Time*, 10 July 1978. Two collections of essays are W. Blackstone and R. Heslep (eds.), *Social Justice and Preferential Treatment* (Athens, Georgia, 1977) and M. Cohen, T. Nagel and T. Scanlon (eds.), *Equality and Preferential Treatment* (Princeton, 1976). Alan H. Goldman, *Justice and Reverse Discrimination* (Princeton, 1979) is a book-length treatment of the ethical issues involved. Notable individual essays include: Thomas Nagel, 'Equal Treatment and Compensatory Discrimination', *Philosophy and Public Affairs*, vol. 2 (1973); Richard Wasserstrom, 'Racism, Sexism and Preferential Treatment: An Approach to the Topics', *U.C.L.A. Law Review*, vol. 24 (1977); Ronald Dworkin, *Taking Rights Seriously* (London, 1977) Ch. 9; and, on the other side, Lisa Newton, 'Reverse Discrimination as Unjustified', *Ethics*, vol. 83 (1973).

Chapter 3: Equality for animals

My views on animals first appeared in *The New York Review of Books*, 5 April 1973, under the title 'Animal Liberation'. This article was a review of R. and S. Godlovitch and J. Harris (eds.), *Animals, Men and Morals* (London, 1972). I elaborated these views in *Animal Liberation* (New York, 1975).

Among other recent works arguing for a drastic revision in our present attitudes to animals are S. Clark, *The Moral Status of Animals* (Oxford, 1977) and T. Regan's 'The Moral Basis of Vegetarianism', *Canadian Journal of Philosophy*, vol. 5 (1975). *Animal Rights and Human Obligations*, edited by P. Singer and T. Regan (Englewood Cliffs, NJ, 1976) is a collection of essays, old and new, both for and against attributing rights to animals or duties to humans in respect of animals.

Bentham's defence of animals, quoted on pp. 49–50 is from his *Introduction to the Principles of Morals and Legislation*, Ch. XVIII, Sec. 1, note.

A more detailed description of modern farming conditions can be found in *Animal Liberation*, Ch. 2 and in James Mason and Peter Singer, *Animal Factories* (New York, 1980). Richard Ryder's *Victims of Science* (London, 1975) is an excellent account of animal experimentation. *Animal Liberation*, Ch. 3, is no substitute for Ryder's book, but contains a fuller discussion of the subject than is possible in this book. The experiments at Princeton University on starving rats, and those by H. F. Harlow on isolating monkeys, referred to on p. 58 of this book, are taken from *Animal Liberation*, pp. 40–4. The original sources are *Journal of Comparative and Physiological Psychology*, vol. 78, p. 202 (1972), *Proceedings of the National Academy of Science*, vol. 54, p. 90 (1965) and *Engineering and Science*, vol. 33, no. 6, p. 8 (April 1970).

Among the objections, the claim that animals are incapable of feeling pain has standardly been associated with Descartes. But Descartes' view is less clear (and less consistent) than most (including myself in

Animal Liberation) have assumed. See John Cottinghan, 'A Brute to the Brutes?: Descartes' Treatment of Animals', *Philosophy*, vol. 53, p. 551 (1978).

The source for the anecdote about Benjamin Franklin is his *Autobiography* (New York, 1950) p. 41. The same objection has been more seriously considered by John Benson in 'Duty and The Beast', *Philosophy*, vol. 53, pp. 545–7 (1978).

Jane Goodall's observations of chimpanzees are engagingly recounted in *In The Shadow of Man* (Boston, 1971). The 'argument from marginal cases' was thus christened by Jan Narveson, 'Animal Rights', *Canadian Journal of Philosophy*, vol. 7 (1977). Of the objections to the argument discussed on pp. 66–7, the first is made by Stanley Benn, 'Egalitarianism and Equal Consideration of Interests', in J. Pennock and J. Chapman (eds.), *Nomos IX: Equality* (New York, 1967) pp. 62ff; the second by John Benson, 'Duty and the Beast', *Philosophy* vol. 53 (the quotation on p. 66 occurs on p. 536 of this article) and related points are made by Bonnie Steinbock, 'Speciesism and the Idea of Equality', *Philosophy*, vol. 53, pp. 255–6 and at greater length by Leslie Pickering, Francis and Richard Norman, 'Some Animals are More Equal than Others', *Philosophy*, vol. 53, pp. 518–27 (1978); the third objection can be found in Philip Devine, 'The Moral Basis of Vegetarianism', *Philosophy*, vol. 53, pp. 496–8.

The quotation from Plato's *Republic* on p. 68 is from Book II, pp. 358–9. Later statements of a similar view include John Rawls, *A Theory of Justice*, Gilbert Harman, *The Nature of Morality* (New York, 1977) and J. L. Mackie, *Ethics*, Ch. 5. They exclude animals from the centre of morality, although they soften the impact of this exclusion in various ways: See *A Theory of Justice*, p. 512, and *Ethics*, pp. 193–5. Narveson also considers the reciprocity notion of ethics in 'Animal Rights'.

Chapter 4: What's wrong with killing?
The case of the mongoloid baby for which a court order was obtained is reported in Anthony Shaw, 'Dilemmas of "Informed Consent" in Children', *New England Journal of Medicine*, vol. 289, no. 17 (1973).

Joseph Fletcher's article 'Indicators of Humanhood: A Tentative Profile of Man' appeared in *The Hastings Center Report*, vol. 2, no. 5 (1972). John Locke's definition of 'person' is taken from his *Essay Concerning Human Understanding*, Bk. II, Ch. 9, Par. 29.

Aristotle's views on infanticide are in his *Politics*, Bk. VII, p. 1335b; Plato's are in the *Republic*, Bk. V, p. 460. Support for the claim that our present attitudes to infanticide are largely the effect of the influence of Christianity on our thought can be found in the historical material on infanticide cited in the notes on Ch. 6, below. (See especially the article by W. L. Langer, pp. 353–5.) For Aquinas' statement that killing a human being offends against God as killing a slave offends against the master of the slave, see *Summa Theologica*, II, ii, Question 64, article 5.

Michael Tooley's 'Abortion and Infanticide' was first published in *Philosophy and Public Affairs*, vol. 2 (1972). The passage quoted on p. 82 is from a revised version in J. Feinberg (ed.), *The Problem of Abortion* (Belmont, 1973) p. 60.

For further discussion of respect for autonomy as an objection to killing, see Jonathan Glover, *Causing Death and Saving Lives* (Harmondsworth, Middlesex, 1977) Ch. 5. and H. J. McCloskey, 'The Right to Life', *Mind*, vol. 84 (1975).

My discussion of the 'total' and 'prior existence' versions of utilitarianism owes much to Derek Parfit. His 'Rights, Interests and Possible People', in S. Gorovitz *et al.* (eds.), *Moral Problems in Medicine* (Engelwood Cliffs, NJ, 1976) reveals only a small fraction of the subtlety and ingenuity of his arguments on this issue. Parfit uses the term 'person-affecting' where I use 'prior existence'. The reason for the change is that the view has no special reference to persons, as distinct from other sentient creatures. I tried to defend the prior existence view in 'A Utilitarian Population Principle' in M. Bayles (ed.), *Ethics and Population* (Cambridge, Mass. 1976) but Parfit's reply, 'On Doing the Best for Our Children', in the same volume, has convinced me that my defence failed.

The issue appears to have been first noticed by Henry Sidgwick, *The Methods of Ethics* (London, 1907) pp. 414–16. Later discussions include, in addition to the articles cited above, J. Narveson, 'Moral Problems of Population', *The Monist*, vol. 57 (1973); T. G. Roupas, 'The Value of Life', *Philosophy and Public Affairs*, vol. 7 (1978); and R. I. Sikora, 'Is it Wrong to Prevent the Existence of Future Generations' in *Obligations to Future Generations*, ed. B. Barry, R. Sikora (Philadelphia, 1978).

Albert Schweitzer's most complete statement of his ethical stance is *Civilization and Ethics* (Part II of *The Philosophy of Civilization*) tr. C. T. Campion, 2nd ed. (London, 1929). The quotation is from pp. 246–7. More modern defenders of rights (including presumably some kind of qualified right to life) for non-sentient life are John Rodman, 'The Liberation of Nature', *Inquiry*, vol. 20 (1977) and Christopher Stone, *Should Trees Have Standing: Toward Legal Rights for Natural Objects* (New

York, 1975). For a contrary view see Joel Feinberg, 'What Sorts of Beings Can Have Rights?' in W. Blackstone (ed.), *Philosophy and Environmental Crisis* (Athens, Georgia, 1974).

Chapter 5: Taking life: animals

The break-through in talking to other species was first announced in R. and B. Gardner, 'Teaching Sign Language to a Chimpanzee', *Science*, vol. 165, pp. 664–72 (1969). Since then the literature has multiplied rapidly. Eugene Linden's *Apes, Men and Language* (New York, 1974) is a popular account of the subject. Peter Jenkins gives a briefer introduction in 'Ask No Questions', in T. Regan and P. Singer (eds.), *Animal Rights and Human Obligations*. The conversational abilities of the gorilla are also now being investigated with promising results: see *Newsweek*, 7 March, 1977, pp. 70–3. For some suggestive but inconclusive evidence about the ability of whales to communicate in a sophisticated way, see John Lilly, *Man and Dolphin* (London, 1962).

The quotation on pp. 94–5 is from Stuart Hampshire, *Thought and Action* (London, 1959), pp. 98–9. Others who have held related views are Anthony Kenny, in *Will, Freedom and Power* (Oxford, 1975) and Donald Davidson, 'Thought and Talk' in S. Guttenplan (ed.), *Mind and Language* (Oxford, 1975).

The experiment on the ability of chimpanzees to grasp the concept of the middle object is reported in F. H. Rohles and J. V. Devine, 'Chimpanzee performance in a problem involving the concept of middleness', *Animal Behavior*, vol. 14, cited in Donald Griffin, *The Question of Animal Awareness* (New York, 1976), p. 43. The description of Figan's thoughtful manner of obtaining his banana is from p. 107 of *In the Shadow of Man*. Jane Goodall's estimate of the number of chimpanzees that die for every one to reach our shores alive is on p. 257.

Leslie Stephen's claim that eating bacon is kind to pigs comes from his *Social Rights and Duties* (London, 1896) and is quoted by Henry Salt in 'The Logic of the Larder', which appeared in Salt's *The Humanities of Diet* (Manchester, 1914) and has been reprinted in T. Regan and P. Singer (eds.), *Animal Rights and Human Obligations*. Salt's reply is in the same article. My own earlier discussion of this issue is in Chapter 6 of *Animal Liberation*.

Chapter 6: Taking life: abortion

The most important sections of the decision of the US Supreme Court in *Roe v. Wade* are reprinted in J. Feinberg (ed.), *The Problem of Abortion*.

The government committee referred to on p. 112 – the Wolfenden Committee – issued the *Report of the Committee on Homosexual Offences and Prostitution*, Command Paper 247 (London, 1957). The quotation is from p. 24. J. S. Mill's 'very simple principle' is stated in the introductory chapter of *On Liberty* (London, 3rd ed., 1864). Edwin Schur's *Crimes Without Victims* was published in Englewood Cliffs, NJ, in 1965. Judith Jarvis Thomson's 'A Defense of Abortion' appeared in *Philosophy and Public Affairs*, vol. 1 (1971).

For an expert opinion on the stage at which the fetus may begin to have the capacity to suffer pain, see the report of the British Government advisory group on fetal research, chaired by Sir John Peel, *The Use of Fetuses and Fetal Materials for Research* (London, 1972).

Paul Ramsey uses the genetic uniqueness of the fetus as an argument against abortion in 'The Morality of Abortion' in D. H. Labby (ed.), *Life or Death: Ethics and Options* (London, 1968) and reprinted in J. Rachels (ed.), *Moral Problems* (New York, 2nd ed., 1975), p. 40.

Bentham's reassuring comment on infanticide, quoted on p. 124, is from his *Theory of Legislation*, p. 264 and is quoted by E. Westermarck, *The Origin and Development of Moral Ideas* (London, 1924) I, p. 413n.

For historical material on the prevalence of infanticide see Maria Piers, *Infanticide* (New York, 1978) and W. L. Langer, 'Infanticide: A Historical Survey', *History of Childhood Quarterly*, vol. 1 (1974). An older, but still valuable survey is in Edward Westermarck, *The Origin and Development of Moral Ideas*, I, pp. 394–413. An interesting study of the use of infanticide as a form of family planning is *Nakahara: Family Farming and Population in a Japanese Village, 1717–1830*, by Thomas C. Smith. References for Plato and Aristotle were given in the notes to Ch. 4. For Seneca see *De Ira*, I, 15, cited by Westermarck, *The Origin and Development of Moral Ideas*, I, p. 419. Marvin Kohl (ed.), *Infanticide and the Value of Life* (Buffalo, NY, 1978) is a modern collection of essays on infanticide.

Further articles on abortion are collected in J. Feinberg (ed.), *The Problem of Abortion* and in Robert Perkins (ed.), *Abortion, Pro and Con* (Cambridge, Mass., 1974). Articles with some affinity with the position I have taken include R. M. Hare, 'Abortion and the Golden Rule', *Philosophy and Public Affairs*, vol. 4 (1975), Mary Anne Warren, 'The Moral and Legal Status of Abortion', *The Monist*, vol. 57 (1973) and the article by Michael Tooley cited in the notes to Ch. 4. See also Jonathan Glover, *Causing Death and Saving Lives*, Chs. 9–12; this includes a section on when the young child can be presumed to have a concept of death (pp. 156–8) and provides further references (on p. 308) to the literature on this subject.

Chapter 7: Taking life: euthanasia

Derek Humphry's account of his wife's death, *Jean's Way*, was published in London in 1978. The quotation on p. 145 is from p. 63. For details of the Zygmaniak case, see Paige Mitchell, *Act of Love* (New York, 1976) or the *New York Times*, 1, 3 and 6 November 1973. Louis Repouille's act of non-voluntary euthanasia was reported in the *New York Times*, 13 October 1939, and is cited by Yale Kamisar, 'Some Non-religious Views Against Proposed Mercy Killing Legislation', *Minnesota Law Review*, vol. 42, p. 1,021 (1958).

Robert Reid, *My Children, My Children*, is a fine introduction to the nature of some birth defects, including spina bifida and haemophilia. For evidence of high rates of divorce and severe marital difficulties among parents of spina bifida children, see p. 127. Another good popular account is Gerald Leach, *The Biocrats* (Harmondsworth, Middlesex, 1972) Ch. 7. Both books describe amniocentesis and other methods of detecting fetal abnormalities with a view to abortion – Reid's has the advantage of being more up to date.

There are many detailed discussions of the precise conditions under which voluntary euthanasia should be permitted. For the views of the British Voluntary Euthanasia Society, see its *A Plea for Legislation to Permit Voluntary Euthanasia* (London, 1970). Yale Kamisar argues against voluntary as well as nonvoluntary euthanasia in the article cited above; he is answered by Robert Young, 'Voluntary and Non-voluntary Euthanasia', *The Monist*, vol. 59 (1976). A. B. Downing (ed.), *Euthanasia and the Right to Death* (London, 1969) is a collection of essays arguing for voluntary euthanasia. It can be contrasted with Jonathan Gould and Lord Craigmyle (eds.), *Your Death Warrant?*, which consists of essays arguing against euthanasia. Marvin Kohl (ed.), *Beneficent Euthanasia* (Buffalo, NY, 1975) contains arguments for and against. See also Jonathan Glover, *Causing Death and Saving Lives*, Ch. 14.

Jonathan Glover discusses nonvoluntary euthanasia in Ch. 15, as does Robert Young in the final section of the article referred to above. The distinction between active and passive euthanasia is succinctly criticized by James Rachels, 'Active and Passive Euthanasia', *New England Journal of Medicine*, vol. 292, pp. 78–80 (1975). Doctors' protests against this attack on their traditional ethic can be found on pp. 863–7 of the same volume, together with Rachels' reply. John Lorber describes his practice of passive euthanasia for selected cases of spina bifida in 'Early Results of Selective Treatment of Spina Bifida Cystica', *British Medical Journal*, 27 October 1973, pp. 201–4. Testimony on the number of defective children allowed to die in the United States was reported in the *New York Times*, 16 June 1974, Pt. IV, p. 7. A representative example of the pious misinterpretation of Arthur Clough's lines occurs in G. K. and E. D. Smith, 'Selection for Treatment in Spina Bifida Cystica', *British Medical Journal*, 27 October 1973, at p. 197. The entire poem is included in *The New Oxford Book of English Verse*, edited by Helen Gardner (Oxford, 1978).

The statistics for survival of untreated spina bifida infants come from the articles by Lorber and G. K. and E. D. Smith, cited above. Lorber's objection to active euthanasia, quoted on pp. 153–4 is from p. 204 of the same article.

The argument that Nazi crimes developed out of the euthanasia programme is quoted from Leo Alexander, 'Medical Science under Dictatorship', *New England Journal of Medicine*, vol. 241, pp. 39–47 (14 July 1949). Gitta Sereny, *Into that Darkness: From Mercy Killing to Mass Murder* (London, 1974) makes a similar claim in tracing the career of Franz Stangl from the euthanasia centres to the death camp at Treblinka; but in so doing she reveals how different the Nazi 'euthanasia' programme was from what is now advocated (see especially pp. 51–5).

On euthanasia among the Eskimo (and the rarity of homicide outside such special circumstances) see E. Westermarck, *The Origin and Development of Moral Ideas*, vol. I, pp. 329–34, 387, n. 1 and 392, nn. 1–3.

Chapter 8: Rich and poor

The summary of world poverty was compiled from a number of sources, including Susan George, *How the Other Half Dies* (Harmondsworth, Middlesex, revised edition, 1977): Hans Singer and Javed Ansari, *Rich and Poor Countries* (London, 2nd ed., 1978); the World Bank's *World Development Report, 1978* (Washington, DC, 1978) and the *World Population Report* issued by Population Concern (London, 1978). The first quotation from Robert McNamara (on p. 159) is from the *Summary Proceedings* of the 1976 Annual Meeting of the World Bank/ IFC/IDA, p. 14; the following quotation is from the *World Development Report, 1978*, p. iii. For the wastage involved in feeding crops to animals instead of directly to humans, see Francis Moore Lappe, *Diet for a Small Planet* (New York, revised ed., 1975).

On the difference – or lack of it – between killing and allowing to die, see (in addition to the previous references to active and passive euthanasia) Jonathan Glover, *Causing Death and Saving Lives*, Ch. 7, Richard Trammel, 'Saving Life and Taking Life', *Journal of Philosophy*, vol. 72 (1975), and John Harris, 'The Marxist Conception of Violence', *Philosophy and Public Affairs*, vol. 3 (1974).

John Locke's view of rights is developed in his *Second Treatise on Civil Government*, and Robert Nozick's in *Anarchy, State and Utopia* (New York, 1974). Thomas Aquinas' quite different view is quoted from *Summa Theologica*, II, ii, Question 66, article 7.

Garrett Hardin proposed his 'lifeboat ethic' in 'Living on a Lifeboat', *Bioscience*, October 1974, another version of which has been reprinted in W. Aiken and H. La Follette (eds.), *World Hunger and Moral Obligation* (Englewood Cliffs, 1977). Hardin elaborates on the argument in *The Limits of Altruism* (Bloomington, Indians, 1977). An earlier argument against aid was voiced by W. and P. Paddock in their mistitled *Famine 1975!* (Boston 1967) but pride of place in the history of this view must go to Thomas Malthus for *An Essay on the Principle of Population* (London, 1798).

Opposition to the view that the world is overpopulated comes from Susan George, *How the Other Half Dies*, Ch. 2, and Roger Revelle, 'Food and Population', *Scientific American*, September 1974. The estimates of population in various countries by the year 2000 are taken from the *World Development Report, 1978*, pp. 106–7. For evidence that more equal distribution of income, better education and better health facilities can reduce population growth, see John W. Ratcliffe, 'Poverty, Politics and Fertility: The Anomaly of Kerala', *Hastings Center Report*, vol. 7 (1977); for more general discussion of the idea of demographic transition, see William Rich, *Smaller Families Through Social and Economic Progress*, Overseas Development Council Monograph No. 7 (1973), and Julian Simon, *The Effects of Income on Fertility*, Carolina Population Center Monograph (Chapel Hill, NC, 1974). On ethical issues relating to population control, see Robert Young, 'Population Policies, Coercion and Morality', in D. Mannison, R. Routley and M. McRobbie (eds.), *Environmental Philosophy* (Canberra, 1979).

A useful general collection is W. Aiken and H. La Follette, (eds.), *World Hunger and Moral Obligation. Food Policy: The Responsibility of the United States in the Life and Death Choices*, edited by Peter Brown and Henry Shue (New York, 1977) is more of a mixed bag, but includes some good pieces, on both philosophical and factual issues.

Chapter 9: Ends and means

Henry Thoreau's 'Civil Disobedience' has been reprinted in several places, among them H. A. Bedau (ed.), *Civil Disobedience: Theory and Practice* (New York, 1969); the passage quoted on p. 183 is on p. 28 of this collection. The immediately following quotation is from p. 18 of R. P. Wolff's *In Defense of Anarchism* (New York, 1970). On the nature of conscience, see A. Campbell Garnett, 'Conscience and Conscientiousness' in J. Feinberg (ed.), *Moral Concepts* (Oxford, 1969).

John Locke argued for the importance of settled law in his *Second Treatise on Civil Government*, especially sections 124–6.

On the sorry history of attempts to reform the law on animal experimentation, see Richard Ryder, *Victims of Science* (London, 1975). The quotation on p. 190 is from the *Bulletin* of the National Society for Medical Research (US) October 1973.

Mill's proposal for multiple votes for the better educated occurs in Ch. 8 of his *Representative Government*.

The quotation from Engels' *Condition of the Working Class in England* (tr. and ed. Henderson and Chaloner, Oxford, 1958, p. 108) I owe to John Harris, 'The Marxist Conception of Violence', *Philosophy and Public Affairs*, vol. 3 (1974), which argues persuasively for regarding 'passive violence' as a genuine form of violence. See also R. P. Wolff, 'On Violence', *Journal of Philosophy*, vol. 66 (1969), Robert Young, 'Revolutionary Terrorism, Crime and Morality', *Social Theory and Practice*, vol. 4 (1977) and Ted Honderich, *Three Essays on Political Violence* (Oxford, 1976).

The issues dealt with in sections i–iii of this chapter are more fully treated in my *Democracy and Disobedience* (Oxford, 1973). Probably the best collection of essays in this area is J. G. Murphy (ed.), *Civil Disobedience and Violence* (Belmont, 1971) although the anthology edited by H. A. Bedau, referred to above, is valuable for its emphasis on the writings of those who practice civil disobedience rather than theorise about it from afar.

Chapter 10: Why act morally?

For attempts to reject the title question of this chapter as an improper question, see S. Toulmin, *The Place of Reason in Ethics* (Cambridge, 1961) p. 162; J. Hospers, *Human Conduct* (London, 1963) p. 194; and M. G. Singer, *Generalization in Ethics* (London, 1963), pp. 319–27. D. H. Monro defines ethical judgments as overriding in *Empiricism and Ethics*

(Cambridge, 1967), see for instance p. 127. R. M. Hare's prescriptivist view of ethics implies that a commitment to act is involved in accepting a moral judgment, but since only universalizable judgments count as moral judgments, this view does not have the consequence that whatever judgment we take to be overriding is necessarily our moral judgment. Hare's view therefore allows us to give sense to our question. On this general issue of the definition of moral terms and the consequences of different definitions, see my 'The Triviality of the Debate over "Is–Ought" and the Definition of "Moral"', *American Philosophical Quarterly*, vol. 10 (1973).

The argument discussed in the second section is a distillation of such sources as: Marcus Aurelius, *Meditations*, Bk. IV, par. 4; I. Kant, *Groundwork of the Metaphysic of Morals*; H. J. Paton, *The Categorical Imperative* (London, 1963) pp. 245–6; J. Hospers, *Human Conduct* (London, 1963) pp. 584–93 and D. Gauthier, *Practical Reasoning* (Oxford, 1963) p. 118.

G. Carlson, 'Ethical Egoism Reconsidered', *American Philosophical Quarterly*, vol. 10 (1973) argues that egoism is irrational because the individual egoist cannot defend it publicly without inconsistency; but it is not clear why this should be a test of rationality, since the egoist can still defend it to himself.

Hume defends his view of practical reason in *A Treatise of Human Nature*, Bk. II, Pt. iii, sec. 3. T. Nagel's objections to it are in *The Possibility of Altruism* (Oxford, 1970). Sidgwick's observation on the rationality of egoism is on p. 498 of *The Methods of Ethics* (7th ed., London, 1907).

Bradley's insistence on loving virtue for her own sake comes from his *Ethical Studies* (Oxford, 1876, reprinted 1962) pp. 61–3. The same position can be found in Kant's *Groundwork of the Metaphysic of Morals*, Ch. 1, and in D. Z. Phillips, 'Does it Pay to be Good?', *Proceedings of the Aristotelian Society*, vol. 64 (1964–5). Bradley and Kant are expounding what they take to be 'the common moral consciousness' rather than their own views. Kant himself adheres to the view of the common moral consciousness, but later in *Ethical Studies* Bradley supports a view of morality in which the subjective satisfaction involved in the moral life plays a prominent role.

My account of why we believe that only actions done for the sake of morality have moral worth is similar to Hume's view in his *Enquiry Concerning the Principles of Morals*. See also P. H. Nowell-Smith, *Ethics*, Pt. III. Hare's distinction between 'intuitive' and 'critical' moral thinking is the subject of his article, 'Principles', *Proceedings of The Aristotelian Society*, vol. 73 (1972–3).

Maslow presents some very sketchy data in support of his theory of personality in 'Psychological Data and Value Theory' in A. H. Maslow (ed.), *New Knowledge in Human Values* (New York, 1959); see also A. H. Maslow, *Motivation and Personality* (New York, 1954). Charles Hampden-Turner, *Radical Man* (New York, 1971) contains a hotch-potch of surveys and research linking certain humanistic values with an outlook on life that is subjectively rewarding; but the data is often only tangentially relevant to the conclusions drawn from them.

On psychopaths, see H. Cleckley, *The Mask of Sanity* (5th ed., St Louis, 1976). The remark about requests for help coming from rela-tives, not the psychopaths themselves, is on p. viii. The quotation from a happy psychopath on p. 214 is from W. and J. McCord, *Psychopathy and Delinquency* (New York, 1956) p. 6. On the ability of psychopaths to avoid prison, see R. D. Hare, *Psychopathy* (New York, 1970) pp. 111–12.

The 'paradox of hedonism' is discussed by F. H. Bradley in the third essay of his *Ethical Studies*; for a psychotherapist's account, see V. Frankl, *The Will to Meaning* (London, 1971) pp. 33–4.

On the relation between self-interest and ethics, see the concluding chapter of Sidgwick's *Methods of Ethics*, and for a useful anthology, D. Gauthier (ed.), *Morality and Rational Self-Interest* (Englewood Cliffs, NJ, 1970). On the more general issue of the nature of practical reasoning, see J. Raz (ed.), *Practical Reasoning* (Oxford, 1978).

INDEX OF NAMES